The Confederate Heartland

CONFLICTING WORLDS

NEW DIMENSIONS OF THE AMERICAN CIVIL WAR

T. Michael Parrish, Series Editor

The Confederate Heartland

MILITARY AND CIVILIAN MORALE
IN THE
WESTERN CONFEDERACY

Bradley R. Clampitt

LOUISIANA STATE UNIVERSITY PRESS

BATON ROUGE

Published by Louisiana State University Press
Copyright © 2011 by Louisiana State University Press
All rights reserved
Manufactured in the United States of America

FIRST PRINTING
Designer: Barbara Neely Bourgoyne
Typeface: Whitman
Printer: McNaughton & Gunn, Inc.
Binder: Acme Bookbinding, Inc.

LIBRARY OF CONGRESS CATALOGING-IN-PUBLICATION DATA

Clampitt, Bradley R., 1975–
 The Confederate heartland : military and civilian morale in the western Confederacy /
Bradley R. Clampitt.
   p. cm. — (Conflicting worlds : new dimensions of the American Civil War)
 Includes bibliographical references and index.
 ISBN 978-0-8071-3995-0 (cloth : alk. paper) — ISBN 978-0-8071-3996-7 (pdf) — ISBN
978-0-8071-3997-4 (epub) — ISBN 978-0-8071-3998-1 (mobi)
  1. United States—History—Civil War, 1861–1865—Psychological aspects. 2.
Mississippi—History—Civil War, 1861–1865—Psychological aspects. 3. Alabama—
History—Civil War, 1861–1865—Psychological aspects. 4. Tennessee—History—Civil
War, 1861–1865—Psychological aspects. 5. Soldiers—Confederate States of America—
Psychology. 6. Military morale. 7. Morale. 8. Motivation (Psychology)—United States—
History—19th century. I. Title.
 E468.9.C558 2011
 973'7'13—dc22

                                                                    2011016236

Contents

Acknowledgments

DURING THE LAST several years I have traveled to numerous archives throughout the South to conduct the research for this book. The bibliography includes the names of these institutions, but certain repositories merit special mention. These are the Mississippi Department of Archives and History in Jackson, where I always enjoy my stay, the Alabama Department of Archives and History in Montgomery, and the Tennessee State Library and Archives in Nashville. Additionally, though they likely would not remember my brief visit, the Special Collections staff at Mississippi State University's Mitchell Memorial Library, in Starkville, deserve special recognition as the friendliest hosts I have encountered during a research trip.

Rand Dotson and the staff at LSU Press have proven immensely helpful and supportive. I would especially like to thank Rand for his early interest in the project. Mike Parrish, editor of the Conflicting Worlds: New Dimensions of the American Civil War series, has worked tirelessly with me through multiple revisions and has supported my work from the beginning. Indeed, at times it seemed that Mike knew exactly what I wanted to express and frequently helped me figure out how to articulate it. His experience and deft touch have improved this book immeasurably since he read an earlier version several years ago.

My colleagues in the history department at East Central University have provided a supportive environment. Linda Reese, Tom Cowger, Scott Barton, Houston Mount, Greg Sutton, and Chris Bean have all provided encouragement. Chris, in particular, has listened to my arguments countless times during our many cross-country drives for this and other research projects. Although he still has not learned how to read an automobile's fuel gauge accurately and his exploits in the buffet line have nearly led to our expulsion from a few restaurants, we always arrive at our destination.

Randolph B. "Mike" Campbell and Richard Lowe are the two finest mentors a historian could ask for, and I count both among my friends. Both taught me how to be a historian, and most of what I know about my craft I owe to these two men. Years ago Professor Lowe (I still cannot bring myself to call him Richard, though I have known him for twelve years) "encouraged" me to take on this topic when he suggested that I could choose another idea that we had discussed or I could tackle this project and write something that "someone would care about." I trust his judgment more than that of anyone in the profession.

Finally, I thank my wife, Diana, for her inexhaustible patience and my son, Theo Jacob, for his inexhaustible energy.

The Confederate Heartland

Introduction

IN THE AMERICAN Civil War the home front and battlefield were insepa-
rable, particularly in the Confederacy, where most of the fighting took place.
Each provided invaluable context for the other. Without attention to military events, any analysis of the home front neglects the central event in the
lives of most southerners, regardless of their stance on the war, for those
four years. Similarly, any military history that neglects the home front over-
looks the fundamental human concerns of home and family, wives, children,
and other loved ones, common to most soldiers in any conflict. Indeed, such
books overlook why most soldiers fought in the first place. This study is not
a military narrative that portrays warfare as though it occurred in a vacuum
without greater social and political consequences. Nor is it an extreme example of new social history that might somehow examine the Civil War
without actually noticing that battles were fought and people were killed.
Rather, it is an examination of one aspect of the conflict—morale in the
western Confederacy during the war's final year and a half—that follows
the lead of the sources. This book focuses not necessarily on issues traditionally raised in Civil War historiography, but rather on issues raised by
Confederates themselves in their contemporary writings as determinants
of morale. At different times military, social, or political events take center
stage because all of those factors influenced morale among both civilians
and soldiers.

This study examines the evolution of Confederate morale, military and
civilian, in three important western states, Mississippi, Alabama, and Tennessee, during 1864 and 1865. In his classic study of the Army of Tennessee,
Thomas Connelly defined the Confederate heartland as that region that included Tennessee, north-central Alabama, northeast Mississippi, and north-
central Georgia. This book draws upon Connelly's definition of the heartland
and expands it to include greater Alabama and Mississippi and examines

northern Georgia during the Confederate defense of Atlanta. As Connelly demonstrated, the region in question formed not only the physical or geographic heartland of the Confederacy, but also the logistical and communications center situated between the eastern and trans-Mississippi theaters. The heartland proved a vital manufacturing center and source of manpower, slave labor, food, livestock, and raw materials. In fact, the 1862 Union capture of much of the region after the campaign that included the capture of Forts Henry and Donelson and the seizure of Nashville, the Battle of Shiloh, and ultimately the loss of Corinth, Mississippi, represented one the Confederacy's greatest logistical losses of the war. Prominent east-west and north-south railroad lines crossed the heartland and connected the area to the Confederate center of government in Virginia. Vitally important rivers such as the Mississippi, the Tennessee, the Cumberland, and the Alabama dissected the heartland. Double-edged swords, those rivers served important economic purposes but also provided highways of invasion into the Confederate heartland for Federal armies. The heartland as examined here also boasted important southern cities, such as Nashville, Memphis, Montgomery, Mobile, Vicksburg, and Atlanta. None of this in any way implies that the heartland was necessarily more important than any other region or that the people there displayed greater dedication or endured greater sacrifice than the residents of any other region of the Confederacy. However, it clearly illustrates the significance of the heartland as a distinct region and demonstrates the potential value of an examination of the morale of the heartland's residents to a greater understanding of the Confederate experiment.[1]

Additionally, a concentration on the heartland of the Confederacy allows a glimpse into the hearts and minds of Confederates who routinely witnessed the defeat of their defenders, the primary Confederate army in that theater, the Army of Tennessee. The soldiers and residents of that region, more than any other, witnessed repeated and successful Union invasions of Confederate soil and frequently found their homelands subject to occupation by Federal forces. Thus, the theater that featured the most consistent Union success and Confederate failure, the theater where many historians contend that the war was won and lost, provides an intriguing opportunity to examine the persistence of the Confederate people. A western focus also provides a perspective in addition to those produced by the many studies of the eastern theater and the legendary and more successful Army of Northern Virginia. A concentration on the relatively brief time period of 1864–1865 presents the opportunity for a deeper examination of the sources than a longer time frame would allow and, more important, permits an assessment of the lingering question of when and why western Confederates recognized and admitted defeat.

Obviously, an assessment of morale requires a clear definition of the term. This book defines morale as a measure of human emotion, including the enthusiasm, loyalty, and especially confidence or lack thereof among individuals with regard to the success of their cause. In this case, it refers to the state of such sentiments among western Confederates with reference to their war for independence. Generally, many factors, such as battlefield results, politics, concern for loved ones, and perceived quality of leadership influenced morale. High morale typically resulted from shared sacrifice or more often from meaningful signs of impending victory, and generally demonstrated significant degrees of satisfaction, group cohesion, and motivation. Low morale could result from dissatisfaction with any aspect of the war effort, especially poor material conditions at home or in the military, or more important, any significant signs of impending defeat.[2]

Because any examination of morale must come to grips with those individuals who persisted in their war effort even after defeat seemed certain, this study recognizes among western Confederates two distinct levels of morale (beyond the generic "high" and "low"). Certain individuals throughout most of the period in question not only supported the Confederacy but genuinely expected to win the war. Those persons exhibited high morale and considerable confidence in their prospects for success and clearly remained dedicated to the Confederate war effort. Toward the end of the period under consideration, among those who had not abandoned the war effort entirely, a second group emerged. Individuals in that group exhibited lower morale and considerably less confidence in the Confederacy's chances for ultimate success, but in their hearts and minds remained dedicated Confederates. In other words, they continued to *desire* southern independence as much as ever, but they no longer *expected* southern independence.

The letters and diaries of soldiers and civilians necessarily serve as principal sources for the analysis of morale in the western Confederacy. As numerous historians have noted, those wartime writings remain the single best source for examining the mind-sets of Civil War participants. Approximately 80 percent of Confederate soldiers were literate, and, regardless of their individual motives or sentiments, all knew that they were involved in something important. This study employs postwar sources only intermittently, because memoirs and reminiscences by southern authors almost always portrayed a more united Confederacy than actually existed, and there is no room for Lost Cause romanticism in a study of wartime morale. Moreover, a memoir written decades after the war is of limited value when assessing the morale of a regiment directly after a specific event or when considering the emotional state of a civilian living under Federal occupation. Collectively, these wartime sources offer insight into the citizens' and soldiers' thoughts and feelings during the war's final months.[3]

If most scholars agree on the principal sources, the same cannot be said for the methodology of how to use them. The study of morale during the Civil War defies quantitative analysis. That approach sounds appealing because of the temptation to label it more scientific and less impressionistic. Similar to a more conventional approach, however, the historian of morale must still choose which sources to sample, which to omit, which phrases to interpret, and how to interpret them. Thus, in examining morale, the quantitative approach proves no more controlled than a more traditional style in the mold of Bell Wiley's classic books about common Civil War soldiers. From a stylistic standpoint, quantitative analysis is simply better suited to certain research topics than others. For the purposes of this study, such an approach threatened to drain the life from a very human subject. Tables, charts, and graphs simply are an inadequate way to measure and describe the experiences of Americans at war.[4]

Moreover, a quantitative approach would have left room for too many variables for the results to be deemed "scientific." Historians employ quantitative techniques in order to be more methodical or systematic. But history, particularly the study of human sentiments in wartime, is not science, able to be replicated in a controlled setting. So the scholar must use what might be called a more qualitative, impressionistic, or literary approach to understand morale. This inquiry employs that approach and relies on what Confederate citizens and soldiers wrote about during the war—military, political, social, or otherwise—to trace their sentiments through 1864 and 1865. Morale naturally varied from one individual to the next, but in most instances clear patterns developed in reaction to major events and at various stages of the war. Differences from the consensus are noted when they arise.

Although this is not a historiographical study per se, a few comments are necessary for context with regard to discussions of the relationship between the home front and the battlefield and issues such as Confederate morale and nationalism. Recent scholarship has embraced the importance of the home front and battlefield relationship, and in the process has redirected decades of historiographical debate that concentrated on an alleged lack of nationalism or unity and other internal problems as fundamental failings that prevented a Confederate victory. Proponents of the internal divisions theses pointed to factors such as the lack of sufficient will among Confederates, conscription, tax-in-kind laws, class conflict, defeatism among women, planter-class greed, and even doubts about the morality of slavery as factors that undermined the Confederate will to fight. Most of those weaknesses indeed existed to one degree or another, and they must have weakened the Confederacy's ability to wage war. (That said, assertions about lack of will, considerable class conflict, and slavery guilt remain unconvincing.) As James McPherson has argued, however, the northern people experienced at least as much division along very similar lines, and the same explanation could have been offered had they lost. Moreover, as many historians have noted, those explanations almost always appear to overlook the role of approximately 2 million heavily armed men in blue. More recent and considerably more compelling scholarship has demonstrated convincingly that battlefield defeats most often caused the loss of will, not the other way around. Thus, historians such as McPherson and Gary Gallagher have reestablished the common-sense notion that although internal factors obviously played an important part in weakening the Confederacy, the North won the war on the battlefield.[5]

Books by those authors, and more recent studies by Aaron Sheehan-Dean and Jason Phillips, therefore have forced historians to grapple with the sometimes-sensitive subjects of Confederate dedication and sacrifice. This study makes no attempt to portray a homogenous South, totally united behind the Confederate war effort. Such unity simply never existed any more than it did in the North. Indeed, historians now frequently and appropriately distinguish between the South and the Confederacy. Just as the much-documented division within Confederate society affected the war effort, at the same time it seems obvious that the enormous sacrifices at home and on the battlefield in the war's major campaigns as late as the end of 1864 indicated substantial commitment on the part of thousands of Confederates. This study recognizes the existence of those sacrifices and a considerable determination on the part of the overwhelming majority of Confederates to achieve their independence. To acknowledge that simple point does not make scholars "neo-Confederates" or defenders of the would-be country that attempted to establish itself on a foundation of human slavery.[6]

Still, some historians have questioned whether these Confederates, despite their demonstrated continued devotion to their cause, shared a common national sense of identity and purpose, or nationalism. Some historians insist that Confederates never formed such a national identity or at least never developed an identity strong enough to win the war. The authors of *Why the South Lost the Civil War*, for example, considered the lack of adequate nationalism an internal weakness that contributed significantly to Confederate defeat, while Paul D. Escott argued that Confederates not only lost the will to sacrifice for the war effort but actually came to resent the Confederacy. Escott placed class tension at the heart of the supposed failure of nationalism. Lawrence N. Powell and Michael S. Wayne found a weak sense of nationalism founded upon common interests but not grounded in a firmly established common culture.[7]

Other scholarship has cast considerable doubt on the idea that a weakness of Confederate nationalism served as a major factor in Confederate defeat. Common themes that run through much of that scholarship include the notion that the wartime struggle for independence helped shape nationalism and that the Confederates saw themselves as the true heirs and defenders of the legacy of 1776. As McPherson has argued, the Confederates believed that the northerners were the ones who had changed. Therefore the Confederates drew from American nationalism and obviously would have had at least as much cultural identity as did their opponents. Drew Gilpin Faust also contended that the southerners claimed 1776 as their own. Faust found religion to be a principal support for nationalism and further found Confederate nationalism not only in the attempt to preserve the old way, but also in the struggle itself. Faust also pointed out the danger in measuring Confederate nationalism primarily by the failure of the rebellion. After all, if certain events had gone differently and the Confederacy had prevailed, would they then have had sufficient nationalism? Similar to Faust, Emory Thomas pointed to the struggle itself and concluded that the fight and sacrifice for independence eventually made the Confederacy an end in itself. In other words, the Civil War experience defined most white southerners as Confederates.[8]

Major obstacles to Confederate nationalism as seen by some historians— various internal divisions and especially class conflict—although they certainly existed, are easily exaggerated. In his excellent study of wartime Virginia, William Blair acknowledged such tensions and public resentment of impressment, high taxes, and conscription. But Blair also found that most citizens actually came to accept those measures as necessities and eventually even called for a strong, active central government. Blair convincingly contended that they received exactly that, a government that actually responded to the needs of the people. The relevance here is that the responsive Confederate government described by Blair not only tried but succeeded to a surprising degree in addressing the needs of its people, thus positively affecting morale in and out of the army. More important, as an extension of that argument, Blair skillfully demonstrated that the Confederate people could grow temporarily disillusioned with their government without wavering in their commitment to southern independence.[9]

Most Civil War historians now recognize at least the existence of Confederate nationalism, though they might disagree on its relative strength. The diaries and letters of western Confederates not only support the existence of a Confederate identity, but also reveal a considerable degree of cohesion or unity of purpose based primarily on the shared sacrifice by Confederates to protect their homes and ways of life from armed invaders. One historian has written that Confederates hating Yankees does not prove the existence of nationalism. Fair enough, but hundreds of thousands of white southerners hating Yankees, whom they perceived as invaders, and the shared sacrifices endured and thousands of lives lost and taken in the attempt to repel those invaders certainly helped form a Confederate identity, even across class lines. As the war dragged on and casualties mounted and invasions continued, Confederates' resentment of the North only increased, and many came to seek independence regardless of issues such as slavery and states' rights.[10]

Somehow, in the study of a war that grew out of the unparalleled hostility of the antebellum sectional conflict and the vitriolic politics of the 1850s and killed approximately 620,000 people, historians sometimes manage to underestimate the animosity Confederates harbored for their adversaries. Even the thousands of Confederates who entered the war without a firm grasp of the larger political issues at stake came to resent and even genuinely hate the people they viewed as armed trespassers literally threatening their homes and families.[11] Future discussions of Confederate nationalism and commitment must come to terms with such widespread enmity. At some point historians must ask which is more difficult to believe, that Confederates of all social classes who fought so hard for so long genuinely believed in what they were doing, or that they fought so hard for so long without substantial commitment to their cause.

The topics of nationalism, sacrifice, and dedication clearly relate directly to the subject of morale. Historians have offered various explanations for the status of Confederate morale throughout the war. Some historians have found a notable decline in morale as early as spring 1862 in response to both internal and external factors, such as the institution of the first military draft in American history, the suspension of habeas corpus, political divisions within the Confederacy, and western battlefield defeats. Traditionally, however, more historians have pointed to the famous summer of 1863 and Union victories at Gettysburg and Vicksburg as the critical point for the downturn of Confederate morale. After the most powerful Confederate army suffered defeat in Pennsylvania and the psychologically and strategically important Mississippi River bastion fell to Union forces, so that interpretation reads, increasing numbers of Confederates lost faith in the cause and gradually accepted the inevitability of defeat. As early as 1934, Charles Wesley offered a combination of those views, noting a gradual decline in popular enthusiasm beginning in 1861 but finding a major deterioration after Gettysburg and Vicksburg. Even in 1934, Wesley wondered how the Confederacy managed to survive as long as it did amid so many divisive forces and with such an apparent loss of spirit. All of those interpretations made a certain amount of sense. Clearly every one of those factors affected morale to some extent, yet the vast majority of Confederates continued to resist effectively for years.[12]

More recently, historians have found among Confederates considerable popular will and commitment remaining well into the war's final year. Most Civil War historians now recognize that, despite periodic highs and lows related to events on and off the battlefield, Confederate confidence remained relatively high as late as early 1864. Even the leading proponents of the idea that Confederates lacked the will to win their independence admit that morale had not yet declined to a critical stage by 1864. (To their credit they acknowledge the importance of military victory and defeat to the shaping of morale.) But what happened next? When and why did most Confederates really give up hope—after the fall of Atlanta and the reelection of Abraham Lincoln, as most historians appear to believe, after the Battles of Franklin and Nashville, or later? No consensus exists regarding Confederate morale in the final year and a half of the war. Therefore this study of morale from early 1864 until the war's end seeks to provide additional perspective on the failure of the Confederate experiment.[13]

Certain fundamental principles provide an important backdrop to the discussion throughout the narrative. First, there was nothing inevitable about Confederate defeat. Even well into the final year, the war might have turned out very differently. Second, modern readers of course know the results of the war and sometimes read every history of the conflict with the surrender at Appomattox in mind.[14] For example, every student of the Civil War knows the results of the Atlanta campaign, but when Confederates evinced high morale in the middle of that campaign, they obviously did so without certain knowledge of the city's impending capture. Everyone who reads about Hood invading Tennessee knows that he and his army marched toward complete disaster. The participants knew nothing of the sort. When they marched into Tennessee in late 1864, they did so at least in part because they thought they would score victories that could help them win their independence. That point lies at the heart of any discussion of why Confederates continued to persist—they did so more than anything else because they believed that they could win. Throughout most of the period in question, Confederate soldiers and civilians alike continued to persist, mutually reinforcing one another in the belief that they could secure their independence on the battlefield.

With those points in mind, this study evaluates morale throughout the period in question by following a primarily chronological approach that blends discussions of home front and battlefront and allows the reader to glimpse the story as it developed. In the formative stages of the project a thematic approach was consciously eschewed in favor of a chronological narrative. Although chapters that individually explore particular themes discussed throughout the narrative would doubtless appeal to some readers, history does not happen in themes.[15] The backbone of this study is the examination of the highs and lows of morale throughout the period, so only a chronological approach seemed appropriate.

Each chapter covers a two-month period, beginning with an assessment of morale as of January–February 1864, including a survey of civilian spirits around the western Confederacy, the beginnings of a rejuvenation of the Army of Tennessee after the disastrous winter of 1863–1864, and the effects of Federal major general William T. Sherman's Meridian campaign through Mississippi. Chapter 2 further analyzes the revitalization of the Army of Tennessee in Georgia during early 1864, explains how the soldiers in that army collectively were "reborn" as a cohesive unit, describes how that transformation affected the civilian population, and examines overall reviving morale around the West during the spring of 1864. The third chapter demonstrates the almost stunningly high morale in early summer 1864 and the importance of Major General Nathan Bedford Forrest and his cavalry to morale and analyzes the status of morale during the early stages of the Atlanta campaign. Chapters 4 and 5 complete the analysis of morale during the Atlanta campaign, and, taken together with chapter 3, challenge some long-held assumptions with regard to Confederate soldier morale during the campaign. In the process, the study adds a new dimension to the generations-old debates surrounding the Joseph E. Johnston versus John Bell Hood controversy. Although the book offers no answer to the question of who was the better general, the soldiers' perspectives are made crystal clear. The remaining chapters reexamine the effects of Lincoln's reelection on western Confederate morale, investigate Hood's Tennessee campaign and its relationship to morale, and conclude with assessments of reactions to peace negotiations and the talk of arming black troops to fight for the Confederacy in early 1865.

In the end, this book provides a corrective to the notions that Confederate morale steadily declined after 1863 and that Confederate morale had reached a critical low after the reelection of Abraham Lincoln in 1864. It answers that lingering question of when and why certain Confederates gave up hope—in this case the crippling failures at Franklin and Nashville. The study details the morale of a group of western Confederate soldiers and civilians during and after Franklin and Nashville and in that way adds to our understanding of those too-often overlooked battles. Perhaps, in its own small way, this book will help to increase the attention historians pay to that crucial campaign. Ultimately, the importance of Franklin and Nashville to crushing western Confederate hopes for southern independence lends further credence to the notion that battlefield results shaped morale more than did any other factor.

The story begins on New Year's Day 1864, during the coldest winter most could remember. Western Confederates had only recently witnessed the embarrassing loss of Chattanooga, Tennessee, and a new commander had recently taken over the largest Confederate army in the West, the Army of Tennessee, camped in northern Georgia. Civilians and soldiers alike found themselves with mixed feelings that winter. At once they hoped for ultimate success in the spring and despaired for what one Alabama poet called "the anguish-stricken land."[16]

1

January–February 1864

HOPE AND DESPAIR

FROM HIS MADISON COUNTY home in western Tennessee, civilian diarist Robert H. Cartmell expressed sentiments common around the Confederate heartland on New Year's Day, 1864. He wrote, "If God be with us, numbers in the end will avail nothing, if God be against us, our destruction is certain. May it be decided quickly." Cartmell understood the odds facing those who still longed for southern independence, but he believed that God would have more than a little say in the war's outcome. Equally important, his diary entry of ten days later revealed that, despite the odds, he believed that his side still stood a legitimate chance and admitted that the conflict would not likely be decided quickly. He predicted, "I look for no peace this spring. I do not think the North is or will be willing soon to agree to separation and I do not think the South is willing for reconstruction." The Civil War was not nearly over in early 1864, and people like Robert Cartmell knew it.[1]

Eighteen-year-old Myra Inman knew it, too. Like so many around the western Confederacy, she found herself with mixed feelings that winter. Surrounded by Yankees in her Union-occupied East Tennessee hometown of Cleveland, she wondered if she was living in the darkest days of the Confederacy. She found cheer in even the smallest of skirmish victories by Confederate forces in East Tennessee under Lieutenant General James Longstreet. After writing that only God could protect them, she wondered if perhaps they could expect better days soon. Despite her conflicted feelings about the state of affairs, her loyalties to the Confederacy clearly had not wavered as she longed for the removal of the "sad emblem" of the U.S. flag that flew over Cleveland and hoped once again to see the "Stars and Bars" wave over her "once happy country." In mid-February, days after arguing with a Union soldier about the merits of slavery and only days before finding herself depressed about the death of one her own slaves, she found pleasure in an opportunity to talk to other Confederates. Such emotional swings were not uncommon for Confederate women during the war. Horrid visions of loved ones dying in battle one minute were often followed by dreams of joyous reunions the next. Thoughts of victory and independence and maintaining the old customs and standard of living alternated with depressing visions of defeat and the changes that it would inevitably bring. The fact that most were essentially powerless to affect the war's outcome only made matters more difficult. In this way, Myra Inman was probably typical of Confederate women, particularly those who lived in such close proximity to Federal troops.[2]

Thousands of Inman's fellow civilians lived under the watchful eye of Union occupation forces. Of course, each reacted in his or her own way, though Confederate morale in occupied areas held up reasonably well considering the frequent absence of supports such as pro-Confederate newspapers and churches customary in other areas. Federal military authorities certainly encountered more difficulty than expected in their endeavor to break the will of Tennessee Confederates. The allegiance of the majority of the white residents to what they considered their new country proved profound and firmly entrenched. Studies of Civil War Tennessee have shown that by early 1864 civilian morale in occupied areas of that state endured, sustained especially by the proximity of Confederate troops and news of military events elsewhere. In the capital city of Nashville, already in Federal hands for two years by February 1864, the majority of residents remained staunchly pro-Confederate and saw no reason to give up hope. In fact, the success of Confederate guerrilla raiders in Middle Tennessee near such a large Union base of operations only encouraged them further.[3]

One would be hard-pressed to find a more headstrong Yankee-hater living in an occupied area (or anywhere else) than the attractive young Ellen House of Knoxville, Tennessee, who wished for Longstreet's men to storm and recapture her city, which she insisted could be done easily. When a pontoon bridge gave way and dumped twenty-five Federal soldiers into the river, she considered it a "pity they were not drowned." She proudly denounced prominent Tennessee unionist William G. "Parson" Brownlow as "the vilest thing ever." During the bitterly cold days of early January 1864, House chafed at the conditions endured by Confederate prisoners of war held in Knoxville, but fumed that those who deserted did not deserve shoes anyway. While her family urged her physically ill brother to take the oath of allegiance to the United States to avoid being taken as a prisoner of war, she angrily retorted that he should have been in the army long ago. House was already "mad as a hornet" that her father had taken the oath just to make things easier on the family. It did not matter to her that to many in Knoxville the oath meant nothing. She found it "humiliating." "It mortified me to death." Intense anger and hatred, of course, do not necessarily reflect high morale, but in the case of Ellen House, as of January 1864 her spirit remained strong and her commitment to the Confederate cause continued unabated.[4]

By February, twenty-year-old Ellen's attitude had not softened, and her confidence in ultimate southern victory had not diminished. When she heard a rumor that Abraham Lincoln had called for one hundred thousand men to take Richmond, she coolly insisted that he would need more and that Jefferson Davis would not let him have the city. After one of her visits to the Confederate prisoners in town, House decided that it would be wise to treat the Yankees at the prison kindly, but never to let them think she was "anything less than a rebel heart and soul." As February faded, House wrote that she hated Yankees intensely, would kill one without hesitation, and insisted that it made her happy when she saw one "with one arm or leg." Despite some historians' claims that Confederates lacked sufficient nationalism to win the war, Ellen House, like thousands of others, certainly demonstrated considerable commitment to the Confederate nation and displayed an unquenchable thirst for southern independence.[5] Nationalism requires not simply patriotism, even extreme patriotism, but also evidence of unifying and defining characteristics among a population. House's desire for independence, coupled with a genuine and increasingly intense hatred for northerners and her view of them as invaders, helped shape her view of herself, the war, and, in her mind, her nation.

Tennessee civilians like Ellen House and Myra Inman who dreamed of independence for their country looked primarily to Confederate armies for their deliverance. Civilians continually looked to good news from the battlefield and an unflagging spirit of determination from their sons, husbands, sweethearts, and brothers in the ranks. They looked to western forces, particularly the Army of Tennessee, at least as much as they looked to Robert E. Lee's more famous Army of Northern Virginia. In part this was because they believed so strongly in Lee's ability that they practically assumed he and his army would prevail in the eastern theater. In addition, western Confederates followed the progress of the Army of Tennessee so closely because that army literally defended their homes. The Army of Tennessee was "their" army. The successes and failures of that army most directly affected the lives of average western Confederates.

Soldiers in Tennessee were not immune to the same feelings of hope and fear expressed by the noncombatants. In fact, such sentiments filled the diaries and letters of men in the only remaining organized Confederate force in the state at the time, Longstreet's command, quartered in the vicinity of Morristown in East Tennessee. "I greet the incoming year with mingled feelings of hope and fear, hope predominating. I have fears lest some mismanagement on the part of those in power may prolong the war beyond the limits of this year and thereby entail more misery upon women and children. While there is life I have hope. I must hope, do hope—I will continue to hope as long as we have an organized army in the field. My honest belief & faith is staked in the triumph of southern arms. 'Pluck will win'—whether in love or arms & Southern Soldiers as a general thing are pluckey but above all I have an abiding faith in the Justness of our cause & consequently in the help of [God]. . . . With such feelings I enter upon the duties & hardships of the Year." So wrote William W. Stringfield, a Confederate soldier camped in East Tennessee, on January 1, 1864. Stringfield's comments, with his amalgamation of cautious optimism and a hint of desperation, proved characteristic of others in the area. From nearby Russellville, for example, another enlisted man reported feeling melancholy about what they faced in the coming year, but he added that the boys were "generally in good spirits."[6]

Soldiers in Longstreet's command that winter endured inconsistent rations and a lack of adequate shoes and clothing—clearly factors that would affect the morale of any man. Writing to his cousin Mary, one soldier who had recently left the area intimated, "Our army suffered more for shoes than anything else and it was a sight that would soften the most callous heart to have seen our brave soldiers marching over the frozen and snow clad ground without any shoes whatever." Rather than bear such conditions, particularly after two and a half years of general war weariness, some deserted their posts. What was worse than desertion to those Confederates who remained committed to the cause and stayed at their stations of duty, some deserters even fled to nearby Union occupation forces and took an oath of allegiance to the United States. One such soldier, who had defected to the enemy only to be recaptured, was executed on February 6 and found little sympathy among his former comrades who witnessed his death. Texan Frank Batchelor lamented that anyone in Tennessee would abandon the cause and noted that future historians would "pause and drop a tear on the page . . . that in our hour of need many deserted and assisted the enemy to forge the chains intended to bind us."[7]

To be sure, most Confederate soldiers in that small stretch of Tennessee did not desert in early 1864. They made the best of camp life, longed for loved ones at home, remained dedicated to their cause, and hoped for the best. Captain Joab Goodson noted that, considering the conditions, including the number of barefoot men, the boys managed "remarkably well." After reading some personal letters captured from a Federal wagon train, James Wilkes and those around him found solace in the knowledge that they were at least as comfortable as their Federal counterparts. Even a soldier who seemingly had given up hope for victory, proclaiming, "We will be subjugated yet sure as abc," acknowledged the high morale of the other men around him. Still another comrade, who was anything but a model soldier and who desperately sought to avoid returning to the front, reported the good health and spirits of his company, too. Longstreet's aide, Major Thomas J. Goree, wrote his mother on February 8 that, despite the despondency of some, he remained confident and predicted a trying but victorious campaign that spring.[8]

Clearly the men of Longstreet's East Tennessee command were weary but not defeated, and as the coming of spring thawed the ground on which many of them slept, their spirits gradually rose to meet the coming campaign season. In late February, one soldier assured his mother that supplies and rations were increasing and that tents captured from the enemy provided adequate shelter. He noted the troops' enthusiasm as the band struck up the right tunes and reported that, despite suffering through several bloody campaigns, the men of his regiment reenlisted for the duration of the war without the promise of any reward, bounty, or even a much-desired furlough. "So you see the spirit and determination the Yankees will have to conquer in the ensuing spring before they can wield their scepter with full sway in the land of liberty and freemen."[9]

Across the border in Alabama, attitudes varied as much as those in Tennessee. North Alabama hosted a pocket of unionist sentiment that drew the attention of Confederate military authorities, who that spring sent part of General Leonidas Polk's Army of Mississippi into the area to hunt deserters and restore order. The state's northern counties in the Hill Country and the Tennessee River Valley provided shelter for Confederate deserters and others who resisted Confederate authority. Some of those individuals were genuine unionists who had never supported the rebellion. Others simply took advantage of the situation to avoid civil authorities or military service on either side. Even among those counties, however, many people supported the Confederacy throughout the war. One study of Lawrence County, a southern community with as much unionist sentiment as almost any, indicated that the residents with Confederate sympathies there held on until late 1864. Although years of war weariness certainly increased the numbers of unionists and others who did not support the Confederacy in the state and ultimately contributed to significant unionist sentiment in the northern counties, "unconditional unionists" remained a marginal segment of the state's population. In fact, one study of Alabama unionism described Union supporters in the state as "a tiny minority marooned in enemy territory, loathed as traitors best expelled or killed." Clearly individuals need not have been unconditional unionists to oppose the Confederacy, but the point remains that the vast majority of Alabamans considered themselves Confederates and supporters of the war effort.[10]

Uncertainty as to the war's outcome marked the diaries of even the most loyal western Confederates, like northeast Alabama resident Sarah Espy, a onetime seamstress and farmer's widow who had four sons in the war. When her fourth left to begin his service, she insisted, "No one can do more for the Confederacy than I have," and few would likely argue. Espy's situation offers an excellent example of the connection between home front and battlefield, and not just because of her sons' military service. Living so near occupied Tennessee and the threatened area of northern Georgia, Espy worried that enemy soldiers would soon overrun her home but hoped that God would "turn them back to their own country to live in peace." Margaret Gillis of south central Alabama was another woman who had grown tired of war. She found it increasingly difficult to see her circuit-riding preacher husband come and go in such times and wondered if their most recent day together would be their last. Gillis, undoubtedly like many other people North and South, looked forward from one month to the next for some major event that might end the war.[11]

In late December 1863 similar weariness and uncertainty manifested themselves in a planned mutiny by a small group of disaffected soldiers at Camp Pollard, the site of an important railroad junction between Montgomery and Mobile. Their attitudes, however, clearly did not reflect the prevailing sentiments among soldiers in the state, or even in their own command. Officers who investigated the would-be revolt determined that the approximately sixty soldiers involved were from poor rural Alabama families, had seen little or no battlefield action, apparently were conscripted or joined the service to avoid the taint of conscription, and began their military service later than did most of their comrades. One report, however, judged them good men who worried about their loved ones in their absence and their families' ability to subsist amid government impressment and tax-in-kind requirements. A soldier who witnessed the scene deemed it a "shameful affair" and assured his wife that "I will not turn Yankee." The potential mutiny at Camp Pollard and the unionist sentiment in North Alabama clearly illustrate that not everyone actively supported the Confederacy or even demonstrated high morale by early 1864. These, however, were exceptions. Most soldiers and civilians in Alabama examined for this study did support the Confederacy and continued to hope for victory and independence.[12]

Mobile resident and famous novelist Augusta Jane Evans remained ardently committed to the independence of the Confederacy and criticized those whom she believed had lost sight of the original cause, which to her mind included independence and a decentralized, state-centered form of government. In her mind, too many people had become willing to consider conditions such as gradual emancipation or to accept the centralization of power around military authorities in order to gain southern independence. She fumed, "The original *casus belli* has been lost sight of; hatred of Lincoln, not love of our liberties, principles and institutions now actuates the masses." In the eyes of Evans, the people remained committed to southern independence, but perhaps they had lost sight of why they had wanted it to begin with.[13]

Optimistic spirits toward the Confederacy's prospects certainly prevailed among individuals living in central and southern Alabama by early 1864, doubtless in part because those areas had not yet been ravaged by warfare. In Montgomery at least the impression of antebellum routine remained into early 1864, and a soldier camped outside the state's capital wrote to his wife, "We are living very hard though we fare about as well as the soldiers generally fare at this stage of the war." Life in novelist Evans's hometown of Mobile, likely more so than anywhere in the Confederacy, remained remarkably close to its prewar standards. Obviously the Gulf Coast city was not unaffected, particularly economically, but parties and social functions such as theater performances and dances continued uninterrupted, and a lighter mood clearly pervades the pages of that city's diarists and letter writers, military and civilian. Confederate nurse Kate Cumming commented on the continued gaiety there and explained that the standard excuse provided was "that there are so many soldiers there away from their homes, and the ladies say they must do what they can to entertain them. Quite a plausible reason!"[14]

In fact, by 1864 Mobile had become a choice assignment for Confederate soldiers. Despite the presence of the Federal fleet outside Mobile Bay, many soldiers and civilians alike considered it the safest city in the Confederacy. Thus an assignment there allowed the loyal soldier the opportunity to perform his duty to his country yet increase his standard of living and his chances for survival. One soldier stationed in Georgia found it difficult to get a recruit, which would earn him a furlough, because, he told his brother, all of the recruits wanted to go to Mobile. After requesting and receiving a transfer to Mobile, native Alabaman Lieutenant Robert Tarleton wrote to his wife from one of the forts defending the bay, assuring her that for all its big guns, the Federal fleet could not capture the city without the reinforcement of a land army. Robert Patrick, who worked as an army clerk, was thrilled to learn that he was being reassigned to Mobile. He confided to his diary that only news of peace could be better. Still another Mobile defender reassured his wife, who was staying nearby, that she should not fear the Federals' big guns, which he confidently insisted could do very little damage from so far away. Doubtless buoyed by the perceived safety of his post, despite suffering a recent illness, he told her that he was never too sick to fight the Yankees and wished that they would only come in a little closer. "I like the fun finely so far."[15]

Another result of the lack of military action and the absence of Union occupation forces in these areas was the continued publication of newspapers loyal to the Confederate cause. Throughout January and February the editors of the *Mobile Daily Advertiser and Register* printed pieces clearly designed to prop up morale. Optimism for the spring military campaigning season emerged as the dominant theme. Much of what the editors printed was true or at least plausible and, this early in 1864 anyway, proved consistent with and representative of the most positive sentiments expressed by individuals around the western Confederacy. The writers pointed to expiring enlistments of thousands of Union soldiers; the enemy's declining interest in prosecuting the war; the North's lack of a strong enough motive to continue the fight; the rising spirits and reenlistments of soldiers in the Confederate Army of Tennessee stationed in northern Georgia; the appointment of Joseph E. Johnston to command that army; and looking ahead to the fall, the probability of Lincoln's defeat in the northern presidential election of 1864. The time to concentrate forces, strike the Yankees, and cripple their war effort would be soon. After all, reasoned the editors, "The Confederacy was in greater danger when [Union general George B.] McClellan stood at the gates of Richmond with 150,000 men; and yet victory followed. . . ." Overall, the sentiments of Confederates around Alabama in the early months of 1864 proved as mixed as those in Tennessee, but a more optimistic sentiment held sway over much of the state.[16]

Meanwhile, Belle Edmondson, a West Tennessee refugee in northern Mississippi who advanced the war effort by smuggling goods through the Union lines around Memphis, evinced an even stronger faith in her nation's prospects. She expected the Confederates to encounter "no trouble out generaling the Yankees" in 1864. Like so many other Confederates, she wrote of God and country, noting that after God, she lived for what she identified as her country—Dixie. She reflected on what the soldiers suffered for people like her and frequently prayed for peace and southern independence. Though she almost certainly never contemplated a definition of nationalism that would satisfy the modern historian, Belle Edmondson nevertheless considered the Confederate States of America her country. She also would have protested any interpretation that blamed Confederate defeat on her loss of spirit. One can only imagine what young, fiery East Tennesseean Ellen House would have said to such a suggestion![17]

Historians have argued that by 1864 Confederate women had begun to think about themselves more than ever before and had become less willing to sacrifice for the war effort. For Edmondson and most of the other women in this study, that simply was not true by early or even mid-1864. Even if one finds the arguments with regard to a loss of commitment among women convincing, at least with regard to women in the Confederate heartland, the time line must be pushed later, certainly beyond mid-1864. Besides, why 1864? If so many women essentially gave up and decided that they had sacrificed enough, to the point that they weakened the Confederate war effort by calling their men home, would that not have occurred earlier? The loss of Chattanooga was important but hardly catastrophic, and nothing dramatic had befallen the western Confederacy in recent months to increase these women's burden significantly. Undoubtedly some women, like some men, gave up hope well before April 1865. More important, however, most in this study did not, and certainly not enough to undermine the Confederate war effort significantly by 1864. Ultimately, like many other women around the Confederacy as of early 1864, Belle Edmondson remained committed to the fight to establish her country's independence.[18]

Elsewhere in Mississippi, a soldier en route to join the Army of Tennessee in northern Georgia assured his wife of his continued health and the good health of his comrades. He did admit, though, that "[w]e have Suffered great with Barefootedness & nakedness I am now Sanscolitis that is with out breeches." Farther south, in the vicinity of occupied Vicksburg, another Mississippi woman railed against Federal forces. Emilie Riley McKinley, a young teacher and an ardent Confederate of northern birth, lamented the desolation of the landscape and saw no prospect of the war ending soon. She thought that no southern man could read the recent address to the people "so ably written" by Confederate president Jefferson Davis and not want to do his part to free their oppressed people living under the "iron heel of despotism." A recent message by Abraham Lincoln, on the other hand, she deemed "ridiculous." Not surprisingly, upon learning of a northern soldier's reported marriage to a black woman, she fumed sarcastically, "What a beautiful state of society we are living in." Her commitment to the cause clearly had not wavered when she met a soldier who, rather than transfer to the infantry, had deserted from the cavalry when his horse died. She told him he should have stolen a mount, because even horse theft was better than desertion.[19]

A circuit judge wrote repeatedly to Davis and Mississippi state officials throughout 1864, informing them of the deplorable conditions and degraded spirits of people in central Mississippi. His letters painted a much gloomier picture than those of other Confederates at the time. Unlike other correspondents, the judge pointed to the depressing effects of impressment and the tax-in-kind requirements on morale, but even he attributed more importance to military defeats than any other factor. A soldier in the same area also encountered much despondency there but found reasons for hope, particularly the "rectitude of our intentions and the justness of our cause. Chattanooga has fallen. Charleston is besieged. But Richmond is still safe." Another combatant in central Mississippi, near Canton, hoped that he would not soon have to face an attack by his adversaries, but maintained that he stood ready if needed to carry out his duty and answer his "country's call." That appeal would come sooner than he expected. Most of the Confederate soldiers in Mississippi spent January resting, but February brought a new challenge in the form of Union major general William Tecumseh Sherman's Meridian campaign.[20]

For essentially the month of February 1864, Sherman and approximately twenty-five thousand Federal soldiers marched across Mississippi and back, from Vicksburg on the western border to Meridian near the Alabama state line, in what amounted to a preview of his more famous March to the Sea through Georgia in late 1864. The plan called for Sherman to be supported by seven thousand Federal cavalry moving south from Memphis led by Brigadier General William Sooy Smith. Already by early 1864 Sherman understood the connection between battlefield and home front and issued an order declaring his right to make war on the Confederate people as well as their armies. He announced his right "to take their lives, their horses, their lands, their everything." On the surface, Sherman's purpose was to destroy the railroad system of Mississippi, particularly the important hub at Meridian that connected it to Mobile and Selma, in order to prevent any concentration of military forces there should General Ulysses S. Grant opt to withdraw a significant number of the Federals who occupied the western portion of the state. The Confederates, after all, maintained control of most of central Mississippi outside of the Vicksburg area. Obviously, railroads were only part of the story. Sherman clearly sought to break the resolve and perhaps the ability of the people to resist. This, he believed, had become the only way to end the war. One student of the campaign in fact deemed it more destructive than Sherman's March to the Sea, while another historian described the Meridian campaign as "an experiment in terror."[21]

Confederate defenders under Lieutenant General Leonidas Polk barely slowed down Sherman's Mississippi march and scattered into northern portions of the state and into Alabama. One soldier pointed to Sherman's numbers and admitted that he and his comrades "had to skedaddle or do worse." The Federals destroyed or took whatever they chose along the route and spent five days wrecking Meridian. The column led by Smith from Memphis, however, never joined in the plunder, having suffered defeat at the hands of Major General Nathan Bedford Forrest's cavalry at Okolona, Mississippi. Forrest's victory and (oddly enough) Sherman's entire campaign in the bigger picture actually improved Confederate morale in the West in areas other than those directly in his path of destruction.[22]

In the northern Mississippi phase of the campaign, Forrest allowed Smith's force to advance slowly into the state from Memphis while seeking an opportunity to strike his more numerous foes. He found his opportunity at the northeast Mississippi town of Okolona. There Forrest's twenty-five hundred routed Smith's seven thousand and quite literally chased them back toward Memphis. Besides derailing part of Sherman's Meridian campaign and temporarily protecting the fertile farmlands of central Mississippi, this victory achieved little in the war's larger strategic picture. The importance for morale in the western Confederacy, however, proved significant. The sight of Smith's frazzled force straggling into Memphis after four days of frantic retreat thrilled those of Confederate sympathies in western Tennessee. Belle Edmondson called it "glorious news," a term she always seemed to reserve for military victories, and cheerfully wrote that the "Yanks are perfectly demoralized. . . . Praise God for this victory." Another Mississippi woman, twenty-year-old Eliza Lucy Irion, coolly wrote that "thanks to Gen. Forrest (under Providence) the Yankees were driven back . . . we once again were delivered from them. The people once more collected their wits & settled down to everyday life." One southern newspaper issued a plea for the people of Mississippi to get behind Forrest and allow him single-handedly to lead them to victory. The success became the talk of the region, raised spirits, and cast the results of the overall campaign in a more positive light. As later months would show, moreover, the legend of Forrest in the Confederate mind would only grow greater.[23]

Meanwhile, farther south, those directly in the corridor of Sherman's march across Mississippi suffered serious loss and their morale dipped accordingly. The campaign disrupted the planting of crops and deprived some planters of slave labor.[24] In the larger picture, however, these developments proved temporary. The Confederates had evacuated great quantities of important supplies and equipment from Meridian before the Federals' arrival, and by April the Rebels were able to repair the damage done to the railroads. More significant, Sherman did not do enough damage to reduce the effectiveness of Confederate forces in Mississippi. Had he accomplished that, he would have more quickly freed his own forces to move east and assist with the impending major campaign in northern Georgia. Most residents North and South presumed that Sherman had more ambitious plans, in particular a thrust toward Mobile or at least Montgomery. Therefore, when he turned back at Meridian, many disgusted northern observers judged the campaign as a failure or at best a waste of time and resources.[25]

Observers with Confederate loyalties, at least those outside the principal path of destruction, came to view the entire episode as a successful repulse of a Federal invasion. Anne Shannon Martin, a Mississippi refugee living in Eufaula, Alabama, wrote, "We are delighted to know that the Yankees are across Big Black [River], and more, and feel particularly glad that it is Sherman who is defeated." Upon learning of the results, a resident of northern Mississippi, much as General Joseph E. Johnston had speculated at the beginning, decided that the entire campaign had been only a feint to draw troops away from Johnston's Army of Tennessee. Moving beyond optimism and approaching the absurd, the editors of a major newspaper declared that Forrest's victory over Smith had saved Sherman by causing him to retreat to Vicksburg. Had the Federals stayed in Meridian only a few more days, so the argument went, Polk's army would have destroyed Sherman's entire force. An officer under Polk's command apparently would have agreed, having written to his wife that the northern army was "baffled and whipped, almost without a battle," and that it marked the close of "one of the most brilliant efforts of the war on the part of a Confederate Genl and his brave little army." That officer obviously grossly overstated his army's accomplishments, but Polk himself proved as immodest, informing his wife that after having been surrounded by the enemy on all sides, "in the name of the Lord I have destroyed them."[26]

Polk's statement was simply ridiculous, but, regardless of the circumstances, what Confederates knew was that the invaders had stopped their march at Meridian and returned to Vicksburg, doing considerably less damage than they might have. More important, they never seriously threatened Mobile (though Sherman never intended to do so) or anything else of foremost strategic importance besides the easily repaired railroads. Morale actually improved around the western Confederacy in the weeks following the Meridian campaign, particularly in light of Forrest's legitimate victory in northern Mississippi and the growing optimism in and about the Army of Tennessee by the coming of spring.

The year did not begin with such optimism for most men in the Army of Tennessee. Fresh off their loss of Chattanooga and the embarrassing defeat at Missionary Ridge on November 25, 1863, the soldiers of the western Confederacy's principal fighting force staggered into winter quarters in and around Dalton in northern Georgia. Here, too, mixed feelings of hope and despair predominated. During that harsh and discouraging winter many soldiers, such as Private Thomas Warrick of the 34th Alabama Infantry, thought primarily of receiving a short furlough so that they could visit wives and families. Letters such as the one Warrick received from his wife, Martha, that described the family's plight without him did nothing to boost his spirits. She recognized his duty and that he would come home as soon as he could, but reminded him that "[Y]ou sae in your letter for mie to kiss the children for you I kiss them for you ever day and I hope tha you will get to com hom to Kiss them you self soune fir it dousnt doue me enny good to kiss them for you and you So far from them."[27]

Despite depleted morale and poor living conditions, soldiers knew that they would have to recover and fight again, and submission was obviously not yet an option for most. Officer Daniel Hundley judged New Year's Day 1864 the "darkest hour of the Confederacy," but continued to expect victory because "there is in the heavens above us a Ruler & Lawgiver, who will yet see the Right cause made triumphant & who will laugh to scorn the boastful power of those who put their confidence in 'the biggest guns & the greatest numbers.'" Enlisted man Isaiah Harlan of the 10th Texas Infantry wished for rest until spring and for the two sides to find a way to end the war, but informed his mother in January, "The feds seem more determined if possible than ever to subjugate us and I do not think that the south can submit to the degradation of yankey rule without one more effort at least which God grant may be a success." Similarly, Flavel C. Barber, a soldier from the 3rd Tennessee Infantry, closed his 1863 diary by summing up the military situation around the country and concluding, "All we can do is fight on and hope and pray for better times next year. Submission has been made impossible by the conduct of our insolent foe; and the only tolerable alternative left us is resistance to the bitter end. We must fight, we can do nothing else, if necessary forever."[28]

Before the army could return to the field of battle, much had to be done. It had suffered approximately seven thousand casualties in the Chattanooga campaign and lost at least one-third of its artillery and an unknown quantity of wagons, caissons, and other supplies on the retreat into Georgia. Many soldiers lacked shoes and adequate weapons, while rations were scant, inconsistent, and often inedible. Organization and discipline were all but non-existent, and predictably, morale plummeted. Living amid these conditions and aware that more fighting would come, one Alabama soldier agonized that he might sacrifice his life "and yet not save his home." Frequent desertions combined with the poor conditions and uncertainty to cast a gloom over much of the army. Even ever-optimistic Tennessean Flavel Barber, a thirty-year-old teacher before the war began, admitted as much. Conditions notwithstanding, he judged the spirits of his comrades too low, all things considered, and deemed it his duty as a true Confederate patriot to "cultivate a hopeful spirit" because "confidence and hope alone will add much to the strength of an army."[29]

The most important event that contributed to the army's recovery occurred even as these soldiers expressed their concerns in diaries and in letters to loved ones. On December 27, 1863, Joseph E. Johnston replaced the embattled Braxton Bragg as the Army of Tennessee's commanding officer. (William J. Hardee directed the army during the month between Bragg's resignation and the appointment of Johnston.) Sources indicate that the vast majority of soldiers greeted the news of Johnston's appointment with overwhelming approval. Although it is possible that any change of commanders at that point would have been generally well received, the appointment of Johnston specifically clearly cheered the troops. All knew of his reputation as an officer who cared for his men and considered their well being his highest priority. A Tennessee soldier noted the emotional response of the men and insisted that the general was "almost worshipped by the troops."[30]

Johnston's appointment almost immediately began the improvement of morale, one of his army's many deficiencies that winter, but his actions during the coming weeks laid the foundation for the rebuilt Army of Tennessee that would defend Atlanta that summer in one of the war's most important campaigns. Upon taking command, the army's new leader improved and increased rations (which required an overhaul of the supply system), procured new shoes and tents for the men, and offered much-sought-after furloughs to those in camp and amnesty to individuals who were absent without leave if they would return to their commands. (Later, deserters would receive harsh punishment, including death in some cases.) The issuing of whiskey and tobacco twice weekly proved especially popular among the troops, as did a reorganization of parts of the army, including reuniting some units with their original officers. Johnston recognized that these steps represented only the beginning of the restoration of the army's morale and fighting spirit. In early January he issued General Orders No. 5 in order to establish discipline among the troops. The order instituted a daily routine for the army, including regular inspections, roll calls, and three hours of drill.[31]

The soldiers responded to these changes positively and understood their value to refitting the army for battle. Edward Norphlet Brown, quartermaster of the 45th Alabama Infantry, wrote to his "Darling Fannie" that if the general's new orders were strictly enforced it would improve the army and have it ready for the spring campaign. Brown was not as immediately enthused about Johnston as most of his comrades were, but warmed to him by February. The quartermaster considered rations the most significant problem to the army's morale. If the ration question was not corrected, he believed, the army was "on the eave of ruin." To emphasize his point, he noted that even the rugged and respected men of Major General Patrick Cleburne's command were demoralized about the lack of proper food. By early February, however, Brown considered the ration problem corrected and deemed the troops in better spirits than he had seen in six months. Isaiah Harlan would have agreed entirely, noting a shortage of food and shoes in mid-January, but describing Johnston as "decidedly a great man. He looks great. I think he is the finest looking man I ever saw. . . . I think that the command of this army could not have fallen into abler hands." The reception of Johnston and the soldiers' responses to his swift actions to stabilize and upgrade the army clearly indicated an improvement in morale, but the actions of the men beginning in late January spoke at least as loudly as their words.[32]

The reenlistment of thousands of soldiers, including those nearing the end of their three-year terms of service, reflects on the improving morale in the army and on Johnston's administrative accomplishments. Certainly some men took the step, at least in part, because extra furloughs were granted to units that reenlisted. This explanation is of limited value, however, at least among those whose enlistments were soon to expire, because even the most homesick soldier was not likely to volunteer for potentially years of additional duty if he was homeward bound in a matter of weeks anyway. Others reenlisted because they saw it as the honorable thing to do, regardless of their feelings about the war or the Confederacy. For example, one soldier noted that a comrade signed on for more service, out of respect for his wife and children, to avoid the prospective embarrassment of conscription later.[33]

The mass reenlistments began before the Confederate Congress passed a revised Conscription Act on February 17, 1864, that obligated most males between the ages of seventeen and fifty to some type of military service. In fact, most diarists and correspondents examined here had little to say regarding the new conscription legislation and certainly exhibited no resentment toward their government or the planter class, despite the commonplace interpretation that conscription caused a plunge in morale among the soldiers and public. As demonstrated by a number of historians, the first Conscription Act, passed in 1862, undeniably hurt morale around the Confederacy, including within the Army of Tennessee. The sudden involuntary extension of enlistments and the addition of men who had evaded service for more than a year and clearly wanted no part of the army disheartened many of the already-veteran soldiers.[34]

But it is difficult to argue that the revised Conscription Act in early 1864 generated the same public outcry and negative consequences for morale as the original, unprecedented 1862 legislation. Many people still did not embrace conscription, but they reconciled themselves to the situation. Even a historian who deemed conscription "contrary to the spirit of the people" admitted that the public gradually if reluctantly came to accept the practice as a necessity of war. Moreover, by 1864 most of the soldiers examined here, and some of their family members, clearly supported the law. After all, by then they had given long and hard service to the war effort and they could use the help, regardless of who provided it. Understandably, one soldier's wife even welcomed reports of the new act because she believed it time for those who had avoided service to do their part, like her husband had. Ultimately, those who reenlisted in early 1864 for reasons other than a renewed commitment were a minority, and the undeniable fact remains that thousands reenlisted and the army's spirits continued to rise accordingly.[35]

Among those scrutinized in this study, most of the men who reenlisted did so because they had begun to find a restored faith in themselves, their comrades, and their cause. They were again beginning to believe that they could win the war. Mississippian Sam Settle wrote home about the reenlistments, including his own, predicted that more men would follow suit, and noted the rising confidence throughout the army. The twenty-eight-year-old son of a farmer admitted that some men were ready to give up, but "the majority are in favor of continuing the war for a while longer yet." Alabama quartermaster Brown believed that favoritism factored into who received the precious furloughs, but he assured his wife that "nevertheless I am in for the war be it long or short." Brown reenlisted thirteen months before his term of service expired because he believed that the country needed signs of encouragement. The press would print news of the reenlistments, he contended, and that would inspire the people, while at the same time showing the Yankees that the fighting was long from over. Thus, the reenlistments were both a result of improving morale and a factor in improving it.[36]

Clearly, the changes made by Johnston improved overall morale in the Army of Tennessee during January and February 1864. Each man experienced the changing sentiments in his own way and in his own time, but during these months soldiers routinely described the rising spirits, confidence, and general happiness of the men in their units. One soldier noted, "The boys in camp seem to have become more lively than usual during the past few weeks and many who were very much discouraged by the affair at Missionary Ridge now seem to be confident." A homesick young Arkansas soldier who desperately wished to fight in his home state wrote his parents regarding the impending clash of arms in Georgia: "I have no fears as to the result if the troops will only do their duty." By the end of February, he found the army "in fine health and the best of spirits." By late February Daniel Hundley noted the improving spirits of his men and found them in "splendid feathers."[37]

Letters and diaries took on a more confident, occasionally even defiant, tone as spring neared. Isaiah Harlan, who considered Johnston such a great man, insisted, "[I]f we all equit ourselves like men . . . I think, I hope at least, that we will be able to hurl back the yankey hordes . . . and inflict upon them such a punishment as will suffice them for all time to come." Another soldier used similar language, noting, "What a proud day it will be . . . when the foe is hurled back from our borders. . . ." An Army of Tennessee soldier on leave in Mississippi confidently predicted that the Federals would encounter great difficulty if they moved toward Atlanta from Chattanooga. He considered the size of the Union forces that would be used to invade Georgia and the problems of feeding, clothing, and supplying such a force in that part of the country. Upon reflection, and accurately predicting at least the circumstances of the campaign to come that summer, he insisted that if "our people bear with patience a retreat of sixty miles, we will whip." A February 27 diary entry by Tennessean Robert D. Smith provided the picture of defiance. As his brigade defended a point two miles from Dalton, he fumed that he would be willing to take on the entire Federal army in that position, "as they *never* could take it from us." Quartermaster Brown also refused to submit to "Yankee domination." He could not imagine life as a "boon at the hands of the hated Yankee—never—never. I will perish first."[38]

Increasingly disciplined, confident, and even occasionally swaggering by February 1864, the Army of Tennessee regrouped considerably under Johnston during his first two months in command. Although it remained far from combat-ready, considering the morale of the soldiers and the tattered condition of the entire operation when he took over, the general's accomplishment ranks as a remarkable feat. Obviously, not every soldier bought into Johnston's efforts, and not every man remained committed to the fight for southern independence. What is more important to note, however, is that most soldiers clearly did both. Improved rations, increased discipline, furloughs, and a strict policy of punishment for deserters stabilized the army quickly. Intense drill and a timely religious revival of larger-than-life proportions that spring would finish the restorative work started by Johnston. Further, the soldiers' reception of Johnston's reforms signaled their recognition of the importance of military discipline and challenges the notion supported by some historians that common Confederate soldiers never fully accepted the significance of discipline in their armies. Most soldiers in the Army of Tennessee by early 1864 were battle-hardened veterans who could easily appreciate the importance of discipline and could recognize how much it had improved their army. They also certainly understood that properly disciplined soldiers rendered more effective service and would more likely survive to fight another day. Given the overwhelmingly positive response to Johnston's actions, it is easier to believe that experienced soldiers accepted strict discipline than it is to believe that they never acknowledged its importance.[39]

In the first two months of 1864, civilians and soldiers around the Confederate heartland expressed mixed feelings about the progress of their war for independence, but most examined here unmistakably had not given up. The winter of 1863 had closed a disastrous year in the West, particularly with the fresh memory of the loss of Chattanooga. Indeed, most of Tennessee had been lost by that point in the war, yet beleaguered Confederates there remained committed to the cause. North Alabama contained pockets of unionist sentiment, deserters, and general lawlessness, but most of the state clearly maintained high morale and dedication to the cause, particularly in its central and southern areas still relatively distant from Union armies. Mississippians survived Sherman's Meridian campaign, even coming to view it as a victory, and boasted Forrest's cavalry among their defenders. The heartland's primary fighting force, the Army of Tennessee, opened the year in shambles but improved in every way under Johnston in January and February and looked toward the spring with improving spirits. Soon those spirits would reach new heights, the likes of which that army had not seen since the beginning of the war. Overall, western Confederates stood poised for a springtime spike in morale as the mixture of uncertainty and despair rather promptly transformed into a rejuvenated confidence.[40]

2

March–April 1864

A NEW BEGINNING

WRITING FROM HIS camp near Lick Creek, Tennessee, John D. Floyd, a common soldier in the 17th Tennessee Infantry, assured his wife of his rising spirits and refusal to surrender the cause and restore ties to the union:

> Of this one thing rest assured that never—no never—will I ever return to that country unless with the victorious army of the south, driving the invaders before it or after the southern confederacy is established and peace restored. Were I to forsake the cause of my country in this hour of her deepest peril; when the enemy is bringing to bear his many resources . . . sending out an armed negro soldiery to conquer us; to destroy our homes, to desecrate our altars and to annihilate ever vestige of liberty and nationality the south ever possessed; I would feel that I was a dishonored, ungrateful, cowardly . . . wretch unfit to associate with a person as pure, sensible and worthy as yourself.

He confidently reported the joyful spirits of the men around him, that soldiers throughout the Confederacy were reenlisting, and that their parents could be proud of the noble set of boys in his company. John Floyd and his comrades had not yielded, and they faced the impending campaigns with mounting optimism.[1]

The spring months unquestionably brought a resurgence of morale in the western Confederacy. As the freezing weather subsided, all were thankful that they had survived another winter of deprivation and relative inactivity and understood that spring would bring the promise of new crops and the early stages of the military campaign season, or as one soldier put it in late April, the "grand tournament of death." Though few relished the thought of renewed bloodshed, the resumption of fighting would mean the opportunity to earn southern independence rather than the uncertainty and frustration of sitting and waiting. Diaries and letters of this period demonstrate the unbreakable link between home front and battlefield. Civilians and soldiers alike recognized the importance of both, but realized that their goal of independence depended more than anything else on the results of battles and campaigns. In the short term they would not be disappointed. The coming months brought news of military victories for Confederate forces in all theaters of the war, a trend that would continue into the summer months. Before season's end, Major General Nathan Bedford Forrest and his cavalrymen would have the undying confidence of the western people that General Robert E. Lee and his Army of Northern Virginia enjoyed in the eastern theater. This theme would only grow more powerful in the summer months. Most important in the overall scope of the war, the Army of Tennessee would be in perhaps its best ever fighting trim, and that optimism spread around the West.[2]

"Daylight is Breaking!" wrote a correspondent for the *Selma Morning Reporter*. General comments illustrating the burgeoning confidence proliferate in diaries, letters, and newspapers for March and April 1864. Citizens, soldiers, and the press all found reasons for buoyancy in things ranging from perceived weaknesses in the northern economy and northern political divisions to the Federals' continued failure to capture Mobile. For some western Confederates, that bastion on Alabama's Gulf Coast seemed to take on a psychological importance reminiscent of Vicksburg, though obviously on a lesser scale. The currency bill passed by Congress in Richmond in February was said to be improving the value of Confederate notes. Newspapers emphasized the looming expiration of northern soldiers' enlistments and the time it would take the Federals to draft and train new, probably foreign-born, soldiers. Meanwhile veteran southern-born Confederates remained in the field led by the likes of Robert E. Lee, Nathan Bedford Forrest, John Hunt Morgan, and Joseph E. Johnston. Even the situation in the trans-Mississippi inspired confidence in some. Texas, western Louisiana, and southern Arkansas remained firmly in the hands of the Confederates, and Union general Nathaniel Banks in New Orleans had never exactly stricken fear in the hearts of many Rebels. By spring 1864, morale around the Confederate heartland was again on the rise, and most Confederates examined here would accept no terms of peace other than independence.[3]

Certain Rebels doubtless drew greater motivation from what the people of the Confederacy had already endured. Despite the difference in resources and manpower, despite the loss of rivers, cities, and millions of acres, the Confederacy survived. Despite attempted offensives against important port cities and William T. Sherman's raid across Mississippi, the conflict continued and the Confederacy stood defiant. Confederates even came to believe that their position might actually be as strong as ever by late spring 1864. In truth, some even believed that they were not only holding on but were in fact winning the war. After all, the Army of Tennessee grew stronger and more confident every day, while the feared Forrest and his cavalry still roamed Mississippi. Looking east, most practically assumed that Lee would handle the Federals in Virginia. All things considered, it is not difficult to see why the Confederates could retain such faith in their cause by early spring 1864.[4]

In the same vein, despite frequent material deprivation and the almost-constant heartache of war, most southern women managed with or without their men, and by early 1864 most of the women whose writings form parts of this study certainly had not succumbed to defeatism. Phillips Fitzpatrick, an Alabama soldier stationed at Mobile, even joked, perhaps worried, that his wife, Mary, had become so self-reliant in his absence that she might no longer need a husband. She frequently provided him with the updates he requested regarding affairs at home, but never asked him to leave his post, though she admitted that the children quite naturally missed their father. In fact, the only request for the soldier to come home came from a male acquaintance who worried about the state of Fitzpatrick's business affairs in his absence. Mary Fitzpatrick, on the other hand, informed her husband on April 24, 1864, "I am not afraid be assured that I get on very well. I feel that I have been endued with strength for this trial, indeed Phillips it is wonderful sometimes to me, how cheerful and contented I am generally." Mary Fitzpatrick's morale in spring 1864 need not be questioned, she certainly exhibited no defeatism, and she most definitely did not undermine the Confederate war effort by calling her husband home.[5]

Another Confederate woman, Eliza Fain of Hawkins County, East Tennessee, also maintained her faith in and commitment to the cause. A member of the planter class and a slaveholding household, Fain entered the war years committed to slavery and, like so many others of her class, found biblical justification for the institution. In her mind, the South's sin was not slavery, but rather the amalgamation of the races. God therefore challenged the South to abandon race mixing and return slavery to a more Christian-like standard. When the war began, Fain expressed paternalistic sympathy for slaves and showed compassion toward the enemy, though she always blamed northern abolitionists for bringing on the conflict. However, as the war dragged on in the vicious guerrilla- and bushwhacker-infested area of East Tennessee where she lived, and southern casualties mounted and her sons suffered in distant northern prisoner-of-war camps, she came to advocate a more unrestrained style of warfare against the Federals. She and her family suffered numerous cruelties at the hands of Union supporters, contributing directly to her growing desire for retribution. Thus, in the case of Eliza Fain, the violence and anguish brought on by the war did not weaken her commitment to southern independence, but rather stiffened her resolve to support the cause and only amplified her hatred for Yankees.[6]

It is not surprising, therefore, that Fain's commitment remained strong and her spirits remained generally high by spring 1864. Although her emotions fluctuated often, sometimes even appearing to follow the weather, in March and April her identification with the Confederacy cannot be questioned. In her diary entry for April 8, for example, she described a letter she received from a wealthy family friend who had remained a Union supporter. The friend invited them to return to his home, despite their differences, perhaps simply to visit or possibly to provide the family a safer environment. Whatever the case, Fain insisted on rejecting the offer because, though she hesitated to doubt her friend's sincerity, he was a unionist and "[t]here is no reliance to be placed in anything connected or associated with Yankee duplicity." Like Mary Fitzpatrick and so many others, Eliza Fain considered herself a true Confederate.[7]

Generally in East Tennessee spirits among Confederate patriots recovered gradually that spring even under Federal occupation and amid continued skirmishes, whereas the soldiers at Dalton, Georgia, rested and refitted for the battles to come, free from the watchful presence of enemy forces. Nonetheless, even in East Tennessee, Myra Inman remained hopeful and confidently insisted that the Confederates deserved to triumph in battle. Meanwhile, Ellen House, among the most dedicated of Confederates, grew frustrated with the Union martial presence in her East Tennessee hometown, and wrote about military news and expectations more than anything else in her March diary entries. As March turned to April, apparently unable to resist, she teased a local Confederate soldier she suspected of turning traitor with a lengthy and pointed April Fool poem. The poem that so clearly reveals the young woman's sentiments and her disgust with those who wavered in their devotion to the Confederate cause began:

> Oh! Tommy dear, you used to talk
> E'er Blue coats came this way
> As if you were the best of Rebs

Why are you Yank today?
You used to say you had no use
For this same Yankee nation
But now after the shoulder straps
You run like all creation
And you were always wont to say
You loved the Rebels dearly.
So a man may change his politics
As he does his dress coat—yearly.[8]

Clearly, in March and April 1864, overall civilian confidence in the western states was on the rise and, like the developments taking place in the Army of Tennessee and other Confederate military units in the western and other theaters of war, the rising spirits represented a new beginning of sorts. The cold months of uncertainty had passed, and all signs pointed to brighter prospects ahead. To this point, western Confederate civilians' writings overall reveal prevailing commitment to southern independence, virtually no defeatist sentiment, and no division among themselves significant enough to undermine the war effort. When the spring campaigns began, these western Confederate civilians absolutely expected victories.

Confederate soldiers still in East Tennessee before their return to Virginia expressed similar optimism and pointed to the battlefield as the only chance to secure independence. A bridge builder working for the Confederate military acknowledged the region's devastated physical condition but wrote his wife, "everything depends on the soldiers." An enlisted man in that region recorded the gradually improving spirits among the troops and, displaying more than considerable self-assurance, somehow judged Lieutenant General James Longstreet's Army of East Tennessee the "flower of the Confederacy." Meanwhile, a soldier at Camp Pollard, Alabama, informed his sister of reenlistments taking place there, assured her that the men remained in fine spirits, and concluded that things looked "better than usual." Overall, the majority of the western Confederates under examination here remained confident in their ability to secure victory so long as they possessed the necessary men and resources.[9]

Imbued with that springtime confidence and coming off the "success" of the Meridian campaign, the dedicated Confederates of the western states, military and civilian, like the bridge builder above, looked to the armies. All expected major campaigns in Virginia and northern Georgia by early summer. From Holly Springs, in northern Mississippi, Robert W. Fort, like other war-hardened Confederates by 1864, knew better than to put too much stock in rumors. Amid the almost constant reports of foreign recognition for the Confederacy, he wrote to his father that "my opinion . . . is not to regard any of these rumors about recognition, but *fight* for our own independence. . . ." Also in northern Mississippi, just across the state line from Memphis, Belle Edmondson unquestionably expected victory for the Confederate armies and scoffed at the Federal presence only a few miles from her home. On March 28, she proudly announced, "I worship Jeff Davis and every Rebel in Dixie," and later insisted that in Virginia, Ulysses S. Grant could not possibly defeat Robert E. Lee.[10]

Indeed, to the surprise of few in the West, Confederates scored victories that spring in all theaters of the war. That for the most part those engagements had relatively little strategic effect on the war's outcome is largely irrelevant here. Confederate diarists and letter writers around the West pointed to these victories with pride and, right or wrong, definitely considered them signs of the Confederacy's improving fortunes and expected northerners to interpret them similarly. The first such victory came in late February 1864 at Olustee, Florida, where Confederates fended off a Federal offensive, the largest campaign in that state during the war. President Abraham Lincoln had authorized the expedition because he believed that northern Florida held a significant number of unionists who could form the basis of a reconstructed state government. The Confederates under Brigadier General Joseph Finegan, however, won the day and an especially satisfying victory against Federal forces that contained three regiments of black troops, routing them from the field in confusion.[11]

Diarists certainly found reason to celebrate this relatively minor success, and April brought victories of more significance. On April 17–20, 1864, Confederates under R. F. Hoke captured Plymouth, North Carolina. More important, in the trans-Mississippi theater, Confederates under Major General Richard Taylor halted the primary column of Federal general Nathaniel P. Banks's Red River campaign force, thus preventing the capture of Shreveport and the planned invasion of Texas. Lincoln again had reconstruction in mind, in addition to discouraging the French imperial presence in Mexico by placing Federal troops in Texas. Among these secondary events, the defeat of the Red River campaign in particular raised the spirits of Confederates around the West.[12]

No battlefield developments raised western morale in the spring of 1864 more than the success of Forrest and his cavalry. Once again, western Confederates took pride in the exploits of a western general and his soldiers and pinned their hopes upon the success of those men. From mid-March to mid-April, Forrest led a raid through western Tennessee and into Kentucky, where he inflicted substantial damage on the town of Paducah. His presence threw a considerable scare into the Federals and unionists in those areas and excited Confederate sympathizers there. In later months, Federal general William T. Sherman at least once referred to the Confederate cavalry leader as "that devil Forrest," and insisted that the Union forces in the Memphis area should "follow Forrest to the death if it costs 10,000 lives and breaks the Treasury. There will never be peace in Tennessee till Forrest is dead." Clearly, the Federal commander appreciated the danger Forrest presented and his ability to affect the entire western theater of the war. By April 1, 1864, most people in the western Confederacy, whatever their sentiments with regard to the war overall, likely would have agreed with Mississippian Robert W. Fort when he wrote his father about the Federals' estimation of Forrest, "whom they know from *experience* is a *gentleman* not to be trifled with." One military diarist even described Forrest as "undoubtedly the best fighter in the Army."[13]

The most recognized and most significant action by Forrest's cavalry that spring occurred on April 12, 1864, when they captured Fort Pillow, Tennessee, at the Mississippi River fifty miles north of Memphis. In the process they killed approximately half of its six-hundred-man garrison of white and black Federal soldiers, including white unionists from Tennessee. At least some of those killed had attempted to surrender. That engagement immediately inflamed emotions on both sides and, because most of those killed after surrendering were black, remains one of the most controversial single episodes of the war. Contemporary northerners portrayed the events as wholesale slaughter and found in the story of Fort Pillow a rallying cry. Confederates insisted that most of those killed had refused to surrender or had attempted to flee. Historians now agree that a massacre took place at Fort Pillow, though disagreement remains regarding Forrest's responsibility for the tragedy. Regardless of Forrest's role, western Confederates cheered the results, which unmistakably served to boost morale.[14]

There can be no doubt that Confederates in the West immediately understood that something controversial had occurred at Fort Pillow, endorsed the version of events as they knew them, and drew encouragement from that victory and Forrest's other exploits. At the other end of Tennessee, Ellen House left no doubt about her views, noting in her diary with grim satisfaction, "General Forrest has taken Fort Pillow, put most of the garrison out of harm's way, killed every officer there. Good for him. I think he did exactly right." Upon learning the results, Tennessee civilian Robert Cartmell described Fort Pillow as a principal harbor for traitors and remarked, "Forrest has pretty well broken up the west, at least for the present." Cartmell described Forrest's dashing and slashing saber tactics, renowned bravado, and growing legend. "He might be picked out amoung hundreds by one who has never seen him as Genl Forrest. He is a terrible man in a fight & one of the best cavalry officers this war has produced." Near Memphis, Belle Edmondson, whose brother rode under Forrest's command, observed with pleasure the Federals' fear of having him so near. The diary of Private W. R. Dyer suggests that Forrest's success in early April provided a boost in recruiting. Diary entries for late April record that, in addition to the continued arrival of conscripts and the return of deserters, many individuals had begun to volunteer, leading Dyer to assert succinctly, "command increasing rapidly."[15]

Regardless of the modern controversy surrounding the former slave trader turned cavalryman, a controversy fueled at least as much by his postwar involvement with the Ku Klux Klan as it is a reaction to his wartime activities, Forrest was nothing less than a brilliant battlefield commander and unquestionably served as a central source of confidence for Confederates and cause of terror for Federals in the West. Before the end of April 1864, at least two newspapers compared Forrest to Moses leading his people to freedom and declared the general easily the greatest hero and fighter of the war.[16]

In a recent, intriguing book, another historian also finds that victories in distant theaters bolstered the morale of at least some Confederates in other theaters, even if the victories were largely inconsequential. However, that scholar argues that some "diehard Confederates" convinced themselves of an exaggerated importance of those victories, at least in part because they *wanted* the victories to be more significant. The Rebel writers cited in this study, however, considered those victories important not because they wanted them to be important, but because collectively those engagements represented a string of victories coming on the heels of the rejuvenation of the Army of Tennessee and of course while Robert E. Lee remained firmly in command in the eastern theater. Moreover, wartime observers could not benefit from hindsight and therefore had no way of knowing that those victories, at least collectively, would not prove more significant to shaping the war's outcome. Nevertheless, similar to the findings expressed throughout

this book, that study eventually and correctly concludes that the idea of ultimate Confederate victory was perfectly realistic to the Confederates themselves. It should be added that, at least as of spring 1864, the idea of overall
Confederate victory was perfectly realistic regardless of the observer.[17]

The fact that Confederate victories in Florida, North Carolina, and Louisiana and Forrest's exploits in Kentucky and Tennessee had relatively little
effect on the war's outcome is irrelevant to the essential fact that the victories boosted western Confederate morale. News of those victories did not
travel in a vacuum, exclusive of other events. Rather, in the minds of western Confederates the reports of distant battlefield success only reinforced
the extant and growing optimism and the belief that ultimate victory appeared increasingly likely. The individuals cited in this study are representative of many other western Confederates, not necessarily more or less committed to the cause than their neighbors. Equally important, they genuinely
believed in the significance of those victories, especially those of Forrest,
and had every reason to do so. Moreover, the western Confederates were not
alone in their views. The grave concerns expressed by Union officers regarding Forrest's exploits serve to reinforce the extent of that general's value to
western morale, both Confederate and Federal.

While Fort Pillow and the other military events so plainly affected public confidence, the thoughts of an officer camped in East Tennessee that
spring reveal the reciprocal nature of the relationship between civilian and
military as it regarded morale. Undoubtedly military events shaped popular
will at least as much as did any other factor, but the comments of Richard
Lewis, a young officer in Longstreet's corps, indicate that civilian attitudes
and behavior significantly affected soldiers. In April he and those around
him looked forward to moving to an area with stronger Confederate sentiment than East Tennessee, a section that had featured a considerable number of genuine unionists since the beginning of the war. He longed for an
area where, during difficult times, the citizens could and would boost the
soldiers' morale with encouragement and their own good spirits. To that
end he noted, "Everything is mockery and derision among the 'Union' in
our cause, and ready to uncoil at any moment and sting you. Though, I
believe, we are to brave the fiery ordeal of a grand and bloody campaign,
wheresoever we are to have our destiny." Lewis experienced firsthand the
relationship between home front and battlefield, yet knew that he and his
comrades would have to earn their independence on the latter.[18]

Securing independence must have seemed increasingly feasible, particularly if the glowing reports about the Army of Tennessee at Dalton, Georgia, recorded by civilians like Alabama diarist Sarah Espy proved true. Throughout March and April morale improved progressively and considerably. Joseph E. Johnston's wintertime improvements had been in place long enough to reap rewards. Edward Norphlet Brown, quartermaster of the 45th Alabama Infantry, proclaimed the ration issue solved. Shoes and clothing abounded, and the soldiers enjoyed quite comfortable shelters. Increased discipline produced a corresponding surge in self-confidence among the men. They competed in sham battles to sharpen their skills, took target practice, drilled relentlessly, and enjoyed their idle hours singing and socializing. Favorite songs included "Lorena" and "Do They Miss Me At Home?" In March the well-known epic snowball fight raged at Dalton, and evidently a good time was had by all. Such events might appear inconsequential to some readers, but they certainly improved the soldiers' collective mood and contributed directly to bolstering morale. The diaries and letters of soldiers in the Army of Tennessee during these months routinely contain the phrases "good spirits," "excellent spirits," and "best spirits ever" to describe the army. Although obviously not every soldier found cause to make merry that spring, there can be no doubt that by the end of April 1864, the Army of Tennessee exhibited virtually unparalleled confidence. Individuals who remained sullen or expected defeat were the exceedingly rare exceptions.[19]

Diaries and letters from this period reflect much more than simple comments on improving spirits. Several definite themes come to light. First, an almost unshakable faith in Johnston as their commander had emerged before the end of spring. Men referred to his military prowess and described him as a genius in letters to their families. One soldier even pledged to execute the general's orders without question and promised to stop assuming that he knew more than his commanding officer. Soldiers came to place an implicit confidence in their general and found a sense of security, no longer fearing defeat or surprise. Just as they knew of his reputation as a general who took care of his men, as illustrated in January and February, they considered him simply superior to Braxton Bragg as a military commander. So good was he in their perception that soldiers no longer feared that they might lose their lives needlessly through a commander's blunder. One would be hard-pressed to find a better morale booster.[20]

Even as their faith in their commander grew, the soldiers' confidence in themselves redoubled as they contemplated the imminent clash of arms. Soldiers frequently referred to their diligent preparations and strong defensive position. Their writings unmistakably demonstrate the return of their fighting mentality. Soldiers grew eager to clash once again with their enemies—not because they delighted in battle, but because they knew that the day must come if they were to vindicate their cause, and they considered themselves better prepared than ever. Assessing the impending operations, R. W. Colville wrote to his father, "I have no fear of the result. I believe we are as certain to whip them as we fight, and if we once get them started back like we did at Chickamauga, Johns[t]on will follow them up and drive them out of Tenn. The whole army is in better health and spirits than I ever saw them." John H. Marshall promised his wife in Mississippi that the soldiers stood ready to meet the "blue devils," and boasted, "Aint us bully we want to whip old Abes boys and we are going to do it too you will hear from us soon." After offering the usual comments on high morale, Isaiah Harlan of the 10th Texas Infantry assured his brother, "All consider themselves in for the war and have made up their minds to fight it out to the bitter end." Harlan's statement points to the growing defiance in the Army of Tennessee.[21]

Of the imminent Federal advance into northern Georgia, Alabama private Thomas Warrick boasted to his wife, "I think tha yankes will Give us A fit be fore minnie Days but if tha Don't lock out tha will Git the worst whippin tha hav had in A long tim." Similarly, fellow Alabaman Edward Norphlet Brown confidently informed his wife, "I guess when he comes that Mr. Johnston will have a few rebels to shoot at him. . . . These hills & valleys around Dalton are full of men and they are about as determined a set as ever shove a musket." Two weeks later he assured her that if the Federals did conquer them, "[t]hey will have to wade through blood to do it." By late April, though he could not guarantee a victory, he continued to predict horrific casualties for the enemy. Another Alabaman, John Crittenden, communicated similar thoughts to his wife, Bettie. If the Federals chose to attack the Confederates in their strong defensive positions, something the southern men routinely hoped for throughout that summer, "woe be to them. They have been so cruel to the citizens above here that the soldiers can hardly be kept within the bounds of prudence."[22]

That comment hints at one of the primary motives for Army of Tennessee soldiers preparing for the summer campaigns—the security of their homes and families. Visions of loved ones dominated soldiers' thoughts that spring. Soldiers often reflected on their wives and children more than anything else and even worried that their youngest might forget them. Receiving letters, packages, or even relayed messages from home frequently proved the highlight of a soldier's day or week. One soldier even wondered how men without women to write to managed army life. An Alabama private wanted badly to see his wife and children, yet remained at his post and hoped for a furlough. He told his wife, "I do want to see you & the dear little ones so very bad I don't know what to do, but I know what I will have to do, and that is stay here & not see you—Kiss them my dear for me. . . . Pray for us & our cause." Another, upon leaving his family to return to service from a furlough, noted how deeply he was moved by the goodbye, particularly in light of the fact that the sight of so much death and carnage no longer fazed him. For even the most battle-hardened and dedicated Confederates, concern for family overshadowed everything else.[23]

For some the visions of their families so far away and without protection during a civil war depressed their spirits and led to desertion. For most of the combatants in this study, however, such factors appear to have fueled their passions to fight. One soldier forcefully expressed common sentiments that captured the troops' disposition when he wrote that it was "not surprising that white southerners would fight the Yankees who try to subjugate his country, sister, wife, mother and give them up to their dusky male servitors."[24]

Considering such emotions regarding the defense of hearth and home, it is hardly surprising that dedicated soldiers in the Army of Tennessee that spring had little sympathy for deserters. Defections from the army overall slowed during that buoyant spring as compared to the gloomy weeks of late 1863. Yet desertion did continue, particularly among a certain group of soldiers unable to resist the temptations of being so close to home. Recent scholarship has revealed a pattern, one that continued throughout the summer as Federal armies under William T. Sherman ground toward Atlanta. The soldiers apparently especially likely to desert from the Army of Tennessee from late 1863 to mid-1864 but before the fall of Atlanta hailed from northern Georgia and Tennessee—the land already lost to or directly in the path of the invading Federal armies. Throughout the coming months, men from northern Georgia counties in particular proved increasingly likely to desert as Union armies overtook their respective home counties. Predictably, other soldiers recognized that such a pattern would result if the army gave up too much land to the enemy. Most studied here condemned desertion and considered it dishonorable to both country and family, but some admitted that they understood the sentiments of those who left because of distress at home. One study of desertion among Georgia troops posited that those who left their posts answered to the "higher duty" of home and family.[25]

The question of desertion that spring provides an interesting glimpse into the motivation of the Army of Tennessee's soldiers. It has been written that "desertion measures morale like a barometer gauges weather patterns." Unfortunately, this oversimplifies the relationship between morale and desertion. If the relationship were so clear, the north Georgia troops who deserted during the Atlanta campaign would have deserted in significant waves at other times as well—for example, after any number of military defeats suffered by western Confederate armies. Obviously, each man deserted for his own reasons. His leaving the ranks might or might not indicate that he had given up on the cause, and his desertion might be permanent or temporary, to deal with family concerns and return to service. Clearly, many north Georgia soldiers, and many from other areas, decided to answer calls from home, whether literal or in their own hearts.[26]

What is just as clear, however, and what somehow frequently gets lost in the historiographical shuffle, is that most of their comrades remained at their posts, condemned desertion, and perhaps most important, considered deserting the army an action that would bring shame upon not only themselves but their families. One soldier, for example, assured his wife that despite the difficulties of being separated from family and enduring the hardships of war, he would always carry out his duties and would never do anything to dishonor her. A doctor from Tennessee assured his wife that "I hope to see the time come when our Army can go into Tenn & route those deserters. I would hate to be a deserter and have to run from home when the good, respectable, & loyal people . . . returned to defend their country. I want to be among the list who can return free from disgrace that would sink not only me but wife & children . . . beneath the dignity of the best class of Tennesseans for all time to come."[27]

The themes of family and home, desertion, and reenlistment appeared in the verses of "Re-Enlistment: The Song of the Patriot Soldier of 1864," published in the *Mobile Daily Advertiser and Register* in April 1864. Attempting at once to praise and motivate the soldiers, it read in part:

> What! Shall we now throw down the blade
> And doff the helmet from our brows
> Now see our holy cause betrayed
> And re prove to all our vows
> When first we drew these patriot swords
> "A nation's freedom!" was the cry

Our faith was pledged in those proud words
And Heaven has sealed the oath on high

Dear are our homes, that smile afar
Off in the weary soldier's dreams
While resting from the toils of war
He sees the light that round them beams
Dear are the loved and lovely maids
Shrined in the patriot soldier's heart
Yet, while the foe, our land invades
In vain the longing tear may start

Then plant the flag staff in the earth
And round it rally every son
Who loves the State that gave him birth
Till her proud sovereignty be won
What though our limbs be weak with toil
What though we bear full many a scar
Huzza! here's to our native soil
We re-enlist, and for the war![28]

All of these issues affected soldiers in the Army of Tennessee, but a religious revival of grand proportions in and around Dalton that spring produced the single greatest boost to military morale during early 1864. Spring 1864 witnessed the onset of momentous religious revivals in armies around the Confederacy not duplicated in the northern ranks or among the public in either section. Explanations for the occurrence of those revivals offered by Civil War historians include the homogeneity of southern religion; greater stresses endured by Confederate soldiers, such as lack of furloughs and more physical deprivation; preexistence of revivalism in southern culture; insecurity in the face of military defeats and the consequent fear of death; and passionate missionary work. Historians have continued to refine the explanations, noting the effects of the Second Great Awakening on mid-nineteenth-century Americans, and that wars typically enhance religious activity. Further, as one historian has observed, if most Americans believed that they could earn eternal salvation, why would not the average Confederate soldier believe that he could enhance his chances of survival in combat through dutiful worship. During a late-February 1864 skirmish with Federals in the hills around Dalton, long before historians examined the source of the revivals, one soldier who was there noticed a sudden change in the activity of many card players and other gamblers and quipped, "I was struck with the missionary influence of the enemy's cannon." None of these explanations necessarily conflict with each other, and examinations of diaries and letters highlight the plausibility of all of these factors to explain the reasons for the intense religious activity in the Army of Tennessee in spring 1864.[29]

"A few months back the preachers could not get a congregation now hundreds are anxious to attend," wrote Alabama soldier John Crittenden on March 29, 1864. The Army of Tennessee had experienced religious activity intermittently throughout the war, but the missionary influence unmistakably peaked at Dalton in spring 1864. Thousands of soldiers took part, to one degree or another, many attending services in town or in camp nightly or even multiple times per day. In fact, the diary of one army chaplain from Tennessee recorded the building of a sixty-foot-long shelter to house services and noted with satisfaction the massive crowds it accommodated every night. One month later he recorded the founding of a Christian association among the troops. Soldiers often worshipped with different denominations, ranging from Baptists and Methodists to Catholics, leading Edward Norphlet Brown of the 45th Alabama Infantry to note the cooperation of the denominations in a letter to his wife and wonder what good such collaboration could do elsewhere. Enlisted men and officers, including the generals, frequently found themselves at the same services and witnessed countless conversions and baptisms. One soldier even noted that the friendly rivalries between units extended to competitions measuring church attendance.[30]

The extent of the revival and church attendance is clear enough, but did so much intense activity in such a brief period actually have a spiritual effect on the soldiers, or was it for many simply a social diversion? Of course not every soldier participated in the revival or found any divine inspiration that spring. Many continued their old ways of gambling, cursing, and whatever else thousands of soldiers do when gathered together for months on end, with hours of idle time on their hands daily. Yet the evidence suggests that thousands of soldiers did undergo meaningful changes that spring. What is more important than how many men truly found religion, particularly as it relates to morale, is that the writings of the soldiers illustrate that *they believed* a significant change had come over the army. In a letter to his wife in Alabama, John Crittenden observed, "Quite a change seems to be coming over the soldiers. They are not near so wicked as they were a few months back."[31]

Like Crittenden, others observed the sincerity and results of the religious activities at Dalton. In a letter to his wife, one soldier illustrated the earnest worship, the nightly services in his brigade, and the reality of camp life that spring, writing, "I reckon it would appear quite odd to you if you could witness one of our Camp meetings with several hundred men sitting on the ground with a preacher in their midst preaching. It looks quite primeval. There is an absence of all show. Noone goes there to be seen. Sober reality is the order of the occasion. . . . I think it would be a great pleasure to you but camp is no place for females." Weeks later he noted that the soldiers observed Confederate president Jefferson Davis's proclamation for a day of fasting more strictly than he had yet seen. On the same day Flavel C. Barber of the 3rd Tennessee Infantry also noted the strict observance of the fast day and beamed that the "revival in the brigade goes on with unabated zeal and success. There seems to be a powerful awakening and seriousness, more than I have ever seen in the army." (Not every soldier observed the fast day, of course. One Alabama soldier, for example, believed that he had fasted enough already.) Overall though, artillery captain Thomas Key, a former private in the 15th Arkansas Infantry, observed "a wonderful reform among the soldiery, for they are leaving off card playing, profanity, and other vices, and are humbling themselves before God. May the good work deepen and widen. I often feel that if all the army would unite as one man in prayer and faith we would never lose a battle and peace would immediately follow."[32]

If the soldiers noticed a change coming over the Army of Tennessee, what did they expect to achieve by it? It is clear that many envisaged the resurgence of faith somehow helping the army on the battlefield. Writing to his mother in Mississippi, B. F. Gentry insisted that because of the new-found religion and constantly improving spirits, the army would be a better fighting force than ever before. Flavel C. Barber recorded the effects of the revival on the soldiers of the 3rd Tennessee Infantry and proclaimed defeat impossible if the army maintained that spirit. Tennessee army chaplain Thomas Hopkins Deavenport recorded in his journal a comment by an elderly slave to the effect that, "If the Yankee let us stay here three months dey can't whip us, if dey could whip us when we were wicked, I know they can't when we got religion." Clearly these men believed that the religious faith fostered in camp and around the town of Dalton would aid them in battle.[33]

In some cases the texts chosen by the preachers for their sermons that spring prepared soldiers for the strong possibility of death that summer and likely contributed to the growing belief that their newfound faith might accord the men added effectiveness or even divine protection on the battle-field. On the morning of March 27, 1864, a preacher from Mobile delivered a discourse from 1 Corinthians 15:26, "The last enemy to be destroyed is death." A few weeks later a Mississippi preacher addressed the same group of soldiers at their makeshift outdoor church with logs for pews. He drew from Ezekiel and asked, "Why will ye die?" One soldier called this one of the finest sermons he had ever heard and noted the substantial interest it drew from the soldiers. The same soldiers heard three sermons the following day. One week later at another part of camp, soldiers heard a sermon titled, "If the righteous scarcely be saved, where shall the ungodly and sinners appear?"[34]

In the same vein as the sermons, a newspaper published in Tuskegee, Alabama, printed the story, probably apocryphal, of an army chaplain who tended to a dying young soldier. The piece, titled "The Christian Soldier in Death," told of the man dying the most honorable death imaginable and speaking of his faith and his mother. The story's dying warrior asked the chaplain to thank God for his mother who taught him so well, for his being a Christian, and for his ability to pass on with grace. Fictional or not, taken with the extent of the revivals, the messages of the sermons, thoughts of home and family, and visualizations of impending combat, this story likely would have influenced almost any soldier who read it that spring.[35]

In a letter rich with detail about the religious activities progressing throughout the army, Edward Norphlet Brown touched on a most signifi-cant aspect of the revival, particularly regarding morale. Writing about the soldiers' newfound faith in the Baptist, Methodist, Episcopal, and Presbyte-rian churches, he asked, "What can it mean? . . . They are getting religion and fitting themselves to die, and I believe they will fight better when the days of battle come. It is reasonable that men who are not afraid to die will fight better than those who have dark forebodings of the future. We are still expecting a fight yet the people seem to care for or dread it far less than ever before." Brown insisted that the army continued to grow more confident and that it was in its finest ever condition. "Let us hope that this good mo-rale will continue to the army and pray God to buckle on his armor in our defense when the clangor of arms shall again be heard on the battle plain. That wicked boastful people, the Yankees, have cried 'now Moab unto the spoil' and I hope that it shall be with them as it was with the Moabites smit-ten by Israel." Without question, increasing numbers of men came to believe that faith in God made them better soldiers.[36]

Soldiers of the Army of Tennessee looked toward those approaching summer campaigns with growing confidence that they were "soldiers of the cross" and "Christian patriots with a sacred mission." The concept of "no cowards among the God fearing" is not new to students of the Civil War. Historians have noted the value of strong religious faith among soldiers who faced death daily. If they genuinely believed that they were fighting with God on their side, obviously they would enter the campaign with more confidence. Moreover, if the men of the Army of Tennessee specifically took the field with the belief that they enjoyed divine protection or, in some cases, that if they died they did so for their family and country and had recently earned eternal salvation anyway, how could this not produce a positive effect on morale? A joint religious experience with their comrades also strengthened group cohesion among soldiers. The fruits of the religious revival at Dalton improved morale significantly in the army that spring, and provided comfort to the soldiers during the wearisome Atlanta campaign that followed, and at least to some extent for the remainder of the war. The soldiers truly believed that their army was transformed in the spring of 1864, and that meant more than a simple shot of extra courage or blind enthusiasm. They looked toward the summer sincerely expecting to win the war and with it the independence of the Confederate States of America.[37]

That confidence proliferated around the Confederate heartland by the end of April 1864. The coldest winter most could remember had passed, and the overall spirits around the West, military and civilian, steadily and unmistakably improved. Confederates had experienced recent success in all theaters of the war and expected that to continue in the great battles that loomed in Georgia and Virginia. Similar to the strong morale in Robert E. Lee's more celebrated Army of Northern Virginia in early 1864, confidence soared in the Army of Tennessee after Johnston whipped it into its best-ever condition and after a religious revival swept the troops.[38] The public witnessed the resurgence of the army and now waited for what they knew would be the brutal and bloody summer of 1864, when they would pin their hopes for independence on the conduct of men like Johnston, Lee, and Forrest, and the thousands who would risk their lives to carry out their orders.

3

May–June 1864

WINNING THE WAR

MAY AND JUNE 1864 brought the resumption of major campaigns in Georgia and Virginia and the renewed reality of civil war. Men and women around the western Confederacy focused their attention on the armies in those two regions, and westerners wrote in their diaries and letters about Joseph E. Johnston and the Army of Tennessee as much as they did about the more renowned Robert E. Lee and the Army of Northern Virginia. They focused so much attention on Johnston's army despite, and to a certain extent because of, the prominence and celebrated status of Lee. The latter general of course defended the nation's capital at Richmond and fought to preserve the existence of his army against a force almost twice the size of his own, but Confederate confidence around the West was so high that most individuals examined in this study, military and civilian, almost assumed that Lee would find a way to hold the city and keep his army intact.

The people also understood the importance of Johnston's defense of Atlanta and the Army of Tennessee to the survival of the Confederacy, only in part because of the importance of the city itself. Interestingly, most of the western Confederates studied here apparently did not think of the defense of Atlanta in terms of its potential effect on the impending northern presidential election. Certainly a relative few hoped that Johnston could hold on to the city at least until the Democrats could nominate a peace candidate in the northern presidential election of 1864, or perhaps even until the election itself. Perhaps a successful Confederate defense of the city could contribute to Abraham Lincoln's defeat in his bid for reelection, though to be sure, the majority of these western Confederates did not think in those terms. They sought simply to hold on to the city and keep the Army of Tennessee in the field. More to the point, if Johnston's army could not hold off and occupy William T. Sherman's armies, those Union forces could not only capture Atlanta but turn toward Virginia, link up with Ulysses S. Grant's army, and amass an assault force against Richmond that even the most diehard Lee proponent could not expect him to defeat. Those facts, the proximity of the campaign for Atlanta to their homes, and of course Sherman's attempt to destroy the Army of Tennessee explain the westerners' focus on the western armies. For the time being they watched with confidence, and this assurance would remain high through the end of June 1864.[1]

Not only did people around the western Confederacy enter the summer with considerable confidence, but many who watched the events from locations other than northern Georgia even expected the two major campaigns to end the war in their favor. From Mobile a soldier wrote that he hoped "[w]e will whip the Yankees badly in Georgia and Virginia, and all living once more in peace and comfort soon." A Texas cavalry officer in Mississippi thought that people discussed Lee and the action in Virginia more than anything else, but predicted success in both campaigns, insisting that he entertained no fears that the northern generals might outfox Lee and Johnston. In mid-May Charles Dubuisson, camped at Canton in central Mississippi, surveyed recent months' reports from the war's various theaters and relayed to his sister Sallie the "glorious news we are continually receiving." Still jubilant from the spring military successes, particularly those of Forrest, another Mississippian, Belle Edmondson, began her May diary entries with the prediction that "a bright day for Dixie is dawning."[2]

Confederates around Alabama expressed similar sentiments. They looked optimistically to Virginia and Georgia, commented on the good spirits of the people around them, and lamented the unavoidable bloodshed to come. From Mobile, throughout the months of May and June, Phillips Fitzpatrick assured his wife of his continued happiness and safety and predicted that the Army of Tennessee would defeat the Federals in northern Georgia. From the same area, Mark Lyons attempted to comfort his wife in his absence, expressed cautious optimism regarding both major theaters of the war, and told her that he would do "anything consistent with honor" to see her. Camped near Tuscaloosa, Texan Elbridge Littlejohn found relief in reports of recent victories from other theaters. Such news made it easier for him to leave his home and family while Federal soldiers roamed the South. From Montevallo, cavalryman William L. Nugent exhibited war weariness but also continued confidence in Johnston and the Army of Tennessee. He wondered why he and others remained in Alabama when they should be reinforcing Johnston. He soon got his wish and, like so many others, found himself assisting in the defense of Atlanta. Clearly the words of these western Confederates attest to their continued faith in their cause.[3]

Predictably, newspapers around the Confederate heartland, particularly in Mississippi, also expressed complete confidence and anticipated victory. The *Meridian (Mississippi) Daily Clarion* printed an extract from a letter "from one of the gentler sex which breathes the true spirit." The author forecast triumph in Georgia and Virginia and peace that summer. The same issue featured a piece from a Union newspaper that decried the blood already spilled in the fight for Richmond even in early June. The editors of a small-town newspaper in Choctaw County, Mississippi, assured their readers that Johnston and his army stood ready for the invaders. The same issue featured a motivational song for the soldiers from Tennessee that concluded with the prediction "Tennessee's own bright eyed daughters, Shall our glorious triumph sing."[4]

Across the state line, Alabama newspapermen refused to be outdone. A Selma newspaper reported the pleasure of hearing men talk of success for the Confederacy and believed that such talk helped lift the spirits of all. A refugee paper from Jackson, Mississippi, then publishing at Selma, confidently pointed to the number of Yankee soldiers buried in northern Mississippi, Alabama, and Tennessee, and hoped that the summer campaigns would increase that figure. From the state's capital and the original capital city of the Confederacy, the *Montgomery Daily Advertiser* printed a preacher's patriotic (if melodramatic) address to the soldiers proclaiming victory near. The preacher apparently sought to encourage the soldiers to look past the numbers of their foes. "Soldiers! [W]e are too near the great events which stir the age in which we live to behold the grandeur of their proportions. Just as when we stand at the base of an over hanging mountain and lift our eyes to the precipices that are beating above, we are unprepared to scan the proportions which are thrown in such gigantic outlines upon the canvas of the sky. . . ." One month later the paper featured a poem titled "Croaker's Dialogue," in which the character of a gallant southern soldier answers the grumbling of a cowardly complainer who doubts the Confederacy's chances. The poem, published on June 3, concluded with "And cheer ye for our Southern braves, And three for Joseph Johnston." That newspapers printed such content and insisted that victory was near is not surprising, but in early summer 1864 their content accurately reflected the prevailing expectations and sentiments among civilians and soldiers around the West.[5]

Western Confederates certainly expected success, but they knew that major campaigns, even successful ones, would also mean enormous casualties. That fact was not lost on nineteen-year-old diarist Myra Inman, who from her East Tennessee home watched the seemingly endless lines of Federal soldiers marching off to begin their invasion of Georgia. The sight of the Federals' numbers and the visions of the terrible carnage that awaited shook her confidence briefly, but she continued to predict success for the southern men. She believed that their gallantry and bravery, along with God's help of course, would be enough to offset the northerners' numbers advantage. She maintained that other girls in the area shared her feelings and that the people there focused their attention on the fighting in northern Georgia because of its proximity to their homes. Meanwhile, a confident resident of Montgomery County in north central Tennessee would have agreed and found plenty of cause for hope.[6]

Similar to the circumstances of the Meridian campaign in February, however, civilians in the path of war found more cause for concern, at least in the short term. For example, Sarah Espy of Cherokee County in northeastern Alabama near the Georgia border, naturally grew more nervous as the sounds of war grew louder. By late May, as northern soldiers approached her house, Espy prayed for protection but noted that her friends in the area remained cheerful. By the early days of June, well into the Atlanta campaign, Espy's confidence rebounded somewhat after Federal soldiers sacked her house and stole whatever they wished. She hoped never to experience such a trial again but seemed to draw comfort from the knowledge that it could have been worse. By the end of June she prayed not to be completely overrun by the northern armies and followed the fighting in Georgia with "fearful anticipation." She closed the month's diary entries with the foreboding notation, "If our army is conquered there, we know we are ruined."[7]

Beyond the press rhetoric, patriotic pleas and songs, emotional diary entries, and defiant letters, Sarah Espy, Myra Inman, and the others ultimately looked to the men in Johnston's Army of Tennessee to protect the heartland of the Confederacy and help win their war for independence. In May many soldiers who were camped in Mississippi and Alabama, some even near their homes, made their way to north Georgia to join the thousands of southerners already there in preparation for their defense of Atlanta. Talladega County, Alabama, resident James Mallory, who had three sons serving in Confederate armies and made cash and crop donations to the war effort, wrote of the "awful conflict" about to take place and recorded the hourly passing of General Leonidas Polk's Army of Mississippi through his community on their way to join Johnston's larger army. Though confident and sincere in their predictions of victory, the men and women of the western Confederacy understood that springtime had passed and that the time to renew the struggle had arrived. Home front and battlefield were never so closely tied as during such times.[8]

A diary entry by Mississippian James Palmer illustrates the mind-set of one dedicated Confederate in early summer 1864, highlights the experience of a common Confederate soldier and his family, and demonstrates again the unbreakable connection between home front and battlefield. In early February, Palmer's unit received orders to leave Meridian, Mississippi, for Mobile, and later Georgia. In order to see his family in Kemper County, fifty miles from Meridian, before leaving the state, Palmer temporarily left his contingent without permission, technically making him absent without leave. He spent approximately five weeks at home, visiting with his wife and children, repairing fences on his farm, and planting a crop for his family, before returning to his unit in mid-May to resume his duty in the field. Of his time at home and the decision to leave his family to return to the army he wrote in his humble grammar, "I enjoyed my family with grate plaisure while I was at home with them it was all moste like tairing my harte asunder to leave my wife and bid them fair well of the deepe ties and bitter tears of my beloved wife on the morning of 16 of May 1864 I never can forget that beloved wife and dear little babes hoo said pray for me but duty called me to my countrys call and I had to go leaving them in Gods cear." Palmer soon made his way east to do his part in the defense of Atlanta.[9]

Another soldier bound for the trenches of north Georgia, I. B. Cadenhead, found himself in a similar situation with the same concerns and outlook on the cause. Unlike Palmer, however, Cadenhead found no opportunity to slip home for a visit, as he lamented in a letter to his wife, Leusa. He asked her not to grieve for him and assured her that he would do his best to stay alive and return home to his family. The soldier asked her to kiss the children for him, reminded her to get her peas planted on time, and comforted her for the loss of her new calf. Four days later he found himself in Georgia and wrote to his wife again, "[D]o the Best you can my deare wife for your self and Children I hope to get home to you Before a grate while . . . I expect to get inn a Battle soon and if I get kiled I feel like in a gust Cus it is for you and our little Children that I am willing to fight. . . ." In the coming months Leusa Cadenhead received two letters from men other than her husband bringing her the news she no doubt dreaded most—I. B. Cadenhead was killed on July 22 in the fighting around Atlanta. There is no doubt about the morale or dedication to the Confederate cause of those two common soldiers, Alabama's I. B. Cadenhead and Mississippi's James Palmer, in May 1864.[10]

Thomas McGuire, an officer who made the trip to Georgia from Montevallo, Alabama, in early May, confessed to being "more completely broken down" than ever before during the trek but soon rebounded in body and spirit. When he recalled the importance of his mission, "It cheered me up and caused me to move with more spirit and with renewed energy." Once he arrived in Georgia and rested up, he found in the landscape around Dalton and the condition of the army cause for continued confidence, asserting, "I feel well and well rested and fully confident of our ability to meet and defeat the enemy at every point of attack."[11]

When McGuire, Cadenhead, Palmer, and the other soldiers reached the Dalton area they found a confident army, eager to face the enemy. The defenders there included a typical soldier, John Daniel Cooper of the 7th Mississippi Infantry. Cooper not only kept a diary during the coming months, he also wrote poems that reflected his thoughts about his family, his cause, and his comrades. From Dalton on May 1, 1864, he wrote:

> And while Im on my long wearisome rounds again
> I think of the wrongs endured and the cause that forces more
> But, alas, I must needs suffer all this that I may stain
> My innocent hands and untainted nature in human gore
>
> Oh, my country it is for thee I these wrongs endure
> I would not be driven from this to any other land
> Nay before I do give up my lovely nation shore
> Destined to fail or conker I do battle with my noble native band[12]

For Johnston's soldiers, exceedingly high morale marked the first twelve days of May, before they evacuated Dalton on May 13 and began the first of what would be many retroactive movements in the face of Sherman's three federal armies bent on the destruction of the Army of Tennessee and the capture of Atlanta. As Sherman weighed his options for how to go through or around the Army of Tennessee on his way to Atlanta, most of Johnston's men continued their daily routines, though all soon realized that the time had come for the clash of arms that they had awaited for months. "I can say to you that the boys are all in high spirits up here at this time We are sorter looking for a fite out here but I can say to you if the yankees come on us at this place they will run a ganst a snag shore as they doo try it for there is some mity strong brest works for them to run over . . . ," wrote Alabama private Thomas Warrick, who admitted that he had grown tired of fighting but clearly had not given up on the cause. Throughout the summer of 1864, soldiers like Warrick recognized the benefit of defensive positions, and the knowledge that they would fight from behind breastworks for most of the campaign, rather than fight in the open or attack fortified positions, clearly bolstered morale. Many of these same men had fought at Shiloh, Murfrees-boro, and Chickamauga. Compared to those bloody experiences, the opportunity to shoot Federals from behind sturdy defenses sounded especially pleasing. After the resurrection of the army beginning in January, followed by its spiritual rebirth and the weeks of diligent training, and armed with the knowledge that they would fight from protected defensive positions, the soldiers stood defiant in the face of superior numbers.[13]

Several themes emerged in the soldiers' early May writings. The religious fervor of the spring had not worn off when the calendar changed to May. In fact, the first day of the month, a Sunday, saw a mass baptism in a creek in one part of the camp that according to one witness drew numbers in the thousands. A soldier from Alabama assured his wife that he expected to enter the campaign with the same safeguard from God that he had enjoyed throughout the war. An officer who observed the continued religious activity assured his wife of the army's preparedness for Sherman, but did not share the previous soldier's confidence in the common soldiers' providential protection, noting, "It is an impressive scene to see such a large mass of sinful creatures standing upon the brink of eternity, worshipping perhaps for the last time in this world."[14]

In addition to religious activity and faith, soldiers frequently wrote of the good spirits among the men, their continued commitment to the justness of their cause, and of course thoughts of their families. An officer in the 17th Alabama Infantry, at Resaca, Georgia, south of the army, wrote his wife, "Kiss the dear children for me. I feel that as danger approaches I love and think of you and them more and more." An Alabama artillerist wrote to his wife on May 4 that he expected Johnston to prevail regardless of Sherman's choice of tactics and that her visit to him that winter did him "a great deal of good." He continued, "I believe I am a better man than I was and Darling to you I owe it all under heaven." The next day, Edward Norphlet Brown of the 45th Alabama Infantry, who predicted victory as long as Johnston had

enough men, pined for his wife and children while he maintained hope for
a quick victory and reunion with them. "Without hope this would indeed
be a warfare of trouble. It is bad enough as it is, but I imagine that I would
be ten fold worse if we did not have hope for better times." Five days later,
another Alabama quartermaster, Joel Dyer Murphree of the 57th Alabama
Infantry, reported the army in good spirits and poised for victory.[15]

Murphree's comment points to a theme that emerged clearly in the soldiers' early May writings—assertive predictions of victory. M. S. Hunter
proudly wrote his sister in Alabama that "I don't believe that a yanky was
ever made to kill me." In the bigger picture, like many around the western
Confederacy, an Arkansas diarist expected the campaigns in Georgia and
Virginia to end the war in favor of his fledgling country. The artillery captain
demonstrated this and the themes above when he assessed Sherman's forces
and the task at hand, "Let them come! In the justice of our cause, with the
memory of dear ones at home and in the name and power of God, we shall
meet them with determined and brave hearts and fight until the God of
Battles shall give us the victory." A Texas private shared similar sentiments
if not style of prose, confiding confidently to his diary, "[W]e are awaiting
the approach of the enemy and if he was to come the boys wold give a warm
recepsion with what is cald the Confederet Blue pill wich is vary poisen to
the Yankees when administered in the proper channel to them so they say."[16]

The final major theme present in soldiers' writings before the true com-
mencement of the Atlanta campaign sheds further light on the reasons for
their confidence, not only in themselves but in the overall war effort. During these optimistic early summer days, and throughout the season, soldiers
routinely commented on successes in other theaters of war, particularly
on Robert E. Lee and the Army of Northern Virginia and their attempt to
preserve that army's existence and defend Richmond. The diary entries of
Tennessean Robert D. Smith for the first week of May express typical sentiments. He continued to draw comfort from the Confederate victories in
the Red River campaign in Louisiana and other smaller victories. On May 6
he mentioned reports of a major battle (the Wilderness, May 5, 6, 7, 1864)
between Lee and Grant in Virginia, noting that he had not yet received con-
firmation of the results but writing assuredly, "We are certain that Lee's
veterans will do their duty." Georgia private Angus McDermid informed his
father, "Old Lee has whipped them 3 days." By May 10 Louisiana soldier
Robert Patrick would have agreed and reported the results of the Battle of

the Wilderness as good news. "Oh, how this cheered my heart and made me feel as if the war was on its last legs," exclaimed Captain Thomas J. Key, the self-assured Arkansas artillerist.[17]

Reports of another battle in Virginia, the clash at Spotsylvania Court House, reached the Army of Tennessee at a convenient time. Conscious of the potential effects on the morale of his men, Johnston issued a proclamation to his troops reporting a Confederate victory and massive Federal casualties at Spotsylvania Court House—the night he abandoned his strong defensive position north of Dalton and began a retreat to Resaca, approximately twenty miles to the south. (Federal officers also reported the Virginia battles to their troops as victories.) During the opening days of May, Sherman attempted to trap Johnston's army by holding his attention around Dalton with the armies of the Cumberland and the Ohio, and with the Federal Army of the Tennessee circling south around the Confederates' left toward Resaca. On May 12 Johnston figured out his opponent's scheme and evacuated his position overnight. During his retreat Johnston received reinforcements at Resaca in the form of General Leonidas Polk's Army of Mississippi, now a corps in the Army of Tennessee, numbering fifteen thousand.[18]

Johnston's decision to abandon Dalton saved his army by avoiding the trap, and the move certainly did not hurt his army's morale. At Resaca he chose to turn and fight Sherman, to the surprise of his foe, who expected him to continue to retreat southward. Johnston sought at least to buy time to get his wagons across the Oostanaula River, and at best to lure Sherman into attacking the Confederates in a defensive position. Sherman also underestimated the speed of Johnston's movements, erroneously believing that he could get between the Confederates and Resaca. Instead, on May 13 he found the reinforced Army of Tennessee firmly entrenched and ready for battle. For parts of May 13, 14, and 15, the two sides fought the first major engagement of the campaign for Atlanta.[19]

The Battle of Resaca brought the reality of vicious combat that the Army of Tennessee soldiers had prepared for all spring. It also brought an opportunity many of them had longed for—the chance to fight a defensive battle against assaulting Federals. "We have splendid entrenchments," wrote one Tennessee soldier. "The best I ever saw and if Sherman will only attack us it will be the ruin of his army for we will give him the worst whipping he ever had. . . ." Johnston's defensive lines faced north and west, and indeed the Union soldiers attacked all across his front. Such an opportunity to strike at their enemies from defensive positions sparked the passions of the Confederates. One soldier described a Federal assault that came out of the woods opposite his position: "We soon commenced 'saluting' them . . . and they retired. A more vigorous charge was made at the same time on the right of the brigade . . . and they came within 50 paces of the works, before being repulsed." One young soldier was genuinely disappointed when the Union forces opted not to launch another frontal assault. "We have been watching and waiting for an advance in our front all day, but they don't seem inclined to repeat the experiment of yesterday." By May 15 he insisted that he had never seen more excitement for battle among the soldiers and claimed that they actually hoped for another attack.[20]

Predictably, Johnston's defending Confederates inflicted relatively heavy casualties on Sherman's attacking Federals. However, typical of the pattern that emerged throughout most of the campaign, Sherman hesitated to launch a full-scale frontal assault on fortified positions. Instead, he sent forces in probing, flanking maneuvers around the Confederates and across the Oostanaula River, threatening Johnston's line of communications to Atlanta, and potentially crushing the army from the front and rear. Overnight May 15–16, again unbeknownst to his adversary, Johnston evacuated his position around Resaca and retreated across the Oostanaula, south toward Atlanta in hopes of finding a position suitable to turn and face the pursuing Federals. After considering stops at Calhoun and Adairsville, he marched his army on to Cassville, approximately twenty-seven miles south-southeast of Resaca. There, Johnston planned to fight Sherman.[21]

The fight at Resaca had indeed taken a physical toll on both sides. Private Hiram Smith Williams of the 40th Alabama Infantry Regiment, a remarkable soldier who frequently appeared disgusted with both sides and war in general, described a scene among the dead and wounded after Resaca:

> How shall I describe the past night? If I live to the allotted period of man's existence, I can never forget the scenes I have witnessed for they are indelibly stamped on my memory. Limbs mangled and torn, much suffering and pain—Oh, Lord! It was truly horrible. . . . The wounded for the whole corps were scattered about on every side. Some in a deserted house, some under rough shelters of brush, some in tents, and others on the cold ground with no covering but their blankets. . . . Here on a rough table the surgeons were amputating a leg, on another one's arm was being taken off, while a score of others just taken from the ambulances were awaiting their turn, with all manner of wounds claiming attention. . . . I saw one poor fellow belonging to a Texas Reg who had his leg almost torn off by a cannon ball just above the

knee, the bones crushed and torn out, only adhering to the trunk by a few pieces of skin. . . .[22]

That soldiers on both sides routinely witnessed such scenes and yet continued to serve demonstrates not only the emotionally hardening effects of war but also strongly united peoples' dedication to their causes and to each other.

During the retreat after the Battle of Resaca, the Confederate troops remained in good spirits. To this point, nothing had occurred to dampen their morale—not the results of the battle or their general's decision to retreat. The soldiers deemed Johnston superior to Sherman, whom they considered afraid to turn and fight them head on. "The enemy will not fight us in our works—It is believed they are trying to flank us . . . ," wrote A. Snodgrass of the 55th Alabama Infantry on May 16. On the same day, another Alabaman agreed, noting, "It seems hard for Johnston to get them to a general engagement. The Yankees keep flanking. . . ." Also on May 16, a Mississippi soldier confidently insisted that Johnston was just too smart for Sherman and would not allow him to choose the battleground.[23]

The soldiers not only retained confidence in their commander, they fully assumed that he would turn and fight at the best opportunity. One combatant believed that they must have been outnumbered, that Johnston made the right decision, and that the soldiers should trust in his judgment. The next day the soldier explained that the army was not discouraged by the retreat because they planned to force Sherman to attack them under disadvantageous conditions and draw him farther from his base, lengthening his lines of communications.[24]

Others recorded similar entries in their diaries and made comparable statements in their correspondence. Tennessean Robert D. Smith initially wondered in his diary why Johnston retreated so far, but decided that the general must be drawing them away from their base, looking for a chance to pounce. "If we can only get him out in a fair open field fight. I have no doubts as to the result for I believe that Johnston will carry them almost if not quite to the Ohio river before he stops." The following day he admitted that the men appeared physically broken down but remained in good spirits. He insisted that he had heard no soldier complain. Even a soldier who showed considerably less confidence than Smith and believed that the Confederates had taken a beating at Resaca by May 18 showed continued faith in Johnston and noted, "The thing is not through with yet and they had better mind how they fool with him for they are getting a long ways from their boats with a good army and a cautious man in front of them."[25]

Upon reaching Cassville the Confederates prepared to fight. Johnston formulated a plan that he expected to cause Sherman to divide his forces, thus allowing the Confederates to defeat the Federals piecemeal. Johnston's confidence soared such that in the early morning hours of May 19 he issued a dramatic order commending his men for their courage and sacrifice and promising to lead them into battle. "Fully confiding in the conduct of the officers, the courage of the soldiers, I lead you to battle."[26]

The announcement rang as music to the soldiers' ears. In their minds, Sherman and his Yankees would not willingly face them in battle, but Johnston would force them to fight on ground of his choosing. A young Alabama soldier who narrowly escaped death in early May did not have the faith and confidence shared by most of his comrades, deeming the northern numerical advantage too great. That combatant's sentiments notwithstanding, the vast majority of men examined here rejoiced at their general's positive declaration. Johnny Green of the famed Kentucky Orphan Brigade reported the satisfaction among the troops. They did not entrench that day, he wrote, because their general had found the appropriate time to attack the enemy. John S. Jackman, a fellow soldier from the Orphan Brigade, recorded that the men loudly cheered the announcement. Later in the day Johnston passed Jackman's group and received their cheers again. A Texas soldier also understood the mood of the day and expected a general engagement if things worked as planned. A doctor in the 56th Georgia Infantry predicted a victory over the "abolition vandals" whether they fought in trenches or not. As of May 19 the soldiers' collective confidence in Johnston remained abundant and their morale high.[27]

Johnston's plan to assume the offensive and attack the Federals went awry when Lieutenant General John Bell Hood, leading the division assigned to attack an isolated portion of Sherman's forces, called off the attack because of the unexpected presence of additional Federal troops. At that point Johnston opted to return to the strategy of assuming the defensive and attempting to lure Sherman into attacking him. He assumed a position south of Cassville and awaited his opponent. Sherman indeed showed himself, and his alignment of his forces, together with a brief artillery bombardment on an exposed portion of the Confederate lines, demonstrated the vulnerability of Johnston's position. After his subordinate generals convinced him that the position was in fact indefensible, Johnston reluctantly ordered another retreat, this time across the Etowah River to the small village called Allatoona. Military tactics and the desire to score a victory notwithstanding, considering the possible effect of the retreat on the morale of his army, Johnston had every reason to hesitate. As one Johnston biographer has shown, the failure of his plan to strike Sherman at Cassville depressed even the general himself. To make matters worse for the general, rumors of his impending removal from command soon circulated in Richmond. More important to the immediate prosecution of the war, what effect would this latest retreat have on his army?[28]

Indeed, the retreat from Cassville marked the first meaningful damage to the overall morale of the Army of Tennessee during the campaign. The retreat, clear to all the result of a last-minute decision, did not proceed with the typical smoothness and efficiency of a movement directed by Johnston. Despite the initial problems and the first signs of noticeable straggling in the campaign, the retreat proved successful as the army marched another eight miles south to Cartersville. Moreover, most combatants examined here, regardless of rank, soon came to believe that the retreat was the only appropriate course of action. Proper or not, the decision not to fight at Cassville momentarily dispirited much of the army.[29]

The overall collective confidence returned almost immediately, but the blow to their spirits at Cassville should not be overlooked, particularly in light of the principal cause of their disillusionment. The problem stemmed not from another order to retreat, but from the soldiers' disappointment after receiving the rousing order for battle only that morning. Over the next few days, soldiers noted their disappointment with Johnston for the order to retreat and showed the effects of the wearisome overnight marches. Some expressed disgust at the Federals' flanking maneuvers, and others allowed signs of doubt to creep into their correspondence and diaries. William D. Cole of the 35th Alabama Infantry, for example, warned his wife to hide money and meat from the Yankees if things got much worse. Yet by May 20–21, the soldiers' spirits had begun to recover in time for a brief pause in the campaign. According to one combatant from the 17th Alabama Infantry in a letter to his wife, although he admitted a degree of uncertainty on his part, most expected "that we are going to demolish them and that soon." Another Alabama soldier assured various relatives that the army remained in excellent spirits despite its retrograde movements. In truth, the confidence he described proved characteristic for the vast majority of the combatants cited in these pages with only days remaining in May.[30]

After the brief pause in the hostilities, the belligerents fought several engagements during the two weeks of May 23 to June 6, between the Etowah and Chattahoochee Rivers northwest of Atlanta. These included major battles such as New Hope Church (May 25), Pickett's Mill (May 27), and Dallas (May 28). Most soldiers spent these days fighting, marching, digging trenches, dodging enemy snipers, and generally trying to stay alive. As the campaign settled into a holding pattern, overall morale in the Army of Tennessee again stabilized and in fact improved, particularly in light of qualified victories scored at New Hope Church and Pickett's Mill.[31]

The former especially ranked as a victory of consequence in the soldiers' minds. The men commented on the severity of the combat and considerable casualties. M. H. Dixon of Tennessee admitted his astonishment at such a spectacle of carnage, noting, "I never saw men lying so thick in all my life." Tennessean William E. Sloan offered a detailed description of the engagement in his diary and judged the Federal casualties "astonishingly heavy." A few days later, enjoying an unusual period of silence, he quipped that the Yankees must have had enough for the time being. On May 25 an Alabama cavalryman expressed his continued confidence and disgust with the Federals' tactics when he wrote to his wife that the Yankees simply flanked constantly, refusing to fight, and that all of the troops remained assured of ultimate success. "God grant that we may . . . rout them completely." Even army musician Albert Quincy Porter, who could easily be described as a chronic complainer, observed the situation in late May and essentially guaranteed a Confederate victory.[32]

Soldiers' writings for this period reflect several themes, including their continued faith in Johnston and their insistence that they were winning the campaign. Thomas Hopkins Deavenport, an army chaplain from Tennessee, noted the soldiers' confidence in their commander and the cheerful attitudes and lack of complaints among the men around him. After the Battle of New Hope Church, Alabaman John Crittenden walked the battlefield and retrieved, among other things, letters written by fallen northern soldiers. He reported to his wife that he could not send her any of them because "I am ashamed they are so vulgar," but assured her that from their content he believed the Federals were worn-out and ready to give up. "I do not believe that God will ever suffer us to be subjugated by such a motly crew of infidels. Our boys are in high spirits. Have the utmost confidence in our generals."[33]

To that point, the soldiers in general refused to view their retreats as anything other than what had to be done. It is fundamentally important to note that the soldiers generally understood Johnston's tactics and strategy in the bigger picture and appreciated his efforts to protect the army overall and their lives individually. A Mississippian, for example, directed his wife's attention toward Johnston's "*great* carefulness in preserving his men from useless exposure to danger. He seems to think more of the life of *one* of his soldiers than Grant does of *100*. For this reason, whenever Gen. Johnston orders a forward movement, this army will step off with an alacrity and good will such as has never before distinguished it under former Generals." The soldiers' endorsement of Johnston's tactics would prove essential to their continued faith in the Confederate war effort. A comment by Alabaman Crittenden further illustrates the soldiers' views of the constant retreating and fortifying. He advised his wife casually, "We may have to fall back further but we will make another stand and fight them again. It only takes about one night for our boys to put up works that will keep the Yankees off." Another soldier advised his wife not to be discouraged by their retreats. Still another insisted in his diary that the retrograde movements did not demoralize the soldiers at all, and found satisfaction in the notion that their defensive tactics daily reduced the Federals' numbers. By early June he noted that the boys considered this the way to "git your independence."[34]

John Daniel Cooper, the soldier-poet of the 7th Mississippi Infantry, put pencil to paper again to express his thoughts on his sacrifice and why he continued to endure it. He penned these lines apparently in late May to early June:

> My loving wife companion dear
> It is for thee that I am hear
> I have some little children
> Two that to me is dear
> While battling for such jewells me think I should not fear
>
> Then I beseech thee pray that we may gain the right
> I will also pray yet I must march and fight
> To end this direful, unjust, cruel, and bloody strife
> Which in the end may cost you dear and me my life
>
> But with you and turn to stimulate and spur me on
> I shall not falter till the last invading foe is gone
> If I fall tell the children their Father in their defince lost his life
> And that you have been truly a faithful soldier's wife[35]

That the Army of Tennessee soldiers under scrutiny here maintained high morale into early June is clear enough. They not only maintained that morale throughout the remainder of the month, but actually saw it continue to strengthen. Sherman soon resumed his march, forcing a return to action by Johnston's Confederates. That action carried the principal fighting into an area northwest of Atlanta marked by several high peaks, including Pine Mountain and Kennesaw Mountain. During the next three weeks soldiers fought heavy engagements in those areas, continued to receive reports of victories in other theaters, including another success by Forrest in northern Mississippi, and closed the month with a momentous and bloody victory of their own at Kennesaw Mountain.[36]

To that point the soldiers' writings continued the common themes of confidence in their commander and, for the time being, belief in the propriety of their backward movements. June 7–9 proved popular days to write home about the status of the campaign. Georgia soldier George Peddy informed his wife that Johnston had already outfoxed Sherman. Alabaman John Crittenden insisted to his wife that despite the harsh conditions the men retained their high spirits. A younger soldier from Arkansas wrote a long letter to his parents that commented on similar themes and attributed the character of the campaign thus far to the cowardly behavior of the Federals, who refused to fight. He also expressed his desire to meet on the battlefield a former schoolmate who fought on the side of the Union. Another soldier supported Johnston's approach thus far and noted, perhaps with a note of sarcasm, or more likely with complete sincerity, his preference for the strategic retreat over getting slaughtered while assaulting breastworks.[37]

Life in the trenches, amid the heat, mud, artillery fire, and stench of dead men and horses, the constant hail of minié balls all around them, and of course the perpetual threat of death all became part of the Confederate soldiers' daily routine by this stage of the Atlanta campaign. Jesse P. Bates of the 9th Texas Infantry, who bathed on June 23 for the first time in weeks, insisted that the hard conditions did not deter his prayers for southern independence. The following day, John Daniel Cooper, poet and infantryman, was at it again and in rare form, describing a midnight scene of June 24, 1864:

> After the fatigues of the day the worn soldier is permitted to lay down to rest his bed being bestuded with prominent bumps and occasionally a stone and natualy very hard at 12 Oclock he wakes up completely refreshed.

He immediately recognises the familiar sound of a well known musket, takes a short glimpse of the horrors of war, the depravity of his fellow man offers a short prayer for his illumination and opens his eyes to find all nature in commotion, the whistle of the gentle breese as it passes through the thick foliage reminds me that man is fallen, the pale moon is draped in mourning as though she would hide the blackness of his crimes

The lonesome howl of the faithful dog say my friends have deserted me. The mournful low of the cow though an animal of inferior grade says that I have more reverence for my kind than man. Oh, man look around and the wisdom from which you are confiding nature waits unpatiently to reclaim you But, alas, you are dead[38]

Mississippian William L. Nugent, whose own spirits appeared to have improved even more after he received a letter from his wife, wrote that at such times the soldiers found themselves "sustained alone by a patriotism that has been purified by fire, in camp he often dreams of loved ones at home. . . ." Whether in camp, in the trenches, or on picket, "covertly seeking a tree to pick off & destroy the Yankee sharp shooters who continually annoy him in a fight, he is actuated by one moving impulse continually and that is to do and dare everything for the independence of his country." The young man from Arkansas put it more succinctly when he told his parents, "[E]verything is born cheerfully for the sake of our Country."[39]

Meanwhile in northern Mississippi, on June 10 Major General Nathan Bedford Forrest, outnumbered more than two to one, scored another victory over Union forces in what came to be known as the Battle of Brice's Cross Roads. Commanded by General Samuel D. Sturgis, with cavalry led by General Benjamin Grierson, the Federals from the Memphis garrison entered Mississippi charged with eradicating Forrest, thereby removing him as a threat to Sherman's long railroad-based supply line, his most obvious vulnerability in his campaign for Atlanta. Black troops who pledged revenge for Fort Pillow and promised to offer no quarter to the Confederates made up more than one-fifth of the infantry. Similar to the February engagement that thwarted part of the Meridian campaign, however, the Confederates sent the Federals fleeing back toward Memphis, many of them in a panic, and captured more than one hundred supply wagons and as many as sixteen pieces of artillery in the process. In the bigger picture, of course, even in defeat, Sturgis had kept Forrest occupied and away from Sherman's supply line.[40]

The big picture notwithstanding, the average Confederate observer, whether military, civilian, or press, delighted in Forrest's victory, perhaps the most impressive of his career. Predictably, the western press went even further and hailed the victory as one of the greatest triumphs of the entire war. One newspaper proclaimed, "The world will be astounded." Another publication boasted that it had become unnecessary to report who had won the engagement because Forrest and victory had become synonymous.[41]

Although such press reports were often intended to boost morale, soldiers and civilians reacted similarly. A Mississippi soldier worried for the safety of his family in Columbus, in the eastern part of the state, until he heard of Forrest's victory. "I think you can rest safely now," he told his wife on June 18. Approximately twenty-five miles to the north, near Aberdeen, writing in her journal on the day of the battle, Jennie Pendleton refused to grow alarmed about the reported presence of Union soldiers nearby. Referring to a worried female acquaintance, Pendleton wrote, "I tried to allay her fears by telling her I did not believe it & that Gen Forrest was between us & the enemy." A few days later she coolly confided to her journal that "Nothing much of interest has occurred only that Forrest gave the Yanks a good whipping and sent them howling from wherever they came."[42]

One Mississippi man's diary illustrates the connection between home front and battlefield and highlights the mixed emotions often experienced by Confederates who found themselves and their homes directly in the war's path. Civilian Samuel Andrew Agnew spent the day of the battle and the night after hiding in the woods, unable to make it back to his home, where the fight raged in his own yard. When he finally returned to his home on June 11, he found his yard full of soldiers and horses, alive and dead, and his house plundered. His diary entry that day offered a perfect summary of what so many southerners must have experienced during the war. "When I saw these things I knew that Forrest had gained a great and complete victory, but my heart sank within me at the prospect of our own losses & found Mother, Nannie, Mary, and Margaret in the back piazza. They were laughing and talking but under their mirth I could see a sadness concealed."[43]

Agnew also initially expressed mixed emotions about the black Federal troops. At first he sympathized with them because he saw so many lying dead, but then he learned that the soldiers had taunted his family as they passed and had predicted that they would become Forrest's masters. At that point, Agnew told his diary, "I lost all my sympathy for the black villains." He wrote two days later about what seemed a great number of black troops killed there, contending, "The most of the negroes were shot, our men being so much incensed that they shoot them wherever they see them. It is certain that a great many negroes have been killed." Those dead men, as well as dead white soldiers and horses, created a stench that lasted for days, possibly weeks, around Agnew's home, further pointing to what many southern civilians endured.[44]

Back in northern Georgia, where morale remained strong after the victory at Kennesaw Mountain, reports of Forrest's latest triumph naturally pleased the soldiers and officers of the Army of Tennessee. Johnston in fact hoped that the success might release Forrest to take his command and launch an offensive on Sherman's supply lines—the plan of action that Johnston had always considered necessary to the defeat of Sherman.[45]

Although mid-June witnessed continued high morale throughout the army, one incident saddened many soldiers. On June 14, while atop Pine Mountain inspecting the terrain with other officers, including Johnston, Lieutenant General Leonidas Polk fell victim to Federal artillery fire. A three-inch solid shot smashed his upper torso and both arms. The loss of the bishop-general briefly saddened much of the army, but truly hurt the spirits of soldiers in his corps, formerly the Army of Mississippi, and those from his home state of Tennessee. As Edward Norphlet Brown of the 45th Alabama Infantry wrote to his wife, "We lost the brave old Genl Polk. . . . He was much loved by the army generally but more especially by the Tennesseans." The death of almost any general officer in combat would elicit an emotional reaction from his troops, but Polk's position as a respected Episcopal bishop made his loss especially poignant. As a factor influencing morale, however, the events of June 14 on Pine Mountain should not be exaggerated. Despite his popularity, most soldiers noted the unhappiness of his passing and moved on. From a purely military standpoint, moreover, it was no secret that most considered him a better bishop than general.[46]

As mid-June became late June, the high-spirited soldiers of the Army of Tennessee continued to predict success. While some might have agreed with a June 19 newspaper report that insisted that Sherman had reached the end of his rope and could advance no farther, many soldiers cited in this study clearly drew confidence from their belief in Johnston and his plan. If they could only force Sherman to launch a direct assault on their fortified positions, they would score a major victory, possibly one to end the campaign completely. The southerners grew increasingly defiant as they actually hoped to be attacked. On June 27 they got their wish.[47]

Claiming that the combatants on both sides had come to believe that he would not employ such aggressive tactics, on June 27 Sherman ordered a direct assault on the Confederates' strongly fortified position on Kennesaw Mountain. Circumstances, he insisted, had forced his hand. Regardless of his motives or the validity of his claims, Sherman asked his men to achieve what was likely impossible, considering that they faced an almost impenetrable position held by veteran soldiers. The decision resulted in the first unqualified victory for Johnston in the campaign and approximately three thousand Federal casualties. Although the casualty figures of larger Civil War battles easily eclipse that number, the northern men nonetheless paid a heavy price to accomplish virtually nothing in an assault that never should have been ordered. Besides the needless bloodshed and the boost to Confederate morale, in the greater scope of the campaign the battle changed very little. Sherman yet enjoyed numerical superiority, a healthy supply line, and still threatened to flank Johnston on the west.[48]

In late June, however, none of that mattered to the soldiers of the Army of Tennessee. In fact, their victory at Kennesaw Mountain marked unquestionably one of the high points, probably the highest point, of morale in the entire campaign. Since the spring they had envisioned the Federals attacking them in fortified positions. In a disturbing illustration of the reality of warfare, Sherman's error in judgment amounted to quite literally an answer to the Confederates' prayers—he had offered up his men to be slaughtered by the entrenched Rebels. Tennessean William E. Sloan wrote of how they "terribly punished" the Yankees, while a fellow Volunteer State soldier confided to his diary, "The slaughter was terrific as our troops literally mowed them down." Without question, the Army of Tennessee emerged from the fight at Kennesaw Mountain a confident fighting force. They faced July with complete faith in their commander, whom one soldier deemed "perfect master of the situation," and with unceasing commitment to their war for independence.[49]

The findings presented here cast considerable doubt on the contention that historians could not make any assertive statements with regard to the Army of Tennessee's morale during the Atlanta campaign because it varied too much from one individual to the next and from one event to the next. A skilled biographer of General John Bell Hood—Johnston's successor as of July 17, 1864, and a traditional target for much blame concerning the loss of Atlanta and the falling spirits of the soldiers—has insisted that proponents of what he called the Johnston school have long held that morale remained high under Johnston and plummeted under Hood. (Johnston's removal in favor of Hood and that decision's effects on morale will be addressed

in the next chapter.) Hood's biographer insisted that adherents to that
school of thought relied too heavily on postwar rather than wartime sources.
Certainly postwar authors knew the disastrous results of Hood's tenure in
command of the army, during and after the Atlanta campaign, and that general's biographer correctly noted that such knowledge would shape those
observers' opinions. He further asserted that historians must admit to their
inability to offer a clear-cut assessment of Confederate morale in the campaign until they could provide overwhelming evidence from contemporary
sources throughout the campaign.[50]

For the portion of the campaign ending June 30, 1864, that evidence is
available. The evidence presented in this chapter, almost entirely from contemporary, wartime sources, demonstrates that morale among these members of the Confederate Army of Tennessee remained exceptionally high
through the end of the month. Nothing indicates that any of the combatants faked high spirits in their letters to keep up spirits at home, a possible
criticism of soldiers' letters. (Such a criticism would be a convenient way
to discredit the value of contemporary soldier letters, while also refusing
to accept postwar accounts.) They certainly had not done this during the
dark winter of 1863–1864, so why should they start that summer? Moreover, many of the soldiers' letters included in this study frequently referred
to the carnage of battle, sometimes graphically, and openly discussed any
number of sensitive issues. Nothing suggests that they would hide signs of
disillusionment now. Besides, to this point in the war, some soldiers did not
hesitate to admit low morale. Later, many more would openly acknowledge
total defeat. Obviously, individuals varied and not every man exhibited high
morale, but then this has rarely if ever happened in the history of warfare.
The army's overall morale at the end of June, even after retreats from Dalton, Resaca, and Cassville, remained strong and certainly presented no impediment to victory. They did not need to fake it, nor did they rely on false
rumors or embellished newspaper accounts. They had scored victories, inflicted severe casualties on the enemy when presented with the opportunity,
and fully appreciated Johnston's ability to keep them alive. Later action in
July and August 1864, both before and after the removal of Johnston, would
lend more support to the contention that morale proved too fractured to
describe straightforwardly.

In the larger picture, popular will around the West as a whole mirrored
the Army of Tennessee's confidence. That these western Confederates, military and civilian, remained committed to their war effort by summer 1864

should be clear enough. In fact, if western Confederate morale for the period from January 1864 to April 1865 could be charted on a graph, June 1864 would mark the high point. May and June brought the return of large-scale combat and casualties, but those months also produced celebrated victories in Georgia, Mississippi, and Virginia. As a soldier camped in Mississippi wrote in late June, "The prospect for our success in Va. is as good if not better than ever. Grant has met with severe chastisement already." Those and other optimistic sentiments of course were not unanimous, but support for the war never had been, North or South. Yet abundant evidence reveals that these residents and defenders of the Confederate heartland generally and consistently remained confident in their prospects for independence. By late June they remained committed to that cause and believed that "We are fighting not only to preserve our homes from desolation but for all that renders life desirable." The coming months, and the Federal armies, would provide the greatest test of those convictions that the Confederates had yet seen.[51]

4

July–August 1864

RETREAT, REMOVAL, AND DOUBT

AMONG THE WESTERN Confederates analyzed in this study, most entered July 1864 with a sense of restrained confidence. James C. Bates, a severely wounded Texas cavalryman hospitalized in Atlanta, expressed typical sentiments. In early July letters to his family he remained optimistic about Richmond and expressed conflicting views on Atlanta—one letter reflected complete confidence, in the next he worried that the city could fall to the enemy. Bates also began to discuss the northern presidential election and mocked the Republican candidates Abraham Lincoln (whom he termed "Abraham Africanus") and Tennessee unionist Andrew Johnson as "a sweet scented pair to save the union." Elsewhere in Mississippi, Belle Edmondson wearily noted the Federals' numbers but continued to insist that God would bless the Confederates.[1]

Just as May and June showed that many believed that they were winning the war, however, July and August brought uncertainty not witnessed in the western Confederacy for at least six months. Indeed the destruction, carnage, and separation from loved ones had begun to wear on civilians such as Alabamans Margaret Gillis, Sarah Espy, and James Mallory, each of whom prayed for a rapid conclusion to the war. Their diaries unmistakably revealed growing war weariness, yet all three remained loyal to the Confederate cause. In some cases, such as that of Tennessean Nannie Haskins, the sacrifice of war seemed only to strengthen the civilians' resolve. For example, in mid-July, in Union-occupied Clarksville, northwest of Nashville, Haskins reflected on the lawlessness and constant violence in the countryside around her. "Every minute of the day we hear of something startling, which four years ago would make us 'shake in our shoes' now merely give them a passing thought. War has hardened us."[2]

During those wearisome summer months, western Confederates directed their eyes more than ever toward Georgia and the campaign for Atlanta, where the Army of Tennessee, for the time being, continued to exhibit exceptionally strong group morale. The contest between Johnston and Sherman completely dominated the diaries and letters of the western Confederates whose writings form the basis of this study. Other events, such as the July defeat suffered by Nathan Bedford Forrest and his cavalry in northern Mississippi, the Federal capture of Mobile Bay in August, and the looming northern presidential campaign, drew secondary interest.

Coming off of the rousing tactical victory at Kennesaw Mountain, soldiers in the Army of Tennessee entered July with unbounded overall confidence. Despite its retreats since Dalton, the army had scored several victories of various degrees and inflicted at least twelve thousand casualties on the Federals (including three thousand at Kennesaw Mountain while suffering approximately seven hundred of their own). To that point, the soldiers had every reason to be satisfied with the results of the campaign. The first week of July proved no different, but during the engagement at Kennesaw Mountain, Sherman's Federals discovered an opportunity to flank the Confederates off of their mountain stronghold. When Sherman acted on the new information, Johnston reacted as usual with a strategic retreat on the night of July 2–3 toward prepared defensive works near the Chattahoochee River.[3]

During the retreat from Kennesaw Mountain to the northern bank of the Chattahoochee River, overall morale remained quite strong. Certainly some soldiers began to express mixed sentiments about the safety of Atlanta, the effectiveness of the Fabian tactics employed by their commander, and the Federals' numbers. Georgian John W. Hagan, for example, noted that the sight of the Federals and their wagon trains disheartened some men, but he dismissed those as the usual grumblers looking for an excuse. He insisted that a good soldier simply fought harder the harder his enemy pushed him. The army's high morale was not universal, and clearly the constant retreating, the sniper and artillery fire, and the summer heat took a toll on some of the soldiers.[4]

As of July 8, however, no momentous drop in the army's overall spirits had occurred. In fact, most of the soldiers in this study remained not only sanguine but steadfast in their predictions of success. Alabaman John Crittenden insisted that the army was not whipped and that no one else should be either. Fellow Alabaman Edward Norphlet Brown admitted that the bullets were getting a little too close for comfort, but informed his wife that he would die doing his duty if necessary. He wondered how any man with a family could not be in the service protecting them and denied any demoralization in the army. Another soldier, perhaps inspired to write on July 4, charged, "Our forefathers fought seven years for independence, and we have only fought for three. Can we stand it the other four? Yes, we will never give up as long as we can sustain an army, but we hope that long before the end of seven years our enemy will withdraw from our country and leave us in the employment of our liberties and under a Government of our own."[5]

Meanwhile, Private Thomas Warrick of the 34th Alabama Infantry reflected fondly on the recent beating they had inflicted on the Federals and wondered if the northerners would attack Confederate breastworks again. Tennessean M. H. Dixon provided perhaps the picture of defiance with his July 2 and 3 diary entries. "If the Yankees intend to eat their 4th of July dinner in Atlanta as they boasted of doing, it is time they were doing something." A day later he continued, "There is one thing that we all know, or think so anyway, that is that we will whip the Yankees whenever and wherever we fight. Our confidence in ourselves and Gen. Johns[t]on is unshaken notwithstanding we have retreated eighty miles."[6]

Dixon's comments provide insight into an important question—why did the soldiers of the Army of Tennessee remain so confident? Similar to earlier stages of the campaign, the men believed in Johnston's course of action that allowed them to score some victories, inflict casualties on the enemy, and stay alive. Soldier after soldier hoped that the Federals would launch another assault headlong into the Rebels' fortified positions, but clearly recognized the Federals' constant attempts to flank them. Furthermore, they absolutely understood and appreciated that Johnston sought to fight only under the most favorable circumstances. The soldiers also continued to hope, realistically or not, that the strategy would extend Sherman's supply line dangerously long and make it susceptible to Forrest's cavalry. Why should the soldiers of the Army of Tennessee not remain confident?

Mississippian Mathew Andrew Dunn illustrated those prevailing sentiments in a letter to his wife. He explained that the Confederates defeated the Federals every time the latter attacked, and that they could hardly ask more of their opponents than to attack "squarely." However, he continued with a hint of frustration, the northerners tended to avoid that whenever possible. He admitted that he could not know exactly how the campaign would turn out, but he knew that Johnston would handle the campaign as well as any general could. In a telling statement, Dunn assured his wife that citizens alarmed by the retreat simply did not know the "particulars," and that his commander knew what he was doing. Later he echoed the spring-time sentiment that Christians made the best soldiers because they faced battle without the fear of death, and he showed that the soldiers recognized that the results of the campaign could directly affect the northern presidential election. He closed by telling her to keep up her spirits and prayed that she never see the horrors of war that he had witnessed. Dunn's lengthy letter, that of a common soldier of yeoman stock, not only reflected the sentiments of the soldiers of the Army of Tennessee, but also demonstrated that at least some of them firmly grasped the importance of their role in the greater scope of the war.[7]

The following day, with his back to the Chattahoochee River, John Daniel Cooper, of the 7th Mississippi Infantry, thought of loved ones at home and wrote the last poem that accompanied his campaign diary:

> I love to be on some quiet stream and sit under the green willow tree
> And think of those that I have seen and wonder if they ever think of me
> But while I undress upon the chatahoochee brink
> And while I am bathing in its waters I shall of other waters think
>
> Ah sweet pearl it is upon thy bank my mind has strayed
> Tis there I often with my Brothers played
> Upon thy bank we've spent many a happy day ·
> But, alas, these days and Brother with me has passed away[8]

Cooper died as a result of mortal wounds he suffered at the Battle of Jonesboro only weeks later.

The events of the next several days again tested the dedication of men like Cooper and Dunn. Parts of Sherman's forces crossed the Chattahoochee River on Johnston's right (east), thus flanking the Confederates yet again and making still another defensive position untenable. Faced with the possibility of fighting the Federals under circumstances he deemed unfavorable and even then allowing some Union forces around him toward Atlanta, on July 9 Johnston retreated across the Chattahoochee River, placing his army near the outer reaches of the city. That move created considerable unrest within Atlanta and caused many citizens to flee. Only one newspaper remained, the refugee *Appeal* originally from Memphis. Its editors remained defiant and insisted that the Confederates would hold the city. More important, in Richmond, Jefferson Davis had grown increasingly apprehensive about Johnston's retreats and refusal to assume the offensive, particularly when the army reached the Chattahoochee River. When he heard of the retreat across the river, the president finally lost his patience with the general, whom he had never liked or believed in anyway.[9]

Such frustration, however, proved limited in the ranks of the Army of Tennessee. Perhaps predictably, as it related to morale, the retreat across the Chattahoochee River virtually mirrored the previous maneuvers. Some soldiers understandably worried that the Federals had pushed them so close to the city. For example, one soldier who remained confident overall and stood ready to fight to the end decided that the army had retreated about as far as it could or should. Another, who by July 12 still found the Confederacy's prospects "cheering indeed," admitted that there were some croakers with every move. On the day of the crossing a soldier wrote that if the Federals could flank them that far, why could they not continue all the way to Atlanta? Still another wrote that Johnston knew better than he and that good spirits generally pervaded the army, but wondered if the army might soon end up in the Gulf of Mexico.[10]

Although those sources clearly show that it was not unanimous, most of the soldiers examined here remained quite confident even after the crossing of the Chattahoochee River. Joseph Branch O'Bryan of the 1st Tennessee Infantry expressed the more typical attitude in a July 13 letter to his sisters. "The army has still the most unbounded confidence in Genl. J. and is not at all demoralized by having fallen back so far. We are satisfied that Gen Johnston will not fight under disadvantages. His men are too precious to be uselessly sacrificed. Whenever he says fight we all will be satisfied that the proper time has arrived. . . ." Only a few days earlier, Mississippian D.R.C. Martin wrote to his sister and expressed remarkably similar sentiments. He insisted that despite the repeated retreats, the troops retained as much confidence as ever in Johnston, "and still think him the greatest man in the army except Lee." On the issue of when and where the ultimate fight for Atlanta might take place, Martin wrote, "I never allow my thoughts to bother me about it I know 'Old Joe' will do the best he knows—whenever he says so the boys will do some heavy fighting—if we can hold our own here & in Va we will probably have peace this year—but there is no telling what Yankee fanaticism will do one day they are against & the next for the war to the last extremity."[11]

Despite the continued confidence of soldiers such as Martin, O'Bryan, and so many others, the soldiers soon received news that without question shocked and saddened most of the army. One of the most momentous decisions of the Civil War soon changed the entire character of the campaign for Atlanta and altered the lives of thousands of soldiers and their families. After months of frustration with Johnston's cautious tactics and numerous retreats, Jefferson Davis finally removed Johnston from command of the Army of Tennessee and replaced him with the younger and more aggressive John Bell Hood. That officer boasted the reputation of a fighter, and his war-ravaged body testified to that characterization. He had suffered a wound at Gettysburg that left one arm useless, and he had lost a leg at Chickamauga. Davis's decision remains among the most controversial of the war and has since provided fodder for the "what if" questions of professional historians and armchair generals alike. Most historians (but certainly not all) consider the removal of Johnston in favor of Hood a mistake, harmful to the Confederacy's chances in the long run. The merits of the decision, however, are largely irrelevant to the status of the morale of western Confederates. For the purposes of evaluating morale, only what the Confederates thought of the removal at the time matters.[12]

The removal of Johnston clearly temporarily lowered the collective morale of soldiers in the Army of Tennessee. But a greater understanding of the effects of Johnston's removal on morale requires a more detailed analysis of the reactions. What soldiers said immediately upon hearing the news differed somewhat from what they wrote over the coming weeks and of course in postwar memoirs. A survey of civilian and press reactions and a comparison between wartime and postwar writings also proves instructive.

The soldiers initially reacted with disbelief and despondency. Diaries and letters written immediately upon hearing the reports portrayed it as the worst possible news. Typical entries expressed love for Johnston, shock at his removal, and near-universal discontent. Some also conveyed disapproval of Hood as the replacement. To be fair to Hood, although some immediately lamented his appointment because of his reputation for rash behavior, most soldiers initially reacted as they did because they had lost Johnston, not because they had gained Hood. Regardless of modern debates concerning the generals' military tactics and who should have commanded the army, the men of the Army of Tennessee genuinely loved Johnston, something that could not be said for their other commanders, before or after him. James Marsh Morey of the 32nd Tennessee Infantry penned a typical entry in his diary upon hearing the news. "The change does not suit the boys at all. Gen Johnston is universally loved by the troops and they all feel as if they had lost their best friend some are even moved to tears. All believe that Gen Hood is too rash."[13]

A member of the 27th Alabama Infantry deemed the change of commanders a "great blow to our cause and has cast a gloom over the whole army." He continued:

> Strong men wept, while others cursed, and not one approved the change. We think it a terrible mistake by our President. While we believe General Hood to be a brave and efficient officer, capable of commanding a division or even a corps, we doubt his capacity to handle a large army opposed by the wily Sherman with three men to our one. No man in the Confederacy, not even Lee himself, could take the place of General Johnston in the confidence and love of the army of Tennessee just at this critical time. When the first shock had subsided, although there was much discontent and grumbling, duty bade us submit and hope for the best. But many of us still believed it the worst calamity that could have befallen us and our cause.[14]

Texan Samuel T. Foster provided perhaps the most famous and emblematic written response to Johnston's removal:

> In less than an hour after this fact becomes known, groups of three, five, seven, ten or fifteen men could be seen all over camp discussing the situation—Gen. Johnston has so endeared himself to his soldiers that no man can take his place. We have never made a fight under him that we did not get the best of it. And the whole army has become so attached to him, and to put such implicit faith in him, that whenever he said for us to fight at any particular place, we went in feeling like Gen Johnston knew all about it and we were certain to whip.
>
> He never deceived us once. It is true we have had hard fighting and hard marching, but we always had something to eat, and in bad weather, or after an extra hard march we would have a little whiskey issued.
>
> He was always looking out for our comfort and safety. He would investigate our breastworks in person, make suggestions as to any little addition or improvement that would make them safer or more comfortable.
>
> Gen Johnston could not have issued an order that these men would not have undertaken to accomplish—
>
> For the first time, we hear men openly talk about going home, by tens (10) and by fifties (50). They refuse to stand guard, or do any other camp duty, and talk openly of rebellion against all Military authority—All over camp, (not only among Texas troops) can be seen this demoralization—and at all hours in the afternoon can be heard Hurrah for Joe Johnston and God D——n Jeff Davis.[15]

The abundant evidence that the soldiers of the Army of Tennessee initially overwhelmingly disagreed with the removal of Johnston should be plain even to readers who consider Davis's decision proper and to the staunchest of Hood devotees. None of the soldiers cited here endorsed the decision within the first couple of days of hearing the news. Texan J. P. Douglas offered the response closest to an endorsement at that stage when he wrote his wife on July 18, "I suppose the President has good reasons for the change. One thing certain, Gen'l Hood will fight the enemy, and I believe he can whip them." Two recent narratives of the Atlanta campaign unfortunately analyze the removal of Johnston without discussion of the soldiers' overwhelmingly negative reactions.[16]

Over the coming days and weeks, the soldiers' overall views changed to some extent. In the letters and diary entries written after the initial shock of the change of generals, opinion was less uniform. To be sure, most soldiers examined here continued to lament the loss of Johnston, but a few actually favored the change of commanders. Edward Norphlet Brown, a quartermaster from Alabama, wrote on July 23 that the removal should have occurred sooner and that the army was now prepared to fight instead of run. (He soon changed his mind and condemned Hood as an army commander.) The next day, fellow Alabaman Robert Croxton wrote to his brother that he had begun to consider Hood better than Johnston. The latter had retreated too far, he reasoned.[17]

But most appeared simply to reconcile themselves to the situation relatively quickly. As a whole they never completely approved of the change, but Hood now commanded them, so they concluded that they might as well make the best of the situation and the positives that Hood offered. After all, whatever their perceptions of his faults, no one questioned Hood's courage on the battlefield, his dedication to the cause, and certainly not his willingness to fight for Atlanta. The thought of becoming the aggressor in the campaign at once worried and pleased many soldiers. They knew that Hood's appointment would mean major casualties, yet turning and fighting provided at least the chance to save the city and claim a victory in the campaign. W. E. Smith of the 7th Texas Infantry wrote a typical letter to his mother on July 31. "Perhaps you have heard ere this reaches you, that Johnston has been superceded by Hood. The troops did not express much satisfaction upon the occasion, but they seem reconciled to the change. Johnston was much loved, and many feared that no one could fill his place as well as he did. Hood is a great military man, and a Texan also, but I cannot say that I prefer him to Johnston. I deem him too impetuous, and many think he lacks prudence, but I hope he will prove successful."[18]

The correspondence of two other soldiers reflects their decision to accept the removal of Johnston and move on. Joseph Branch O'Bryan, a Tennessee soldier who wrote detailed letters to his sisters during the summer of 1864, on July 24 wrote of the removal, "It was very unexpected & it took everyone by surprise. No one knew what to make of it." Later in the same letter he stated that the soldiers initially disagreed with the decision, "but after more mature deliberation they think it is best to fight where we are." Still, he closed the letter with yet another comment about how much the soldiers appreciated Johnston. A Georgia soldier communicated similar thoughts to his wife, insisting that all regretted the loss of their beloved commander, but assured her that they were satisfied with Hood. They now expected to drive the enemy away from Atlanta.[19]

The soldiers' wartime reactions to the change of commanders differed from their postwar reflections on the subject primarily in that the later writings neglected to mention that the soldiers came to reconcile the change reasonably quickly. Although most never favored Hood over Johnston at any point during the war, postwar memoirs and reminiscences tended to portray the change of commanders only as a disaster. Postwar soldier accounts frequently portrayed Johnston's dismissal in favor of Hood as the administrative decision that killed the Confederacy. Such explanations indicated that the army never seemed to recover and, perhaps more important, implied that the soldiers at the time somehow knew that Johnston's removal marked the deathblow. Obviously, the soldiers who wrote after the war cheated by way of hindsight, particularly with regard to Hood. The veterans knew that Hood led the army into three major bloody battles around Atlanta almost immediately upon taking command. More important to the shaping of their postwar opinions, they knew that he virtually destroyed his own army that winter in the near-suicidal climax to his Tennessee campaign. Of course they knew none of that in mid-July 1864. In the veterans' defense, however, regardless of the decade, they knew that "Old Jo Johnston" never did anything like that and never would have.[20]

Reaction to Johnston's removal outside the Army of Tennessee proved largely similar to the soldiers' opposition but unmistakably less emotional. Predictably, the press offered a mixed reaction overall to the change of commanders. One newspaper editor decided that it would be improper to comment on the appropriateness of the change, though he noted that confidence remained high and judged that a tribute to Johnston. Western Confederate soldiers outside the Army of Tennessee also opposed the change of commanders. A soldier in Mobile, for example, on July 21 assured his wife that all looked hopeful for the Confederacy with the exception of Johnston's removal. Nine days later from a hospital bed in Auburn, Alabama, a wounded cavalry officer informed his family in Texas that the removal created "great dissatisfaction . . . not only in the army but in the whole country."[21]

That Texan's comment raises the question of civilian reaction. Like others outside the Army of Tennessee, the western Confederate civilians cited here regretted Johnston's removal, but reacted without great emotion and certainly saw no disaster in the decision. Frances Woolfolk Wallace, a soldier's wife in Meridian, Mississippi, noted that everyone around her regretted Johnston's removal. West Tennessean Robert H. Cartmell recorded in his diary the country's confidence in Johnston, but surmised that Davis must have removed him because he retreated so much during the campaign. Confederate nurse Kate Cumming insisted that no one knew why Davis changed commanders. It is tempting to assume that civilians, particularly those in the West, would rejoice at the decision to replace the always cautious Johnston because even the military novice knew that Hood would fight for their homes rather than retreat. Indeed some probably reacted exactly that way. Yet others bemoaned the removal of Johnston, because they genuinely believed that he was doing the best job possible. Perhaps more important, as in the case of Julia Davidson, a soldier's wife living with her parents in Atlanta during the campaign, civilians recognized the soldiers' feelings for Johnston and the effect of his dismissal on their morale.[22]

Overall, wartime sources clearly demonstrate the evolution of western Confederate sentiments regarding the removal of Johnston. The soldiers in particular genuinely mourned his loss, but most soon moved on and continued the fight. Understandably, the army's confidence in mid-July could not match the heights it had reached early in the campaign. Nevertheless, the majority of the soldiers remained confident and optimistic about their prospects for defending Atlanta. Moreover, to assert that the army's overall morale declined steadily, "with every step" southward, is simply incorrect. In a recent narrative of the Atlanta campaign, Richard McMurry, noted Hood biographer and historian of the western theater, insisted on this declining morale thesis, though he also has contended that no definitive statements could be made about the true status of morale throughout the campaign. McMurry has done much to rescue Hood's reputation as Army of Tennessee commander and has argued persuasively that, though extremely aggressive, Hood had very few choices when he assumed command and, at least in the battles around Atlanta, was not necessarily reckless and careless with the lives of his soldiers. The point here, however, remains that whatever the merits or flaws of Johnston's Fabian strategy or Hood's aggressive approach, and whatever side one takes in the debate over the change of generals, as long as Johnston retained command, the army as a whole was not demoralized, it did not disintegrate, it did not suffer traumatic casualties, and the soldiers stood ready to fight whenever he ordered. Moreover, Davis's removal of Johnston from command on July 17 genuinely outraged and saddened the vast majority of the army.[23]

By mid-July, probably neither Johnston nor Hood could have held Atlanta. Sherman's numbers and relentless flanking movements likely made that impossible. Thus, historians are left to ponder other questions, such as whether Johnston might have held the city until the northern presidential election, thereby denying Lincoln a major coup that helped him secure re-election. That, too, is impossible to answer for sure, though most likely he could not have. Conjecture aside, another question can be answered: once Hood assumed command, did his change in tactics affect morale?

To the surprise of no one, Hood almost immediately attacked the Federals, leading to the three hard-fought bloody battles of Peach Tree Creek, Atlanta, and Ezra Church, due north, east, and west of the city respectively, during the closing days of July 1864. Hood lived up to his reputation as an exceptionally aggressive fighter, but Johnston had left him little choice anyway. The Army of Tennessee could retreat no farther and maintain possession of the city. Hood now sought to strike the Federals when and where he considered them most vulnerable, during their turning maneuvers around the city. All three battles were Union victories, though Hood very nearly scored a significant success in the engagement known as the Battle of Atlanta on July 22. Despite the defeats, Hood showed his enemy, his soldiers, and the Confederate people that Atlanta would not fall without a severe fight. July closed with Hood still in possession of Atlanta but having suffered approximately thirteen thousand casualties in little more than a week.[24]

Obviously both sides fought hard, as Alabaman Thomas Smyrl described in a letter to his wife, Mary Jane. On July 25 he wrote of a Confederate assault during the previous days: " . . . [W]e are confident of whipping them when we fight our men is striking death blows they [the Confederates] don't fight like common men they fight like demonds & charge like wolfs on green beef. I am anxious to see this desperate war come to an end." In a series of letters written in late July, another Alabama soldier, Robert A.

Croxton, wrote to his parents and brother and sister about the death of an-other brother. He described in graphic detail how a shot struck his brother's head, relayed his sibling's dying moments, reminded his sister of a soldier's continuous vulnerability, and, as if to reassure them that he sought ven-geance, explained how he killed two northern soldiers immediately after his brother's death. Hood's aggressive approach certainly suited Croxton, who fumed, "I want ninety-eight more chances just as good before I am satisfied with the trifling Yanks."[25]

The idea that they would fight for the city temporarily proved popular among the soldiers. Hood and General Braxton Bragg, sent to Georgia by Davis to inspect the situation and apparently to gather information to sup-port the case for removing Johnston, predictably claimed that the more ag-gressive tactics boosted morale. Some soldiers' writings support the gener-als' claims. Alabaman Croxton assured his family that Hood would fight and that the Yankees would find great difficulty in taking the city. A Mississippi infantryman closed his July correspondence to his mother with a prediction that, despite his own disapproval of the change of commanders and the Yan-kees closing in around the city, the Confederates would repulse the enemy. Another Mississippian agreed, admitting that the Federals might maneuver the Rebels out of Atlanta, but they could never whip them out. He decided that the Federals wanted to "play Vicksburg" again.[26]

Although Hood's decision to fight revitalized some soldiers, the results of his decision, particularly the casualties without reward, soon weakened general morale. One soldier described the Union breastworks, behind which "a man is almost perfectly secure. They are as high as a man's head, and have a large log laid on the top, with skids under each end, thus leaving room enough for the rifles between log and dirt." After the carnage at Peach Tree Creek accomplished virtually nothing, one Confederate soldier compared Hood to Union general Ulysses S. Grant—in his opinion neither showed any concern for the lives of their men. A week later, the same soldier wor-ried that Hood would soon kill his entire army. Another combatant practi-cally echoed those sentiments and wondered about the wisdom of a weaker army charging a stronger foe. On July 28, after the Battle of Ezra Church, he quipped that more such affairs would leave Hood with no army at all. He contended that Hood's actions that day had done more to demoralize the army than three months' service under Johnston.[27]

Hospital records for both sides indicate that more than twice as many Confederates as Federals were treated for gunshot wounds during Hood's approximate tenure (17,260 Confederates compared to 8,021 Federals). Those data are hardly surprising, considering Hood's tactics, and the numbers certainly pale compared to the carnage many larger Civil War battles produced, but such losses by a smaller, supposedly defending army must have hurt morale. An Alabama infantryman offered a fitting summary of the situation when he insisted that the Confederates could not afford to swap man for man with the Yankees and that whatever else happened, considering Hood's aggression, if Atlanta fell no one could blame the common soldiers.[28]

After the Battle of Ezra Church, the campaign entered a month-long lull in major engagements. Hood's army physically could not take the offensive anytime soon, and Sherman found that he could not sever or take control of the important Macon & Western Railroad with his cavalry alone. Moving enough infantry to do the job would require exposing his supply line deep in enemy territory. That left the armies to face each other without a general engagement for a month. That lull, however, did not mean peace along the lines. Deadly sniper and artillery fire continued all along the front, and Union forces continued to lob artillery shells into Atlanta itself. A member of the 9th Texas Infantry grew tired of the constant sniping by late August, and wrote home that "we are nevr saft her no plase." An understandably exasperated sergeant in the 1st Mississippi Artillery confided to his diary on August 3, "Several shells bursted over our works this evening and two ps. passed through my fly. . . Thank God my dear ones were well."[29]

Despite that soldier's near miss, however, during the August lull Hood's embattled Army of Tennessee recuperated, wrote letters home, and turned much of their attention toward issues elsewhere. Soldiers' August diaries and letters predictably revealed increasingly mixed sentiments about the possible outcome of the Atlanta campaign and the war overall. For example, one Mississippian admitted some demoralization among the troops, but insisted that no army had ever held up better under such circumstances. He judged Hood a good general but lamented that he could not keep up spirits like Johnston could. Clearly, months in the trenches, constant artillery and sniper fire, questions about their leader, and the casualties suffered in late July had worn on them, particularly by late August. Until then, however, the prevailing sentiment among the soldiers studied here remained cautiously sanguine of their chances to save Atlanta, and most certainly retained their hatred for the Federals.[30]

In a letter written August 10, an Alabaman assured his wife that "I am as ardent a hater of the whole Yankee nation as anybody to be found and had rather kill one than any other thing into which God has breathed the breath of life." Later in the month he found added indignation from the sight of the destroyed landscape and homes around Atlanta. He judged the site of flames all around sufficient "to make a Southernor's blood boil. They may burn every house in the city but it will not hurt the army. They are only making war on private property, as other savages have done." Despite what must have been disheartening scenery and the sight of the Federals closing in, that soldier and many others continued to predict success for the campaign. Tennessean Joseph Branch O'Bryan reasoned that Atlanta could be held as well as any other point, while Linson Montgomery Keener wrote to his brother in Texas that all expected the Federals' campaign to fail. Myriad other soldiers echoed those predictions of victory and wrote about difficult but endurable conditions and generally steady or even improving spirits among the troops. Throughout most of August 1864, men in the Army of Tennessee continued to believe that they could hold Atlanta and ultimately achieve southern independence.[31]

The lull in major activity allowed many soldiers to focus on their concerns for home and family. George Peddy of Georgia hoped to survive the war so that he could repay his wife for her sacrifice. Alabaman Joel Dyer Murphree wished to make it home to show his wife how much he appreciated her and worried that the continued loss of loved ones could tarnish their happiness even if all else progressed well. Fellow Alabaman Thomas Smyrl wrote to his wife, "Janey My Dear do you think I have forsaken you No not so for I study daily about your welfare. . . ." A common theme that ran through such correspondence pointed to the soldiers' belief that they literally fought for their homes and loved ones. Mississippi cavalryman William L. Nugent wrote to his wife Nellie, "A cruel, relentless war is waged for our annihilation, and unless we present a bold front to the enemy, contesting every inch of ground, we may expect nothing but vassalage and slavery all our lives. Our rights and privileges will be totally destroyed and military governors and Yankee judges will govern us, while our lands will be parceled out among a horde of foreign adventurers and mercenary soldiers. This is a fate to which we can never submit." There can be little doubt why Nugent fought or that he remained committed to southern independence.[32]

Similar sentiments about home and family abound in other soldiers' letters from August 1864. Edward Norphlet Brown, quartermaster of the 45th Alabama Infantry, admitted to his wife that he preferred to remain behind the lines rather than enter the frontline trenches, but insisted that he would "go cheerfully and do all I can to drive the accursed foe from Atlanta and if I am killed I will endeavor to leave a memory behind that will not be a reproach to you & our babies. . . . The grave of a soldier fighting in such a cause as that of the South is a hallowed spot, and if I were allowed to choose the most honorable grave I should take that of the brave southern soldier who died in defense of his native land with the consciousness of having done his duty and of being remembered with affection by his wife and children."[33]

Other soldiers worried and wrote specifically about the conditions of their families in their absence. Thomas Warrick, a private in the 34th Alabama Infantry, instructed his father on what to do if the Yankees came, while another soldier, dodging shells as he wrote, asked his family to understand when the government agents or other soldiers impressed their cattle in order to feed the army. Grant Taylor, a reluctant Alabama private, enlisted in 1862 primarily to avoid conscription. In that way, he was atypical of the soldiers cited here. His concerns for his family, however, proved characteristic of probably every common soldier. On August 3 the thirty-something soldier wrote to his wife and four children, "I am glad you get plenty to eat. Have you ever bought any wheat or flour yet? Did you make any wheat at all and how are your hogs getting along. Have you a pretty good chance to make your meat next winter. And has the government taken any of your meat yet. These are little things but I would like to hear all about your little matters. Though small they are important and whatever is for your welfare is interesting to me to hear about."[34]

Meanwhile, those families at home also recorded their observations about the war that August, and many remained as defiant as ever. From Memphis, soldier's wife Frances Woolfolk Wallace insisted that her husband and his comrades would fight harder and seek revenge if they knew of the conditions the Confederate people faced under Union occupation. A week later she fumed, "If I were a man how quickly I would join the Southern army and how savagely I would fight." From Athens in East Tennessee, Robert F. Bunting, the patriotic chaplain of the 8th Texas Cavalry (Terry's Rangers) and a frequent correspondent to Texas newspapers, found numerous reasons for encouragement and insisted that the Yankees had more reason than the Confederates to fear demoralization. Although his message smacked of a pep talk, and he probably exuded too much confidence, he wrote nothing unrealistic. In Mississippi, Belle Edmondson wrote in late July, "God is with us, and the light of independence now glimmering in the distance will soon burst forth with a halo of unfading light and glory." Another month, however, would weaken even Edmondson's resolve.[35]

Although most of the civilians studied here clearly continued to believe that the Confederacy could win the war, they generally showed considerably less confidence than the soldiers. By mid-August, East Tennessean Myra Inman lamented about what a sad journal she kept for a nineteen year old. In a more extreme case, Alabaman Sarah Espy, a widow, mother of four Confederate soldiers, and owner of a farm overrun several times by soldiers of both sides during the Atlanta campaign, by late August focused on simple survival and understandably showed diminishing concern for the Confederate war effort.[36]

Spirits also took a hit in northern Mississippi, where Union forces scored a rare victory over the feared and hated cavalry leader Nathan Bedford Forrest at Tupelo on July 14. In skirmishing during the Federal movement back to Memphis, Forrest suffered a wound that put him out of commission for a month. The defeat at Tupelo and the wound kept Forrest away from Sherman's supply lines permanently, thus effectively neutralizing one of the western Confederacy's most potent fighting forces. From nearby New Albany, Elizabeth Jane Beach experienced the aftermath of battle. Although she interpreted the engagement as a Confederate victory because the Yankees returned to Memphis without going farther south, she wrote to her parents about northern soldiers, white and black, ransacking her house and eating everything in her garden. "I *can't begin* to tell you how they treated *every body*." She certainly remained committed to the Confederacy, as her comments throughout the letter attest. Beach continued to write for pages with disdain about what the northerners did to her property and that of others in the vicinity, and how slaves took what they could and followed the Federal army north. The same day Beach wrote her letter, farther south in Kosciusko, Mississippi, diarist Jason Niles observed more accurately that Forrest had been "badly whipped." Regardless of how Confederates chose to interpret the battle, the Federals accomplished their objective, and the tangible results plainly shook the collective confidence of people in the region.[37]

Two other issues drew the attention of western Confederates in August 1864—the Federal threat to Mobile Bay and the impending northern presidential election. In early August a combined army and navy force led by Federal admiral David G. Farragut attacked the Confederate fortifications that guarded Mobile Bay, one of the Confederacy's most important remaining ports and a prime target for blockade-runners. Many Confederates in the Mobile region had grown comfortable and until early August never expected an attack to materialize. When it did, the Confederates met the Federals with confidence. Despite the defenders' self-assurance and three strong fortifications at the entrance to the bay, however, Farragut purportedly issued his famous "Damn the torpedoes! Full speed ahead!" command on August 5 and battled a small Confederate squadron in the bay itself. By August 23 the Confederates had surrendered Forts Powell, Gaines, and Morgan, and the Federals controlled Mobile Bay.[38]

The Federal capture of Mobile Bay cut off blockade-runners and thus deprived the Confederacy of a major source of materials. As it related to morale, however, the entire episode ranked as a nonissue. Union commanders chose not to attempt to capture the city itself in part because they lacked sufficient land troops in the vicinity. More interesting, Sherman preferred to see a Confederate garrison there rather than Union troops tied down defending Mobile. Besides, Sherman reasoned, if northern forces controlled the city, importation would continue unabated and the goods would eventually make their way into Confederate hands. Thus to the western Federal brain trust, Mobile might have been more valuable to the northern war effort in southern hands. Of course, Confederates likely never thought of it that way. They regretted the loss of the bay to be sure, but they also knew that Mobile remained safely southern. That likely explains the relative dearth of written reactions of any kind to the loss of the bay among Confederates cited here. Mississippian Belle Edmondson, for example, worried greatly about the battle for the bay, but clearly focused on the city itself. Edmondson discussed Mobile in the same terms as Richmond and Atlanta. All things considered, it is not surprising that the loss of Mobile Bay did not significantly weaken western Confederate morale.[39]

Away from the battlefields another matter garnered western Confederates' attention that August. Although the topic became much more prominent in the coming months, even before the fall of Atlanta westerners began to talk about the upcoming northern presidential election and how it would affect the war. Most, but certainly not all, Confederates assumed that the election of a Democratic candidate in the place of Abraham Lincoln would be best for the Confederacy. While the Democratic platform remained unknown, the reelection of the Republican Lincoln would unquestionably mean a continued northern war effort and would illustrate an unceasing northern commitment to the war. A Mississippi cavalryman expressed a typical sentiment, and illustrated that some soldiers clearly understood the bigger picture beyond their segment of the battlefield, when he wrote his wife that the Army of Tennessee needed to hold back the Yankees until the Democratic convention could name a peace candidate. One week later he speculated that the Federals approached Richmond and Atlanta so slowly and cautiously for political reasons, apparently hoping to avoid major casualties or decisive defeat, thus facilitating the reelection of Lincoln. Others also hoped for a peace candidate to secure the Democratic nomination and initially approved of the nomination of former Union general George B. McClellan. As August closed, however, McClellan and the Democrats had not yet made public a campaign platform, and to their credit, most western Confederates knew better than to assume that the party would advocate peace.[40]

With thoughts of the election and their families, and with knowledge that Mobile Bay had fallen, the Army of Tennessee prepared for what shaped up to be the final clash for Atlanta. Although morale had diminished after Hood's three bloody battles in late July, it had recovered somewhat during the August lull. Despite the heavy casualties, Hood was not without admirers in the army, even in late August. Edward Norphlet Brown of the 45th Alabama Infantry insisted that the general would have held the mountains around the city if only he had been placed in command sooner. Brown reasoned that Hood had held Atlanta for more than a month and saw no reason why he should not continue to hold it.[41]

Others showed considerably less confidence in Hood, and Brown soon joined their ranks. On August 28 another Confederate soldier resolved that Hood's time had come to make his name or to be derided as a failure—he predicted the latter. On the same day, Sherman acted aggressively to end the campaign once and for all by capturing the railroad south of the city. With all but one corps of his three armies, he marched around Atlanta's western side and on the last day of August met the Confederates at the Battle of Jonesboro. Hood sent Lieutenant General William J. Hardee and two corps to come to grips with the Federals. Hardee's southerners fought that engagement with an uncharacteristic lack of zeal discerned by several observers. The dispirited Confederates' half-hearted attack against Federal major general Oliver O. Howard's Army of the Tennessee failed miserably, and Hardee found his forces separated from the rest of the Confederates by the other two Union armies—the Army of the Cumberland and the Army of the Ohio. The soldier who had predicted Hood's failure wrote in his diary on August 31, "The ordeal is past and JB Hood is gone under. . . . Our infantry

reached here, and charged the enemy in their works as usual, only to be repulsed with heavy loss. This horrid useless waste of human life, this wholesale butchery is terrible and should damn the authors through all time."
With news of the failure at Jonesboro and knowledge that the Federals had
captured the railroad and thus cut his last line of supply, Hood spent the last
night of August contemplating the evacuation of Atlanta.[42]

So concluded the month of August and for all intents and purposes the
summer 1864 campaign for Atlanta. Three Federal armies stood poised to
march into the city within one day, leaving Hood's battered Confederate
Army of Tennessee in a temporary state of limbo, unsure of where to go or
what to do next. More important, the imminent Union capture of Atlanta
would shift the focus of eyes North and South beyond the battlefield and
onto the northern presidential election of 1864.

Miles away from the action, in Cleveland, Tennessee, Myra Inman
closed her August 1864 diary entries with the perceptibly tentative note,
"This is the last day of summer and Atlanta and Richmond are still ours."
Two months earlier few predicted such a state of affairs. Western Confederates entered the summer of 1864 with exceptionally high morale, holding
the line in Virginia and Georgia while inflicting thousands of casualties on
northern armies in both theaters. In Virginia the indomitable Robert E. Lee
held off Ulysses S. Grant from the capital city, kept his own army in the
field, and retained the faith and confidence of virtually everyone in the Confederacy. Farther south, the Army of Tennessee entered July on the heels of
a significant victory at Kennesaw Mountain and retained almost unbounded
devotion to their commander, Joseph E. Johnston. Over in Mississippi, Confederates fully expected Forrest to continue to embarrass seemingly incom-
petent Union forces, while back in Alabama, Mobile seemed the most secure city in the Confederacy. All things considered, a lack of confidence in
summer 1864 would have been more surprising than such widespread high
morale.[43]

By the end of August, however, mixed feelings reminiscent of winter
1863–1864 replaced the tremendous buoyancy of previous months. Justified
or not, most of the Army of Tennessee never warmed to Hood as they had
to Johnston, and now those soldiers faced the almost certain loss of the city
they had so skillfully defended for months. Although the loss of Mobile Bay
never hurt Confederate morale like the loss of the city would have, it served
as yet another loss of southern territory. Even Forrest suffered a stinging
defeat in Mississippi, putting him out of action for at least one month, and

by summer's end Confederates found Lee bottled up between Petersburg and Richmond. As was so often the case, the emotions of a southern woman perhaps best expressed the situation and illustrated the morale of the Confederate heartland. In July, Belle Edmondson had written from Mississippi about "the light of independence now glimmering in the distance." By late August, she grieved for her "poor bleeding Confederacy."[44]

5

September–October 1864

UNCERTAINTY AGAIN

ON SEPTEMBER 4, 1864, Alabaman James H. Finch recorded a rambling, downhearted diary entry about the fall of Atlanta. "One more of our cities has fallen into the hands of the enemys yes one more is gone forever. rather discouraging to our brave soldiers some of our brave Soldiers have fallen . . . Husband Brothers sons sacrifices their lives there to the demand of their country many seats around the fire side are vacant never to be filled any more by the loved ones that have fallen at the fated city of Atlanta." The entry continued in the same vein to describe the anguish of lost loved ones and countrymen and employed the rhetoric of brave men fighting for freedom and defending home soil against invaders. Finch took the loss of Atlanta harder than most western Confederates and worried that that defeat might ultimately doom his country's chances for independence. But by September 1864 the mixed nature of his comments—nationalistic language contrasted with uncertainty after the loss of Atlanta—proved typical for the western Confederates examined here.[1]

Only three days earlier the Confederate Army of Tennessee under John Bell Hood had begun its evacuation of Atlanta amid chaos, fires, and munitions explosions, set off by the Rebels to keep the materiel out of enemy hands. The evacuation took place just before Federal soldiers entered the city that they had fought so hard to capture. Atlanta had indeed fallen, or rather had been taken, but now what? How would this momentous defeat affect the overall war effort and the Army of Tennessee specifically, and how would people North and South react? Only time and more bloodshed could answer the former question, though hindsight tells us that William T. Sherman's Federal armies later marched almost unopposed through Georgia and the Carolinas. As for the Army of Tennessee, after a few days of continued skirmishing south of Atlanta and a Federal withdrawal into the city, Hood attempted to gather his beleaguered army, once scattered over a thirty-mile area. Later in the month Hood moved back into northern Georgia in an attempt to strike at Sherman's long supply lines and force his adversary to withdraw to Chattanooga.[2]

Armies and battlefields notwithstanding, the reactions of the individuals involved are most important in a study of morale. In his masterful study of the Atlanta campaign, historian Albert Castel demonstrated that northerners celebrated the capture of the city as a sign that they could and probably would win the war. The victory reunified behind Abraham Lincoln what had been a divided Republican Party and weakened the once formidable Democratic Party by eliminating the possibility of a legitimate campaign platform that called for anything less than victory in the war and complete reunion. In short, Sherman's capture of Atlanta probably assured Lincoln's reelection and therefore the continued U.S. commitment to its war effort. Castel also showed that people around the Confederacy predictably took the news hard. The press continued in their attempts to prop up morale, but Castel contended they protested too much. He insisted that the loss of Atlanta essentially crushed overall Confederate hopes, particularly because it occurred at a time when so much had been going their way.[3] The fall of Atlanta unquestionably inflicted a major blow on the Confederacy's war effort and the spirits of its people, but in the western theater it fell short of the decisive event in devastating Confederate morale.

To be sure, for some western Confederates like Alabaman James H. Finch the loss of Atlanta shook their faith in the Confederacy to the core. Finch worried that the defeat might have doomed the fledgling nation to failure, and indeed an undetermined but significant number of Confederate soldiers deserted in the days just before and after the fall of Atlanta. Although desertion cannot be considered a clear-cut indicator of morale, a substantial surge in desertion directly related to such a significant military defeat must be considered at least a sign of deteriorating overall army morale. Interestingly, however, western Confederates' writings from the period of early September 1864 indicate clearly that the morale of the soldiers in the Army of Tennessee held up better than did that of the public.[4]

Among those studied here, western Confederate civilians, particularly women, clearly exhibited more despondency at the news than did the soldiers. The women's reactions are somewhat surprising, considering the emotional strength most of them showed up to September 1864. Days after the city fell, despite her father's insistence on downplaying the defeat, a female relative of a soldier finally issued to her loved one the famous call to come home. Elsewhere, Sarah Espy, northeastern Alabama widow, mother of four Confederate soldiers, and witness to the campaign for Atlanta, recorded the news in her diary with more than a hint of depression: "This is bad for it is an important place. It seems that the Lord is indeed shutting us up in the hand of the enemy for they are all around us." Similarly, young Myra Inman in East Tennessee responded to the news with "a very quiet cry over our country and absent friends," while ten-year-old Atlanta resident Carrie Berry witnessed the evacuation of most of the city's civilians and proved as capable as anyone of noticing how sad everyone appeared.[5]

Hundreds of miles away, another child diarist, nine-year-old Belle Strickland of northern Mississippi, also discerned the sadness, though she heard at least one adult predict that the Yankees could not hold Atlanta for long. That notion proved common and pleased one East Tennessee diarist and allowed some who took the loss so hard to maintain a sense of hope. Farther south in central Mississippi, a northern couple who had relocated to Georgia, only to be forced to flee that state, observed among the people a sense of dejection that they had never before witnessed in the Confederacy. Meanwhile, another Georgia woman refused to move and found her house surrounded by dead horses and mules, lived amid an overpowering stench that prevented her from taking a breath of fresh air, and in the aftermath of battle struggled every day to find enough food for her family. She understandably despaired and struggled not to give up hope. Nurse Kate Cumming, perhaps living in a state of denial impossible for the previous Georgia diarist, admitted the importance of Atlanta, but engaged in a somewhat transparent attempt to put a positive spin on the defeat. She insisted that even Georgians cared little about the loss of the city because of the prevalent wickedness there.[6]

The wife of an Alabama soldier provided one of the most extreme reactions. Malinda Taylor and her farmer husband could never have been described as much more than reluctant Confederates. But while he lamented the loss of Atlanta, by September 1864 she had tired of the war she never truly cared about anyway. While caring for five children (including an infant) and the family farm in her husband's absence, Malinda delighted in reports of increased desertion around Atlanta. She, like many soldiers to be discussed below, blamed Hood for what she deemed unnecessary loss of life. Hood was so mean, she wrote, that perhaps someone should aim a gun at him.[7]

Malinda Taylor's emotional response was not typical of most western Confederate civilians in this study, but it vividly demonstrates one extreme example of public sentiments by September 1864. Most of Malinda Taylor's fellow westerners after the fall of Atlanta experienced a period of dejection and uncertainty but still had not wholly given up on southern independence. A frustrated Alabama resident was probably typical of many when he observed in his journal in mid-September that neither victories nor defeats appeared to increase the likelihood of peace. Lieutenant General Richard Taylor, then recently given command of the Confederate Department of Alabama, Mississippi, and East Louisiana, toured and assessed the condition of his new department in September. Throughout his excursion he noted visibly weakened civilian morale in the aftermath of Atlanta's fall, which most civilians, he insisted, blamed on the removal of Joseph E. Johnston from command of the Army of Tennessee.[8]

Some civilians even remained optimistic despite the loss of Atlanta. One Mississippian admitted, "It is a dark dark day for our little Confederacy," but through the gloom he found a "gleam of sunshine." Despite many great ordeals, that civilian's faith in the Confederacy never wavered, and overall, he reasoned, "The health of the Confederacy is generally very good." Similarly, the wife of a soldier in the Army of Tennessee assured her husband of her high spirits, thanked him for his admirable service, and explained that she was glad to be the wife of an honorable soldier, unlike the unfortunate families of other soldiers who dishonored their loved ones by deserting. By late September, even a woman who initially refused to believe the news remained confident that the wearisome times would not long continue and, assessing the greater scope of the war, insisted, "I do trust that our Father is not going to give us into the hands of our enemies."[9]

At the same time that citizens reacted to the news from Atlanta, they heard reports of the death of Confederate brigadier general and cavalry raider John Hunt Morgan on September 4, 1864, at Greeneville, Tennessee, allegedly after a woman betrayed the officer by revealing his whereabouts to Federal troops. Interestingly, the raider's death produced more reaction among civilians than from soldiers. Morgan's death certainly was not a major factor in shaping morale, particularly in the bigger picture, but western Confederates who wrote about the event seemed as much annoyed as they were saddened. The loss of Morgan appeared to anger and further motivate those who took notice. Nurse Kate Cumming declared Morgan a martyr, while East Tennessean Eliza Fain proclaimed, "Thus has fallen another defender of the South. His blood will cry for vengeance on her who was his betrayer." Another East Tennessean who called for revenge sought it from Federal soldiers, and her comments, at least in part, illustrate some civilians' interest in Morgan's death. Sixteen-year-old Alice Williamson thought that the citizens should mourn for the fallen soldier and worried that Morgan was the only officer who cared for the Confederates in the occupied areas. The fiery young Williamson insisted that the Federals "had better stop rejoicing," because Morgan's men remained in the field.[10]

Like those hopeful civilians who refused to see the fall of Atlanta as the end of the Confederacy, the soldiers of the Army of Tennessee obviously recognized the defeat as a severe blow to army morale, but most of the men persevered and continued the war effort for the same reasons they had always fought. Moreover, the soldiers exhorted their families to remain defiant and loyal to the Confederate cause. One soldier wrote to his father immediately after the evacuation that the loss of Atlanta had not demoralized the army as much as he might suppose. Another, a member of the 6th Alabama Cavalry, wrote to his wife on September 2 from the small Georgia town of Oxford, west of Atlanta, that she "must cheer up & not be so low spirited." The boys remained in high spirits and expected peace and homecomings soon, he assured her. Yet another found a certain amount of comfort in the knowledge that the Yankees had lost so many men while trying to capture the city. Perhaps the most optimistic outlook came from a Texas cavalry officer in Mississippi who typically retained higher than average spirits and frequently found a way to put a good spin on almost any circumstances. He coolly assured his mother that the railroad connecting Atlanta to Richmond was the only real loss and that Sherman probably could not hold Atlanta anyway. Besides, he insisted, if the Confederates could not find a way to cut Sherman's dangerously long communication and supply lines, perhaps they should just give up the whole thing.[11]

Without question, some soldiers took the loss harder than these men did, and they too recorded their observations about their comrades' lowered spirits. Even men who took the more negative view of the defeat, however, typically did not consider it the fatal blow to the Confederacy. Robert Patrick, a clerk in the quartermaster and commissary offices, found the defeat and more particularly the disorganized retreat perfectly disgusting, disheartening, and dishonorable. He even questioned whether the army would ever be the same again. But before the end of September, even Patrick carried on and hoped for the best. Whatever his apprehensions about the army, he certainly did not give up all hope because Atlanta had fallen. Generally, the soldiers of the Army of Tennessee viewed the loss of Atlanta as damaging but not fatal and marched away from Atlanta with what one Mississippi artillery sergeant called their "characteristic fortitude." Others around the West perceived that mentality among the troops. For example, one soldier stationed in Mobile wrote that he was glad to learn that the loss of the city had not demoralized the army, and he proudly argued that only for the cause would men endure so much.[12]

The soldiers of the Army of Tennessee maintained, or in some cases recovered, their relatively high morale after the fall of Atlanta in part because, unless they chose to surrender, desert, or give less than their full effort toward independence, they had no other alternative. Second, those men who believed that they fought to defend their homes and families against invaders could not suddenly forget or forgo that motivation. Third, they had suffered defeat before, more than most armies in fact, and they had always lived to fight again. In that regard the loss of Atlanta was no different. After all, as some northerners noted with regret, Sherman had not destroyed the Army of Tennessee when he captured Atlanta. The army suffered, but it remained in the field and regrouped to fight on—in the soldiers' minds they had to. Finally, as the western soldiers had done throughout the war, they looked to each other to maintain their spirits. Once again, in their comrades they found reason to continue their struggle.[13]

Regardless of how harmful the soldiers considered the Atlanta defeat, the tendency to blame Hood emerged as a prominent theme in many of their contemporary writings. One historian has written that the bitter postwar writings of soldiers unfairly shaped Hood's reputation as an army commander. To an extent that was certainly true, but as was the case with the change of commanders in July, soldiers who wrote during the days directly after the loss of Atlanta had little praise for their commander. One soldier rightfully admitted that the uninspired effort by soldiers at Jonesboro could not be laid at Hood's feet, but beyond that admission and the typical recognition of his courage and tenacity, most of Hood's men whose writings form part of this study expressed little admiration for his abilities as a commander. For the loss of Atlanta, the soldiers clearly blamed Hood and to a lesser degree Jefferson Davis for appointing the general. On the day Atlanta fell, one Texas soldier even wrote that the Federals should thank Davis for replacing Johnston with Hood. That some soldiers anywhere anytime would blame their commanding officer for a failed campaign is hardly surprising, but it is especially relevant to the morale of soldiers who never experienced much success at any stage of the war and, for the most part, never approved of that particular commander in the first place.[14]

During and after the war Hood frequently blamed others for his short-comings. For the Confederate failure to hold Atlanta he blamed subordinate officers, the supposedly detrimental effect that Johnston's Fabian policy had had on the soldiers, and even the soldiers themselves for purportedly lack-ing the spirit and manhood to hold the city. He alleged that his aggressive tactics in the battles around Atlanta actually improved morale and showed a "manful" effort to protect Atlanta. However, the words of his own men, and not only those written after the war, contradict his claims. The name and image of Joseph E. Johnston that haunted Hood after the war already loomed in the last few months of 1864. Even days after the Federals marched into Atlanta, common Confederate soldiers knew that Hood blamed others for the failed campaign. Tennessean Joseph Branch O'Bryan, who composed detailed letters to his sisters during the campaign, wrote on September 12, 1864, that Hood attempted to blame Lieutenant General William J. Hardee, particularly for the uninspired performance at Jonesboro. O'Bryan, however, insisted that Hood's efforts to evade responsibility "could hardly succeed."[15]

Most of the other soldiers in this study clearly would have agreed with O'Bryan, as demonstrated by two common themes that emerged in their September writings. First, they insisted that Sherman simply "outgeneraled" Hood. Second, and probably more telling, they routinely contended that such a failure never would have happened with Johnston in command and that the army could never be as good under Hood as it was under Johnston. Fair and accurate or not, that is a powerful statement about the mind-set of an army. The loss of Atlanta made the soldiers of the Army of Tennessee miss their beloved Johnston and appreciate his abilities, or at least their percep-tions of them, more than ever. Much like the soldiers' reactions to Hood's replacement of Johnston in July, as it relates to morale, whether the sol-diers were correct about Johnston is entirely irrelevant. They wrote and they genuinely believed that Johnston would not have directed such a failure.[16]

The soldiers' writings are not entirely clear about whether most believed that Johnston could have actually held the city for any significant duration, let alone long enough to make any meaningful difference, such as depriving Republicans of the major battlefield victory they so desperately needed to help reelect incumbent Abraham Lincoln in the northern presidential elec-tion. By September, even Johnston's ardent admirers among the soldiers of the Army of Tennessee probably could not sincerely make such a claim. But the soldiers were unambiguous in their contentions that the army would have come away from Atlanta in immeasurably better condition under Johnston and that it would not have suffered as it did under Hood's command in July and August. The Federals almost certainly would have captured Atlanta either way, but there can be no doubt whom the soldiers blamed.

Even Alabama quartermaster Edward Norphlet Brown, one of the relatively few who initially supported the appointment of Hood, changed his mind by early September. In fact, two days after the fall of Atlanta he not only doubted his commander's ability but wondered if Hood even had a plan at all. In a statement that reveals much about the concerns of a Civil War soldier and illustrates the link between home front and battlefield, Brown warned his wife that after the defeat at Atlanta the war might now make its way toward her and their children in Barbour County, on the Georgia border in southeastern Alabama. Meanwhile, another Alabaman and dedicated Confederate soldier, Private Thomas Warrick, also worried more about the Federals reaching his home near Montgomery than about the loss of Atlanta. The Atlanta issue certainly dominated the writings of most Confederates, but the thoughts of even dedicated Rebels like Brown and Warrick never strayed too far from home and family.[17]

Traditionally, historians have agreed that the Federal capture of Atlanta inflicted a severe blow upon Confederate hopes, and the writings of Confederate civilians and soldiers certainly support that contention. But some historians see the fall of Atlanta as tantamount to the fatal blow not only to Confederate hopes but also to the overall Confederate war effort.[18] Although sensible and capably argued, such contentions go too far when they point to Atlanta as the event that dashed Confederate hopes in the western theater. Even if hindsight affords much perspective on the military and political significance of Sherman's victory, Confederates and Federals did not foresee the end of the war the following April. Moreover, the vast majority of Confederates studied here refused to admit defeat even after the reelection of Lincoln. As historian Thomas L. Connelly wrote, Confederates had experienced significant defeats before, including the loss of major western cities, such as Nashville, and yet the rebellion always continued. More to the point, Herman Hattaway and Archer Jones demonstrated that despite suffering significant symbolic and logistical losses with Atlanta, the Confederates maintained an east-west railroad line and manufacturing centers at Selma and Augusta, and in the bigger picture, Confederates more than held their own in Louisiana and, more important, Virginia. The capture of Mobile Bay proved relatively inconsequential with regard to morale, particularly because the city itself remained in Confederate hands, and overall Union military commander Ulysses S. Grant's vision of capturing the city of Mobile as part of his plan to advance simultaneously against the Confederates on multiple fronts never materialized. An Alabama newspaper printed a general update on the state of the war on September 1, while Federal forces prepared to march into Atlanta, and concluded, "On the whole, the news is quite cheering." Although that statement is an obvious exaggeration, the writer addressed some of the same points raised later by Hattaway and Jones. Finally, and perhaps most important, Hood's beleaguered Army of Tennessee remained in the field with the opportunity to strike a major blow for the Confederate cause.[19]

Long before Civil War historians debated the significance of Sherman's capture of Atlanta, Confederate soldier E. H. Rennolds recorded in his diary a fitting summary of the defeat's effect on morale. On September 4, 1864, he wrote, "It is a severe blow, but is bravely borne by all." In subsequent entries he admitted seeing despondence among some soldiers but hoped and expected morale to improve. Within the month and in succeeding weeks, he noted improving spirits throughout the Army of Tennessee. Rennolds's characterization is consistent with the general spirit depicted in soldiers' diaries and letters following the loss of Atlanta. The loss clearly demoralized civilians and soldiers more than any other event since 1863, but most Confederates refused to concede the war just because Atlanta had fallen. Citizens generally took the loss harder than did the soldiers, but even the civilians typically did not consider it a crippling blow. Whether historians see it as fatal or not, they agree that the loss of Atlanta hurt morale significantly because of the loss of an important city, the loss of munitions and other supplies, the encouragement provided to Republicans in the upcoming northern presidential election, and the psychological blow of losing not just another city but one that the Confederates had fought so hard to defend.[20]

The loss of Atlanta proved significant for all of these reasons, but in assessing morale, the psychological aspect warrants closer scrutiny. Although Confederates did not write explicit explanations for why the loss of Atlanta hurt morale, certain points emerge clearly from the sources. The significance lay not merely in another, albeit momentous, military reverse, but rather in the circumstances of the loss. Confederates knew how much, materially and emotionally, they had invested in Atlanta's defense and realized that they had fought under more favorable conditions than many Confederate forces had encountered throughout the war. The defeat therefore forced many, possibly more than ever before and certainly more than at any other time since 1863, to question their overall position in the war. With few exceptions, Confederate authorities had virtually stripped Mississippi and Alabama of soldiers, and the coveted lands of Tennessee had at least temporarily become an afterthought. During the campaign the Rebels fought the Federals from the defensive for the most part and, though outnumbered, they were not dramatically out-manned.[21] The mountainous terrain of northern Georgia appeared to provide ideal natural support for a defensive campaign. In short, in the bigger picture Atlanta could have been more competently defended, or at least held for a longer period, and the Confederates knew it.

Therein lies the larger significance. Despite the circumstances (if not favorable, they were at least no more overwhelming than other Confederate armies had encountered), despite the emphasis the national government at Richmond, officers, soldiers, citizens, and press placed upon holding the city, and despite the massive effort in materials and lives expended, the Confederates lost. Over the coming months western Confederates must have at least wondered about the relative strengths of the battered Army of Tennessee and the western Federal armies, and by extension, the relative strengths of the two belligerents. Yet, as soldier E. H. Rennolds and so many other western Confederates wrote, the loss of Atlanta was painful but hardly fatal. The Confederates had suffered significant defeats before and they had always carried on. The Army of Tennessee survived (thus depriving Sherman of his goal of destroying Hood's army), other armies of varying strengths remained around the Confederacy, and of course the Confederates still boasted Nathan Bedford Forrest and Robert E. Lee.

As one western Confederate wrote, after the fall of Atlanta most people North and South turned their attention to the northern presidential election, and for many Confederates that contest seemed to provide an excellent opportunity for a peaceful and favorable settlement of the war. Western Confederates had long talked about the election, not just after the Atlanta campaign, but the defeat in Atlanta changed their outlook considerably. One Alabaman predicted that the recent Federal triumph would likely sweep Abraham Lincoln back into office, but he expected the war to continue almost regardless of the election's outcome and wondered whether the election really mattered to the Confederate cause anyway.[22]

In the North, Abraham Lincoln had secured renomination for the presidency despite deep divisions within his own party, in part over the perceived leniency of his reconstruction plan for the postwar South. Moreover, at least until the fall of Atlanta, many northerners regardless of party allegiance questioned his ability to lead the country to victory in the war. The capture of Atlanta and the lack of any other suitable option unified the Republicans, who during the 1864 campaign dubbed themselves the Union Party in order to attract those Democrats committed to the war and unionists from the border states.[23]

To oppose Lincoln, the Democrats proposed a familiar name, former Union general George B. McClellan. The most important plank in the Democratic platform, announced from Chicago only days before news of Atlanta's capture made headlines, called for an immediate armistice and a peaceful solution to the war. Such a stand effectively pronounced the war a failure. Until the fall of Atlanta, many people, including Lincoln, believed that the Republicans would lose the presidency. But Sherman's triumph in Georgia obviously undercut the Democrats and their peace platform. Moreover, McClellan accepted the nomination after the fall of Atlanta and, in light of the recent Federal military success and as a military man, found himself in a difficult position. In his acceptance letter, the former general explained that he could not tell his fellow soldiers that their efforts had been in vain, and therefore, if elected, he would see the war through to victory and reunion. The Democratic nominee thus had renounced the central plank in his party's platform, and the Republican Lincoln won the election handily.[24]

It is widely agreed that, during the months leading up to the election and especially before the capture of Atlanta, most Confederates hoped for the defeat of Lincoln. After all, although a Democratic victory clearly would not have guaranteed peace, a Republican victory certainly would have demonstrated continued northern commitment to the war effort. Until September most believed that any Democratic chief executive would be more likely than Lincoln to entertain proposals to end the war at the negotiating table rather than on the battlefield, and any such settlement would likely include terms favorable to the Confederacy. After all, that new president probably would be elected based on northern opposition to the Lincoln administration's conduct of the war and, to a degree, opposition to the war itself. Like most northern Democrats, many western Confederates initially cheered the nomination of McClellan as a legitimate contender and potential peace advocate, but even that sentiment was never unanimous, and his letter of acceptance obviously shattered that notion.[25]

McClellan's letter definitely flustered some western Confederates and dramatically affected their perspectives on the election and that contest's relationship to morale. The general, or whomever the Democrats might have nominated, had represented a legitimate chance for peace with southern independence achieved and slavery intact. Most quickly understood, however, that McClellan's announcement combined with the fall of Atlanta virtually guaranteed Lincoln's reelection. More important, many western Confederates examined in this study found little difference in the candidates if both publicly committed to the war effort. By September, in the minds of an increasing number of western Confederates, it made little difference which Yankee won the presidency. That revelation of course fundamentally altered many observers' positions on the election generally and on Lincoln specifically. Many even began to consider the heretofore paradoxical possibility, argued by a small minority even before the fall of Atlanta, that the election of Lincoln might somehow be better for the Confederacy.[26]

Two examples of that argument are instructive. One written by a typically optimistic Texas cavalry officer, James C. Bates, at Auburn, Alabama, reeks of post-Atlanta spin or damage control. In mid-October the cavalry captain conjured up five reasons why he preferred Lincoln to McClellan. Bates concluded that Lincoln's policies of confiscation and emancipation would further unite southerners; that the president had frequently proven his general incompetence; that Lincoln's opponents in the North would unite against him and work against his war policies; that McClellan's election would breathe new life into the northern war effort; and that McClellan might offer terms of reconciliation that to one degree or another honored southern rights and therefore might attract southern support. After his treatise, Bates offered confident predictions for the election but admitted what most western Confederates increasingly and perhaps had always understood, that they probably would have to fight for their independence regardless of who won the election.[27]

Some Confederates announced their preference for Lincoln long before the fall of Atlanta, when the war was going relatively well for the Confederacy. In April 1864, five months before Sherman's Georgia victory, a Mobile newspaper published a piece titled "Our Best Friend—Abe Lincoln," in which the editors argued that a Republican Party triumph that fall would be the best possible outcome for the Confederacy, in part because no foreign power or significant, organized political group in the North had yet advocated official recognition of the Confederacy. Therefore, fighting for independence and recognition against "the same corrupt imbeciles that have managed the war for the last three years" seemed as desirable and as likely to succeed as any other alternative. To support that statement the editors pointed to alleged northern weaknesses ranging from the national treasury to the lack of strength and character of the Federal armies. Second, they insisted that Lincoln's reelection would further unify the Confederate states by revealing a northern popular endorsement of the president's declarations and policies about slavery and emancipation, thus making any peaceful reunion and reconstruction impossible. Third, a Lincoln victory would keep northern military and administrative power in the hands of those the Confederates had repeatedly defeated and surely would defeat again. Finally, the editors blamed Lincoln for preventing a peaceful resolution to the sectional disputes, starting the war, and changing the object of the struggle from a war to preserve the union to a war for black slaves. If reelected, therefore, Lincoln would someday receive his due punishment when his "deluded people fully comprehend" that the war had been conducted not for the good of the country but rather for party supremacy. The Mobile editors went on at length, but ultimately asked their readers why any Confederate should favor anyone other than Lincoln as an opponent. More important, they concluded what most others realized months later, that "peace and separation can come only by victory," and they rejected "all the babbling folly about *negotiation*."[28]

The election would not be final until November, but in September and October 1864 the western Confederates considered here already understood its significance, or lack thereof, to their cause. Most of the rank and file remained committed to their struggle for independence, and they knew that if they were to achieve that goal they would have to fight for it. The election would not change that regardless of the outcome. Although Lincoln's reelection helped to secure a Union victory in the Civil War as much as any nonmilitary event, as of October 1864 his expected victory had not demoralized these residents of the Confederate heartland. One Alabaman who recognized the likelihood of Lincoln's victory continued to insist that God could not allow the Confederates to be "subjugated by such a race of people as the Yankees," while a Texan preferred war to a "degrading peace." In late October a soldier who had been disgusted and disheartened by the retreat from Atlanta had recovered in spirit. He concluded that Lincoln would certainly win the election, looked toward possibly another four years of war, and confided to his diary, "Well, let her rip, I say. It is better to fight always than to give it up."[29]

Regardless of the pending election and the loss of Atlanta, the Army of Tennessee remained in the field and its officers and soldiers indeed intended to fight. Even a soldier who occasionally showed lower morale than his comrades and was more than ready to go home insisted, ". . . I can never let a Yankee boast of whipping us to me I will shoot him when ever he does it . . . let it be as it may. . . ." After the fall of Atlanta the army fielded approximately thirty-nine thousand men fit for duty, including infantry, cavalry, and artillery, following the loss of an estimated fifty thousand men killed, wounded, missing, captured, fallen ill, or deserted during that campaign. The hasty evacuation of the city forced the army to leave behind or destroy immense quantities of artillery, small arms, ammunition, supplies, rail cars, and even food. During the next few weeks, the army rested and recuperated while Hood plotted his next move. The general ultimately relocated his army to Palmetto, Georgia, a railroad village twenty-four miles southwest of Atlanta. There Hood planned a campaign that would take his battered forces back into northern Georgia in an attempt to cut Sherman's communication and supply lines in hopes of drawing the Federals out of the state. Also at Palmetto, Hood received a visit from Confederate president Jefferson Davis, who intended to inspect the army and give a number of morale-building speeches to soldiers and civilians around the West.[30]

During the early September days between the fall of Atlanta and the Davis visit on September 25, the army's overall morale could be described as mixed but gradually improving. Certainly some soldiers expressed low morale and doubted their chances, but most recovered from the loss of Atlanta and thought of home and family, wondered what the winter would hold, and pondered future campaigns. During the first weeks of September, soldiers talked about northern politics, continued to criticize Hood, and called for the return of Joseph E. Johnston. Religious activity also picked up again in the lull between major campaigns. By mid-month, Jesse P. Bates of the 9th Texas Infantry noted improving rations and increasing numbers of soldiers because of the use of slaves in noncombat positions, thus freeing up more white men to enter the ranks. Bates expressed what was once again becoming an increasingly typical sentiment when he told his wife, "Our army is generally in good spirits and determined to be free or sacrifice their lives trying." Overall, the men of the Army of Tennessee expressed a more cautious or reserved confidence than before but remained committed to their fight for independence.[31]

Besides those general points, two other related themes ran through many soldiers' writings. Common anger and hatred of the northern invaders, whom they blamed for the war to begin with, continued to provide motivation. Because the army was located so near some of the battlefields around Atlanta, the soldiers walked those fields and saw the devastation wrought by the contest for that city. For many, the carnage and desolation provided constant reminders of why they fought. One soldier, for example, wrote to his father that he had found his brother's partially buried remains on an unnamed battlefield. Another described to his wife an area littered with partially buried soldiers' remains. That soldier admitted his doubts about the army's ability to defeat the Federals and defend the Confederacy's heartland, but maintained, "I think we should fight them to the last & kill all of them we can." Even this man who admitted demoralization found a degree of motivation in the opportunity to kill as many Federals as possible. Sherman's famous order that forced citizens to evacuate Atlanta only angered these soldiers more and fueled the hatred that helped form the common bond between western Confederates.[32]

On September 25, 1864, Confederate president Jefferson Davis arrived at Palmetto to visit with Hood, inspect the army, formulate a new strategy, and bolster morale. The army held a grand review for the chief executive, who, according to some soldiers, appeared noticeably gaunt and worn. With predictably mixed results, Davis addressed and attempted to inspire the soldiers. Although one postwar account recalled how Davis's message uplifted and inspired the men, wartime sources show that the soldiers generally greeted Davis with varying degrees of enthusiasm, but the mood was hardly celebratory. One diarist observed that some men chose not to cheer Davis not because they had any problem with him, but because they simply did not feel like it. On one hand, even if they questioned his leadership and particularly his removal of Johnston from command of the Army of Tennessee, the soldiers recognized and appreciated Davis's efforts and dedication to the cause. On the other hand, some soldiers refused to forgo such an opportunity to make their opinions heard. As the president and other high-ranking officials and officers rode in front of the troops, according to wartime sources, groups of soldiers yelled for the return of Johnston, despite advance orders not to do so. As one young Arkansas soldier wrote, although many among the public appeared discouraged, "[T]he Army is in fine spirits. All they want is a leader."[33]

During those late September days at Palmetto, the soldiers' morale indeed continued to recover. An Alabama infantryman exhibited continued confidence in a September 25 letter to his wife. In his broken grammar, Thomas Warrick told his wife, "[T]he yankes is still at atlanta yet but they ant no telling when they will come down on us but we are ready for them when they do." Another Alabama soldier's diary reflected steadily improving morale from late September throughout October, while a Texas cavalryman embellished somewhat when he wrote that the troops were "in as good Spirits as ever it apear like nothing wont dis hearten them." That Texan's braggadocio notwithstanding, the men in the Army of Tennessee still believed that they could win the war. That such men would continue to believe in themselves and their cause is hardly surprising. After all, those soldiers at Palmetto were the ones who were still there. Moreover, Army of Tennessee historian Larry J. Daniel described western Confederate soldiers as "a rough looking set" who bore hardship patiently throughout the war and typically drew their spirit not from their leaders but from each other.[34]

Despite their continued commitment, however, they were also undoubtedly fatigued, cranky, tiring of war, and increasingly dissatisfied with their leadership. Some soldiers recognized Hood's attempts to address living conditions and morale, particularly improvements in the form of increased and more consistent rations and requisitions to pay the soldiers money the government had owed them for months. All of those actions helped sustain the soldiers' spirits, but money, rest, steady meals, and patriotic speeches could not restore the army to its pre-Atlanta form. Something greater would be required to reinvigorate the army's spirits to that degree.

Hood provided the needed spark to morale on October 1 when he launched a campaign into northern Georgia and northern Alabama designed to threaten Sherman's lines of supply and communication and force the Federals to withdraw from the state or attack the Confederates in prepared defensive positions. Hood would receive the support of Nathan Bedford Forrest's cavalry, recently ordered by Davis to strike at Sherman's communications. As Hood and Davis expected, Sherman moved north from Atlanta to protect his communications, delaying what would become his March to the Sea, but no major engagements occurred north of Atlanta. Instead, Hood achieved moderate success in damaging Sherman's railroad supply line and consciously avoided involving his army in any major clashes with his stronger adversary. Ultimately, by mid-October, Hood moved his army west into northeastern Alabama, where it paused briefly at Gadsden. From there Hood prepared to launch a more ambitious campaign that observers recognized would either bring him glory or destroy his army.[35]

Although Hood's foray north of Atlanta accomplished relatively little in the greater scope of the war, the return to active service clearly helped the collective morale of the Army of Tennessee. A degree of uncertainty remained, particularly regarding the soldiers' perceptions of Hood's leadership, but soldiers genuinely rejoiced at the decision to take action rather than sit in camp. One Tennessee soldier confided to his diary in early October that he was "jubilant" to advance again, that he had never seen the army in better spirits, and that civilians along the way cheered their arrival. Others echoed his assessment of improved army morale. Even a soldier who took the loss of Atlanta especially hard and initially worried that the army marched toward failure at the beginning of the early October campaign changed his mind within the first week, exhibited higher spirits, and considered the brief campaign a success.[36]

Two articulate men who frequently provided vivid expressions of soldier sentiment once again summarized their comrades' morale in early October 1864. Going beyond the simple comments about good or improving spirits, Edward Norphlet Brown, a quartermaster from Alabama, probably spoke for many when he described his mind-set as "hopeful but fearful." He and most other soldiers knew that Hood envisioned a more grandiose operation into Tennessee, and Brown expected that campaign to result in the ruin of someone's army. He insisted that the Army of Tennessee had never been in better spirits, delighted in the notion that Sherman might have considered them defeated, and hoped that Hood could somehow draw Sherman out of Georgia.[37]

An equally observant and expressive comrade, army clerk Robert Patrick, also evinced feelings of hope and fear. Clearly less optimistic than quartermaster Brown, Patrick lacked confidence in Hood as a leader, proclaiming, "He is a good, rough fighter, but when that is said, all is said. He hasn't the knowledge of military affairs that Johnston possesses." Within the first few days of October, however, even Patrick found signs of hope during the campaign in northern Georgia. Perhaps Hood had "out-witted" Sherman. Yet, throughout those first two weeks of October, Patrick's appraisal of the army's chances fluctuated. He remained committed to the cause, found more than ample joy among the young ladies in the area, and seemed to look for a reason to be as hopeful as most of his comrades, but he clearly could not completely overcome his doubts about Hood.[38]

The coming weeks provided ample opportunity for Hood to gain the approval of his soldiers. On October 22, the army marched northwest out of Gadsden, Alabama, beginning the campaign that would be the ill-fated invasion of Tennessee. Hood planned to recapture Nashville and possibly even invade Kentucky or Ohio. Those actions and continued assaults on Sherman's communications would either draw the Federals out of Georgia or at least, believed the Confederate brain trust, Hood could do more damage in Tennessee and farther north than Sherman could do in Georgia. Sherman, of course, essentially left Hood to George H. Thomas's Union forces in Middle Tennessee, and soon began his March to the Sea through Georgia. In a strange turn of events, two major adversarial armies now marched in opposite directions. To Hood's credit, it was clear to most observers then, and most Civil War historians agree today, that the initial move toward Tennessee improved morale because the army assumed the role of the aggressor after months of reacting to their opponents' maneuvers and because so many soldiers from the Volunteer State rejoiced at the opportunity to return to and retake their homeland.[39]

The soldiers themselves definitely noticed a spike in morale when the movement toward Tennessee began. Diaries and letters abounded with comments pointing to good spirits and enthusiasm. In addition to the return to the offensive and the opportunity to "liberate" Tennessee, the soldiers pointed to their perceived success in attacking Sherman's railroad supply lines in northern Georgia, their recent payday, and an issue of shoes and clothing. Some soldiers had been barefoot for more than a month. One Alabama soldier credited Hood with showing improved leadership but still breathed easier when Confederate general P. G. T. Beauregard arrived at Gadsden with the somewhat ambiguous new title of theater commander. All things considered, the men of the Army of Tennessee began their march through northern Alabama with rather high spirits. Material deprivation, almost impassable roads, freezing weather, and one of the Confederate military's most disastrous evenings of the entire war would soon change that.[40]

Like January–February 1864, September–October marked uncertain times for the western Confederates analyzed here. During that previous winter, the impending spring, the rejuvenation of the Army of Tennessee, and the reputation of eastern Confederate forces provided reasons for hope.

By fall 1864, to a much lesser degree and more so for soldiers than for the public, the imminent invasion of Tennessee provided some sense of hope. By October, East Tennessean Eliza Fain routinely found the "news so calculated one hour to elevate, the next to depress," while other civilians such as northeastern Alabaman Sarah Espy had seen their homes plundered by soldiers from both sides and conditions only continue to worsen. Similarly, Tennessee civilian Robert Cartmell witnessed depredations by both Federal and Confederate forces to the point that he cared less and less about the outcome. He still hoped for peace "on the best terms it can be had." The chaos and lawlessness of wartime Tennessee prompted Cartmell to long for order and "a government . . . any government is better than no government. . . ." That yearning for better leadership proved increasingly typical.[41]

Overall morale among those western Confederates whose writings form the basis of this study, by October 1864, resembled the mixed feelings of hope and despair exhibited in early 1864, though civilian morale clearly dwindled more rapidly than did soldier morale. In an attempt to encourage persistence and Confederate unity, soldiers encouraged their families and friends to chastise and even condemn disloyal civilians. The civilians' inability to affect the war's outcome directly, the increased speculation after the fall of Atlanta, and general war weariness that resulted from a devastated landscape and material deprivation explain the lower morale on the home front. Still, the bond between the civilians and their defenders remained unbroken. There is nothing in the different morale trajectories between civilians and soldiers that in any way undermines, limits, or strains the bond between home front and battlefront. Civilians and combatants simply responded differently to diverse events and circumstances, as one would expect from groups of people who lived and operated under such disparate conditions. They shared their passion for their cause, but some lost hope before others. As bleak as the situation had grown in the eyes of many, at least the soldiers still had a say in the matter. A successful march into Tennessee or beyond could very well change the course of the war and revive southern spirits one more time.[42]

The loss of Atlanta weakened morale in both groups and certainly made some acquiesce and admit defeat, but most western Confederates examined here still hoped for the best and had not yet given up on independence. The nomination of two war candidates in the impending northern presidential election made that contest a less significant factor in western Confederate morale than it otherwise would have been. McClellan's commitment to carry on with the war if elected, in part a result of the Federal capture of Atlanta, hurt morale in the sense that it eliminated the possibility of the election providing a peaceful settlement favorable to the Confederacy. But that Democratic former general's position also made the election's actual results almost immaterial to morale in the Confederate heartland. Finally, Hood's army stood poised to cross the Tennessee River at the end of October. The army's fate in Tennessee would settle things, one way or the other, for the western Confederacy.

6

November–December 1864

SUNSET AT FRANKLIN

BY NOVEMBER 1864, after three and a half years of warfare, and in the aftermath of the fall of Atlanta, civilian morale in the western Confederacy reached a new low for the year. To be sure, most westerners studied here continued to desire southern independence, but fewer and fewer actually expected to achieve it. Recent campaigns had failed, much of the landscape appeared desolate with winter looming, and Federal armies marched virtually at will through parts of the Confederate heartland. Confederate currency and government bonds were almost worthless. Civilians such as Alabaman Sarah Espy now dreamed of peace and happier times and thought more about survival than winning the war, while fellow Alabaman James Mallory wondered if the southern armies could hold together much longer. Mallory still hoped for Confederate victory, but like many other noncombatants in the West, he struggled to find reasons for optimism. Formerly, during hard times western Rebels recognized and admitted difficulties, but always found reasons to predict better times. By late 1864, fewer sanguine predictions followed those acknowledgments of hard times. Western Confederate civilians as a whole had not yet submitted, but increasing defeatism unquestionably undercut their confidence in the cause.[1]

Even in the face of weakening confidence, some steadfast western Confederates remained as committed as ever to the idea of southern independence. Tennessean Nannie Haskins recorded in her diary the story of a local man captured by the Federals and labeled a spy. The man's father attempted to prevent his son's execution by insisting that the younger man was not a spy but rather a Confederate deserter. Revolted by even the concept of deserting the cause, Haskins wrote, "Great Heavens I would rather be shot twenty times and hung as many in addition as a Confederate spy than be branded a deserter."[2]

Haskins's desire for southern independence is clear enough, but perhaps pales in comparison to the continued fire and passion of twenty-year-old northern Mississippian Martha Tipton. Just across the Tennessee-Mississippi state line south of Memphis, Tipton kept a relatively brief diary, making infrequent but detailed and emotional entries. In her November 1864 entry, the young woman railed against those who appeared to have given up on Confederate independence. She considered anyone who contemplated reunion a turncoat who lacked self-respect and deserved a "traitor's doom." She longed for the power to "build up a wall of fire between Yankeedom and the Confederate States, there to burn for ages as a monument of the folly, wickedness and vandalism of the puritanic race." The Mississippian insisted that she would rather see her entire homeland destroyed by "fire and sword" than "reunite with such people."[3]

Tipton remained confident in her country's chances in the war and claimed a willingness to take to the battlefield herself. Referring to those who considered submission, she seethed, "When the men of the south shall become such base cowards as to wish for such reunion, let JEFF DAVIS call upon the women of the south to march to the field, and there in the name of the God of justice, bid them fight under the banner of southern liberty. The call would not be in vain." Tipton clearly exhibited no defeatism and was not about to call any southern man home from the battlefield. The diary entry continued at length with the rhetoric of blood-soaked fields of honor, noble mothers and fathers, martyrs for liberty, and the sacred cause. More important, Tipton remained supremely confident and insisted, "We have little cause for despondency—nor for despair. . . . If we are only true to ourselves, true to the memories of the past, our homes and firesides and true to our God, we cannot, we will not be conquered. In any and ev'ry event, let us prefer death to a life of cowardly shame."[4]

Martha Tipton wrote in November 1864 as though it were April 1861. The fiery young woman's hatred of Yankees and her desire for her version of freedom reflected the sustained sentiments, if not the expectations, of most of her contemporaries cited throughout these pages. She blamed Abraham Lincoln and any other northerner she could think of for the war and Federal depredations against Confederate citizens. For all of the death, destruction, theft, and lawlessness that frequently occurred in the Civil War's western theater, she sought retribution. She closed the month's entry with the notation, "Vengeance is mine saith the Lord. I will repay." It was confidence, not hatred or desire, that distinguished Tipton from most of her contemporaries that winter. Most of the western Rebels examined here still *wanted* southern independence. Martha Tipton still *expected* it.[5]

Similar to the disparity between Tipton and her fellow civilians, the western press displayed different degrees of dedication to the cause and confidence in its success. A Jackson, Mississippi, newspaper joined the call for an end to the war and a negotiated peace in October, while a Troy, Alabama, newspaper insisted that the Confederacy had more than held its own in recent months. A larger publication in the state capital of Montgomery remained defiant and reminded readers that any consideration of peace overtures by Confederates would show signs of weakness and indicate a retreat from the struggle for independence.[6]

The press and the public also shared a keen interest in John Bell Hood's campaign into Tennessee. No one knew for certain the army's exact destination, but apparently everyone in the region knew of the impending invasion of the Volunteer State. Consistent with overall western civilian morale as exhibited here, most hoped that the campaign would succeed in some measure, further the war effort, and revive spirits, but they did not necessarily expect success. Indeed, despite their continued longing for independence, some civilian observers expressed little faith in the army's chances to achieve a significant victory. Nurse Kate Cumming, for example, admitted that she knew nothing about military matters but remarked that Hood's plan just did not sound good. A Mississippi diarist reported hearing about "the various mishaps of Hood" searching for a route of invasion.[7]

In late October a Mississippi newspaper reported on the Army of Tennessee's northward movement toward the Tennessee River in northern Alabama and endorsed the embattled general's strategy. "Gen. Hood has at last struck the right chord, and comprehends the true policy." The writer, who correctly noted the high morale among the troops, lauded the commander for taking the aggressor's role and moving forward. "No matter what the critics may say—no matter what the books may say—no matter what silence may say—we lose more in retreat than we do in advancing." The editor's thesis is debatable, but his assessment of troop morale rings true. The soldiers exhibited higher spirits than did their civilian counterparts because they were returning to the offensive, looked forward to recapturing Tennessee, and believed that they could still affect the war's outcome. For the time being, Hood's aggressive plans and movements definitely helped improve morale. One historian has written that the demands of maintaining Confederate popular will also at times mandated an aggressive military policy. At least for the moment, the soldiers in the Army of Tennessee and the editor of that Mississippi newspaper clearly would have agreed.[8]

Hood's Tennessee campaign ultimately became an extreme example of an aggressive military strategy, but it hardly began that way. After a smaller Federal force prevented the Confederates from crossing the Tennessee River at Decatur, Alabama, on October 26, Hood's army began crossing the river during the last two days of October farther west at Tuscumbia and soon occupied the town of Florence on the north side of the river. At that point, however, the would-be invasion halted for approximately three weeks while Hood waited for supplies. The army did not begin its ill-fated northward march into Tennessee until November 21. In the meantime, scattered Federal forces converged on the Nashville area under the overall command of Brigadier General George H. Thomas, who would be promoted to major general during the campaign.[9]

Soldiers routinely described the area in the vicinity of their river crossing as barren, a once-idyllic and bountiful area ravaged by war. Tennessean E. H. Rennolds expressed the sentiments of his comrades when he wrote in his diary, "It makes the heart sick to pass through this once beautiful country and see it so desolated by the hand of the unfeeling vandals. Almost every house and fence burned, the negroes taken off, and the citizens left to seek homes elsewhere. They [Federals] will be repaid." Clearly Rennolds and others blamed the Federals for the devastation wrought by war and in the process largely overlooked the role of black agency in emancipation. Scenes such as that described by Rennolds only fueled the fires in the bellies of western Confederates and intensified their hatred of northerners. It appeared to the soldiers that the war had displaced most of the residents in one way or another, and those who remained apparently made varying impressions on the soldiers. Some soldiers, such as Rennolds and Alabaman J. M. Lanning, reported enthusiastic greetings, especially from the ladies of the area. Others, such as young Arkansas soldier Alex Spence, admitted to his parents that some people did not "rejoice" at the army's arrival.[10]

During those three intervening weeks between the river crossing and the advance into Tennessee, the soldiers rested and wondered what the near future held. Although some soldiers knew all along that a major campaign into Middle Tennessee awaited them, others at least initially assumed that they would enter winter quarters soon after crossing the Tennessee River. Hardened Confederate veterans such as John Crittenden of Alabama and Texans Samuel T. Foster and Elbridge Littlejohn at first expected the army to advance no farther than northern Alabama that winter. The young Arkansan Alex Spence agreed and apparently had more faith in his commander's judgment than did most of his comrades. Spence, who by November desperately sought a furlough to visit home, wrote to his parents, "I can't think we will remain in Middle Tenn long because the Feds are concentrating their forces there very fast & Gen Hood sure does not intend to fight a battle on this campaign." Spence was killed only a few weeks later at the Battle of Franklin.[11]

Morale remained high among the troops scrutinized here in early November and only improved as the time to march north approached. Living conditions easily could have undermined morale. After all, besides the lack of pay for some soldiers and the dearth of winter clothing and supplies for most of them, some men marched literally without shoes. Soldier diarists of course noted the harsh conditions but often seemed only to draw further motivation from their sacrifice and that of their comrades. A Tennessee chaplain certainly thought so when he observed, "I see the poor soldier as he toils on, sustained by the hope of better days and by the love he bears for those far away. I saw but yesterday the Captain commanding his regiment barefoot. Such men will not be conquered. I cannot give the history of this campaign language to describe its suffering." A Texas soldier insisted that he did not mind doing without because it seemed that the officers did the same. That viewpoint was exactly what Hood expected from his men. According to the general, the soldiers' sacrifices were no cause for complaint, but instead should motivate them to fight harder for their cause.[12]

Hood and other officers, such as Major General Nathan Bedford Forrest and the popular division commander Major General Patrick Cleburne, delivered speeches designed to inspire the troops as they prepared to invade Tennessee. With or without the speeches, the soldiers stood ready and willing to advance, though Hood remained generally unpopular with his men. More important, the soldiers still did not truly trust his judgment as an army commander. Yet for the men who remained in the Army of Tennessee by winter 1864, surrender obviously was not yet an option. Joe Johnston was not around, and Hood commanded the army. They would stand by him and keep fighting. When the marching orders came down on November 21, the soldiers as a whole headed north with a qualified confidence. Inspired to be taking the offensive and by the opportunity to "liberate" the Volunteer State (the homeland of many of the men), most of the soldiers cited here genuinely expected to score some kind of meaningful success in Tennessee.[13]

That confidence of course was not unanimous. Alabaman Edward Norphlet Brown expressed the strongest reservations about the impending campaign. In a letter to his wife, the quartermaster fretted, "I had not believed all the while that the army would go into Tennessee, and even now it seems almost absurd to me, but I am now forced to believe that the move will be undertaken. How many of us will ever recross the River no one can tell, but I clearly foresee hard times & disaster to the army. I have never in my life felt so much opposed to a move. But I will try to be reconciled & hope for success." To a lesser degree, others also expected difficulty in Tennessee. Brigadier General Mark Perrin Lowrey worried about the condition of the men even before the campaign began and worried more that Hood had told him that the Confederates would attack regardless of the Federals' numbers.[14]

Once the northward march began, those apprehensive soldiers clearly constituted a minority. Most soldiers examined here continued to improve in spirits and confidence as the army advanced. Although conditions were far from ideal and none knew exactly what awaited them, soldier after soldier, in wartime and postwar accounts, wrote about cheerful comrades and buoyant spirits during the last week of November 1864 as they approached and crossed the Tennessee state line. At the Alabama-Tennessee border, several soldiers noted a handmade sign that, depending on the account, read, "Tennessee a Soldier's Grave or Free Home."[15]

In addition to the opportunity to "liberate" Tennessee and the usual dynamics that sustained morale for the Army of Tennessee, two other factors in late November boosted the soldiers' spirits. First, at least some men marched under the impression that Hood would not attack against superior numbers. Second, and at least as important, more so than in northern Alabama, soldiers noted an enthusiastic welcome by Tennessee civilians. On November 27 the army approached Columbia, Tennessee, approximately forty-five miles southwest of Nashville. Several accounts described Tennesseans there as loyal Confederates who openly celebrated the Rebels' arrival.[16]

Also on November 27 at Columbia, Hood's army encountered approximately thirty-two thousand Federals under the command of Major General John M. Schofield, charged with the task of delaying the Confederate advance toward Nashville until Union forces could concentrate there. By the next day the Union commander correctly ascertained Hood's intention to maneuver between the Federals and Nashville in an attempt to cut Schofield off from the state capital and the remainder of the Union garrison under the command of George H. Thomas. (It is possible, however, that Hood did not even know that another significant Federal garrison occupied Nashville.) To prevent Hood's maneuver, Schofield crossed to the north bank of the Duck River, just north of Columbia. Hood countered with another attempt to get between Schofield and Nashville and marched northward to the small community of Spring Hill. Hood's exact goal at Spring Hill remains unclear, though he likely sought either to strike Schofield as the northern general brought his force up the main road to Nashville or perhaps simply to out-run the Federals to the long-occupied Tennessee capital. In their excellent study of the Battle of Franklin, historians Thomas L. Connelly and James Lee McDonough pointed to the latter interpretation. Once Hood reached the heavily fortified city, even with Schofield's force still in his rear and with or without knowledge of Thomas's troops, he apparently intended to storm the works around Nashville.[17]

Whatever Hood's intentions, in one of the most celebrated oversights of the war, the Confederates failed to secure Spring Hill or the turnpike that ran through it directly to Nashville. As if written for a Hollywood movie, during the night of November 29–30, Schofield's Federals eluded Hood's Confederates, many of them by walking along the pike within a few hundred yards of Rebel camps. Although the event remains shrouded in mystery— exactly what happened, why, and who was to blame—even the common Confederate soldier in the ranks knew immediately that something had gone awry at Spring Hill.[18]

Several historians have demonstrated that Schofield had alternate routes to Nashville and that the Federals could simply have fought at Spring Hill with every chance to fend off the Rebels. Therefore, for the Confederates the Spring Hill fiasco represented a missed opportunity and certainly an embarrassing lack of organization and discipline, but not the elusive golden opportunity to seize control of the western theater. At the very least, the Confederates might have fought the Federals piecemeal with some realistic chance for success rather than contend with the united forces of Schofield and Thomas that they would later battle outside Nashville in mid-December. More important, Hood perhaps would not have grown angry enough, as some historians contend, to order the suicidal assault at Franklin the day after what became known to history as the Spring Hill Affair.[19]

"Hood is at Columbia—they are fighting—My God! How I pray our men may succeed." So wrote Tennessee civilian Nannie Haskins from occupied

Clarksville, northwest of Nashville. Haskins and others of course knew that the Rebels had arrived in Middle Tennessee and hoped for their success, but few could have predicted what happened next. On November 30, the day that Haskins prayed for Confederate victory and the morning after the Spring Hill Affair, Hood marched his army toward disaster. At the town of Franklin, thirteen miles farther north and halfway between Spring Hill and Nashville, Hood caught up with Schofield, whose Federals occupied strong defensive positions.[20]

While Schofield's engineers repaired bridges necessary for the Union troops to cross the Harpeth River on their way to Nashville, Hood chose to attack his entrenched foes, despite the absence of most of his artillery and an entire corps yet to arrive from Columbia. In one of the most questionable command decisions of the entire Civil War, at 4:00 P.M., against the advice of most of his subordinate officers, Hood ordered a frontal assault with virtually his entire available force of eighteen thousand (of approximately twenty-five thousand, including those who had not yet arrived at Franklin) against Schofield's approximately thirty-two thousand Federals. For the next five hours, soldiers in the Army of Tennessee marched to their deaths across an open field. Without significant artillery support, the Confederates advanced in the face of Union artillery and attacked an entrenched enemy infantry, many of whom were armed with repeating carbine rifles. When the Confederates viewed the battlefield the next morning, the numbers and carnage told most of the story. Approximately 1,750 Confederates were killed, at least 5,500 wounded or missing, six generals killed or mortally wounded, and several others wounded or captured.[21]

Several factors contributed to Hood's ill-fated decision to order the suicidal attack. His anger over the Spring Hill embarrassment clearly played a role, and in the larger picture, he apparently believed that if Franklin fell, so too would Nashville. Additionally, Hood acted out of a delusional belief that his men needed a boost of spirit or manliness. He believed that Joseph E. Johnston's defensive tactics had softened the men of the Army of Tennessee and that he would toughen them again. Yet the actions of Hood's men that evening left no doubt about their bravery or willingness to fight on the offensive. One study of the Battle of Franklin noted an unusual ferocity and determination among the Confederate soldiers that day. Perhaps the return home affected some of them dramatically. (Some of the men hailed not only from Tennessee but from that exact area.) Perhaps they found motivation in the opportunity to recapture Tennessee, invade Kentucky, and threaten the Ohio River, a long held Confederate goal. Probably, too, they continued to fight for each other, as they always had. What is certain, however, is that the soldiers of the Army of Tennessee remained committed to their cause and that, when they launched those fateful attacks, they still believed that the war could be won.[22]

That the men of the Army of Tennessee began November 30, 1864, with confidence and high overall morale is clear. What is equally apparent is that the Battle of Franklin affected even hardened veterans in ways that none of them would have predicted. Their diaries and letters reflected the thoughts of men stunned by the carnage—carnage ultimately without meaningful reward. Even for hard-bitten veterans of countless skirmishes, battles, and campaigns, Franklin seemed to defy words. Man after man described it as the worst battle the Army of Tennessee had ever experienced, and they hoped never to see anything like it again.

Samuel King Vann, a young soldier who wrote mostly love letters to his teenaged future wife during his service, took time out from his epistles of adoration to describe what he saw on that Tennessee field: " . . . [T]here we fought one of the bloodiest battles yet known, commencing about 3 o'clock in the evening and ceased about midnight. They were well fortified and we had to charge their works, so we put out through shot and shell, driving them from three lines of breastworks, though many of our gallant men fell on the field. Oh! you cannot have the slightest imagination of how many men were killed. They were lying heaped up all over the battleground. Such a slaughter of men was never seen before on neither side. I counted 30 dead Yanks in a space of ground not larger than a common dwelling house." Probably referring to the famous incident of soldier Tod Carter, who was mortally wounded within yards of his family home, the young Vann wrote, "Some of the brave fellows from Tenn. were killed right at their homes, and one poor fellow was killed right in his yard; the next morning after the fight ceased his wife came out of the cellar where she had been for protection and found her husband lying at the doorsteps dead. . . ."[23]

The dramatic descriptions of what the soldiers witnessed—the overall scene, the battle, and the death—could fill pages, but two common themes emerged in the soldiers' writings in the immediate aftermath of the battle. First, the unbelievable carnage and suffering the men witnessed unmistakably affected them deeply. Second, despite what they witnessed and described, some of the soldiers *initially* considered Franklin a victory because the Federals "retreated" that night toward Nashville and left significant amounts of supplies and many of their wounded on the field. Even the stunned young Samuel King Vann initially thought, "We lost as many killed as the Yanks but we gained a complete victory, driving them to Nashville." One Alabaman wrote his wife, "Thank God I am yet alive, but thousands of our brave men are sleeping their last sleep tonight. The most terrible battle that this army has ever fought was fought on the ground where I now write, on yesterday afternoon & last night, and our loss has been frightful, yet we gave the enemy a signal defeat. . . . The Division is cut all to pieces and Cleburne's Division will be known no more except in history." Most soldiers in this study avoided language that referred to Franklin as a "signal" victory, but frequently wrote in terms of a victory dearly bought.[24]

Even those who initially viewed Franklin as a success almost immediately recognized and commented on the severity of the slaughter. More important, they quickly realized that they had not scored a victory. On the ensuing march toward heavily fortified Nashville the soldiers realized that they had won nothing. With the benefit of daylight, they recognized the devastated condition of their army and, of course, understood that Schofield's Federals awaited them in Nashville. Overall army morale at that point could be described as mixed at best. The army was not completely defeated, and some of them continued to write about their confidence in ultimate victory. Alabaman Thomas Smyrl found himself down but not broken and worried more about his family than anything else. Fellow Alabaman Edward Norphlet Brown, who had predicted disaster before the army entered Tennessee and the day after the battle was thankful simply to be alive, wrote the next week that as a southern soldier he had grown accustomed to hardship. He assured his wife that he and his comrades retained their confidence and stood as defiant as ever. "These poor rebel soldiers are having a hard time of it now. We have but little protection from this severe weather, no shelter & a scarcity of clothing & shoes, yet the men seem as cheerful & as defiant as ever, & if the Vandal horde of Lincoln does not believe it let them come out from their forts & ditches in Nashville & try the poor 'rebs.'"[25]

Yet for every confident and defiant Edward Norphlet Brown, there was a bitter, shaken, or even defeated Confederate. Thousands of others lay dead or wounded on the field at Franklin and an undetermined number deserted during or after the disaster. Texan Samuel T. Foster, a captain in the immensely popular Irish-born Major General Patrick Cleburne's division, penned perhaps the most damning wartime assessment of Hood's direction of the campaign. Incensed by the carnage suffered by the army, Hood's misleading promises to the troops before they entered Tennessee, and doubtless by Cleburne's death at Franklin, Foster wrote:

> Gen. Hood has betrayed us (The Army of Tenn). This is not the kind of fighting he promised us at Tuscumbia and Florence Ala. when we started into Tenn.
>
> This was not a "fight with equal numbers and choice of the ground" by no means. And the wails and cries of widows and orphans made at Franklin Tenn Nov 30th 1864 will heat up the fires of the bottomless pit to burn the soul of Gen J B Hood for Murdering their husbands and fathers at that place that day. It can't be called anything else but cold blooded Murder.
>
> He sacrificed those men to make the name of Hood famous; when if the History of it is ever written it will make him *infamous.*
>
> He had near 10,000 men murdered around Atlanta trying to prove to the world that he was a greater man than Genl Johns[t]on—Because Johns[t]on said that Atlanta was untenable, and could not be held with the men he had against the men that Sherman had. And how small he must have felt when he had to leave there in the night to keep from being captured.
>
> And now in order to recover from the merited disgrace of that transaction he brings this Army here into middle Tenn. and by making them false promises and false statements got these men killed—Put them into a fight where the Yanks have three lines of breastworks; the second or middle being lined with artillery.
>
> The men have a right to believe he told the truth and go forward to certain and sure destructions; but "Vengeance is mine Sayeth the Lord" and it will surely overtake him.[26]

Foster's seething assessment reads more like Confederate soldiers' postwar rants than the wartime diaries and letters of his comrades. The Texan's diary was published years after the war and might have received some postwar editing. Regardless, those who wrote about Franklin after the war certainly cursed and blamed Hood more strongly than did those who wrote on-the-scene. A survey of those postwar accounts reveals that many surviving soldiers viewed Franklin as the darkest day in their army's history and Hood as little better than a butcher. They pointed to the slaughter at Franklin as the deathblow to the army's chances for victory, its morale, and to the army itself. In their memories nothing equaled Franklin, in part because of the carnage, but more so because it was all so unnecessary. Decades after the war a Mississippi veteran revisited the scene and lamented the events in Middle Tennessee, "for which I could hang Hood even now. . . ." Another former soldier doubtless expressed the sentiments of many comrades when he deemed Hood's decision an "inconceivable folly."[27]

Why did Franklin traumatize the soldiers so much? The Confederates suffered more killed there than the Federals lost during the entire Seven Days Battles or at Chancellorsville, and Hood's army endured more than two and a half times the number of casualties it inflicted on its enemy (6,252 C.S.A., 2,326 U.S.A.).[28] But by Civil War standards, the number of men engaged on each side and even the total casualty figures seem unremarkable. Even the Army of Tennessee itself suffered more casualties at Shiloh, Chattanooga, and during the Atlanta campaign. Other armies had also survived frontal assaults and lived to fight another day without apparently suffering the trauma described by Confederates at Franklin. In that regard, and in foolishness, the Confederate assault at Franklin hardly differed from the Federal attacks at Fredericksburg and Cold Harbor.

Yet the soldiers' writings during and after the war make it clear that in their minds Franklin was different. Several things likely explain this. The soldiers' frequent references to bodies lying in "heaps" point to both the relatively small and contained killing field at Franklin and the fact that so many men perished in just a few hours. Too, Hood had told the men before entering Tennessee that he would fight only under advantageous circumstances, so the suicidal attack must have been a shock to the system and likely created feelings of bitterness and a sense of betrayal from the moment the orders were given. They knew that Joseph Johnston never would have done this to them. Finally, and perhaps most important, the soldiers obviously recognized the bigger picture effects of the slaughter at Franklin. They had given so much to the Army of Tennessee and endured so much for it, but it barely existed anymore. Many of their comrades continued only as memories, and those who survived recognized that they were fortunate to be alive. Simply put, after three and a half years of war, it seemed as though the Army of Tennessee had met its destruction in one brief, unnecessary battle.[29]

At Franklin, Hood's foolish tactics crippled his army. His decision to continue on to the outskirts of Nashville positioned the Army of Tennessee for its definitive deathblow, delivered by George H. Thomas's Federals. To be fair to Hood, most historians of the campaign contend that by that juncture Hood had few realistic options. He probably intended to find a strong defensive position and lure the Federals into attacking. Retreat at that point likely would have caused wholesale desertion, at least among Tennessee soldiers, and Hood's army lacked the supplies and ability to bypass Nashville. So, with what remained of his once mighty army, Hood approached arguably the most heavily fortified city in the entire Civil War. The embattled but determined general almost certainly remained unaware that Thomas had amassed approximately seventy thousand men to defend Nashville. Within two weeks after the Franklin slaughter, Hood's army stood in a virtual no man's land. The December 14 thaw after a freeze that approached single-digit temperatures muddied the roads back to Franklin, making a retreat even more unlikely, and slowed resupply and potential reinforcement of his exhausted army. His numbers wholly inadequate to launch an offensive, Hood had put himself in the helpless position of awaiting his opponent's next move.[30]

Civilians and common soldiers alike understood the difficulty of the situation. Moreover, they knew that even Hood would not assault the defensive works around the city. Nashville resident Mary L. Pearre recognized that the city was "too formidable a place to be taken by force of arms. They say Hood will not storm it and the loss of life would be frightful. Our boys were literally piled in heaps at Franklin. . . ." An Alabama soldier also believed the Federal line too strong for the Rebels and contended, "It would seem the quintessence of folly in Hood to assault it." Nannie Haskins, a resident of Clarksville, northwest of Nashville, attempted in vain to remain hopeful as she witnessed thousands of Federal reinforcements marching toward the Tennessee capital. The men in blue still feared Forrest, she reasoned. Perhaps he could find a way to salvage the campaign.[31]

On December 15–16, Thomas and the Federals took the initiative and removed any remaining uncertainty as to the results of Hood's invasion of Tennessee. In two days of battle, the Federals left their defensive positions and with an overwhelming numerical advantage launched repeated assaults on the thin Confederate lines. On the second day the Confederate left broke in chaos, and the near disintegration of the Army of Tennessee ensued. Federal cavalry under the command of Major General James H. Wilson chased the fleeing, ragged Confederates southward until the remnants of the once-proud army crossed the Tennessee River in late December. During the Battle of Nashville and the pursuit afterward, Hood's army lost another six thousand casualties, most of them captured in the commotion near Nashville. In a revealing anecdote, Federal major general John Schofield later recalled asking a captured Confederate when the Rebels knew that they were defeated. The soldier reportedly responded that he and his comrades knew nothing of the sort until the Federals overran them at Nashville.[32]

Soldier after soldier commented on what they considered the unprecedented confusion that marked the Confederate defeat at Nashville. In their minds they had never seen such a disorganized collapse, and near wholesale dejection spread quickly throughout what remained of the army. Perhaps even worse than the defeat, the most demoralizing scenes experienced by the Army of Tennessee during the entire war followed as ragged, half-starved, and frequently barefoot men marched southward out of Tennessee and away from their dreams of conquest.[33]

During the retreat the men of the Army of Tennessee expressed their disgust with Hood in verse, sung to the tune of "The Yellow Rose of Texas":

> And now I'm going southward,
>   For my heart is full of woe,
> I'm going back to Georgia
>   To find my Uncle Joe [Johnston].

> You may talk about your Beauregard
>   And sing of General Lee,
> But the gallant Hood of Texas
>   Played hell in Tennessee.[34]

As 1864 wound to a close, what remained of the Army of Tennessee gathered in northern Mississippi. During the respite, the scenes of the campaign's aftermath, the Christmas holiday away from their families, and the coming of a new year caused soldiers to reflect on the disastrous campaign and ponder the Confederacy's future. Frequently throughout the war soldiers in the Army of Tennessee had dealt with defeat and setbacks of all kinds, but they almost always concluded their assessments with statements that they would yet find a way to win. Regardless of the circumstances, they would persevere. Not so after Franklin and Nashville. The disasters in Middle Tennessee ended western Confederate hopes for independence. The army that had fought at Shiloh, Chattanooga, Chickamauga, and Atlanta was but a shell of its former self. By January 1865, death, wounds, capture, desertion, and the actions of their leader had depleted the ranks to fewer than twenty thousand total, and perhaps half of those were considered armed and effective.[35]

Alabaman Edward Norphlet Brown, long an ardent and confident Confederate, expressed the thoughts of many when he wrote to his wife, "Our army is entirely demoralized and has straggled to this point. . . . I think now that the cause of the South is sadly on the wane & I fear we shall be subjugated. I am more despondent now than ever before, but let me not think of it." Another soldier, James H. Finch, spent the days around Christmas reflecting on the thousands of former comrades who had sacrificed their lives for the Confederate cause, never to return to their loved ones. He found it impossible to celebrate the coming of a new year. A Tennessee captain who missed the campaign but returned to the army immediately afterward found only the "skeleton" of his command and legions of barefoot, wounded, frostbitten, and entirely demoralized men, while another soldier despaired for the Confederacy's fate if it depended on what remained of the Army of Tennessee. Even a higher-ranking officer, Brigadier General Claudius Wistar Sears, who lost his lower left leg at Nashville, admitted that the campaign and retreat had "almost annihilated" the Army of Tennessee.[36]

Desperation and despondency marked even the most optimistic soldiers' writings in the aftermath of the Tennessee campaign. Even articulate Tennessee soldier Joseph Branch O'Bryan, a steadfast Confederate who wrote myriad letters to his sisters during his military service, admitted the wretched condition of the Army of Tennessee and the gloom that the campaign had cast over the men who remained. O'Bryan urged his sisters not to despond and insisted that he and all "true patriots" remained committed to the fight for southern independence, but the dedicated soldier admitted several telling details: the army's horses and mules could do no more without an extended rest; the same held true for the remaining soldiers, and the condition of the command was "disgraceful"; the army was so scattered that it was hard to tell how many survived, deserted, or were captured; Sherman probably could not be stopped in his march through Georgia; and the country's overall prospects looked gloomy in what O'Bryan deemed the Confederacy's "darkest hour." The soldier ultimately concluded that only a total reorganization of the Army of Tennessee from top to bottom could save it. In the bigger picture, the Confederacy could survive only if the government could inaugurate some new decisive policy to deal with the enemy in the spring of 1865.[37]

Clearly O'Bryan and his comrades understood the significance of the failed Tennessee campaign and recognized that their army now bore only a passing resemblance to a Civil War army. Just as the soldiers recognized it, western Confederate civilians, those who had not given up after the fall of Atlanta, comprehended that Hood's disastrous campaign marked the beginning of the end of the Confederacy. Their writings in December 1864 reflected a gloomy sentiment, a loss of fighting spirit, and in some cases a noticeable shift toward thinking about the future and how they and their families might best survive rather than how to win southern independence.

Alabaman Sarah Espy, for example, noted that Confederate taxes no longer concerned her because she had nothing to give anyway. She lamented her inability to celebrate a joyful Christmas, living as she did in "the bosom of destruction." Espy somehow resolved, "We should be thankful that it is no worse with us than it is." The previous year she had wished that in the next year things would not get worse. "Vain wish! for since this time we have lost nearly everything." She closed her 1864 diary with yet another wish that things get no worse and that she and her family would survive to see peace.[38]

Other western Confederate civilians expressed similar sentiments. Tennessean Nannie Haskins mourned the failed attempt to "free" Nashville and the horrific loss of life during the campaign. Haskins's disappointment was matched only by her continued bitterness toward the Federals. Her Christmas Day diary entry read: "Damned dark and cloudy, instead of jubilation in our hearts our hearts are filled with mourning. . . ." She admitted that her disappointment overcame her and that "I wait and hope. But my God how long will we have to *wait*." A fellow Tennessean, Nimrod Porter, witnessed the passing of Hood's army on December 17 and described them as "the worst looking and most broken down looking set I ever laid eyes on." He, too, recognized that the end was near, yet retained his palpable hatred for Federal soldiers, whom he described as "the blackest vilest robbers I ever heard of. . . ." Porter half-heartedly joked that he might yet be conscripted at the age of seventy-four and longed for a "river of fire" to separate the North and South. For his family's Christmas dinner he killed a fox that made the mistake of wandering too close to the Porter home. For all of this he blamed the Yankees. Like Nannie Haskins, for Nimrod Porter the loss of his spirit to resist and recognition of impending defeat in no way changed his views about North and South.[39]

Even two civilians who refused to acknowledge defeat in December found little to cheer. Nurse Kate Cumming claimed that she would never yield, chastised those who had, and pointed with wounded pride to Edmund Kirby Smith's trans-Mississippi army and to the continued Confederate possession of Richmond and the Carolinas. Yet she recognized the disaster behind the reports of a "victory" at Franklin. She had heard accounts of Confederate soldiers lying in "heaps." Cumming described a gloomy Christmas and wrote in terms of the "fearful odds" the Confederates faced and the scenes of "woe and desolation" around her. Meanwhile, in western Tennessee, Robert Cartmell believed that, considering the comparison of resources between the two belligerents, the Confederacy had already offered an "unparalleled" resistance. In evaluating his country's chances for ultimate victory, Cartmell wrote, "There is a limit to human endurance . . . when it will be is covered in mystery."[40]

By December 1864, Cartmell and Cumming were the optimists among the western Confederates examined here. Fewer and fewer individuals even bothered to keep diaries for the remainder of the war, and fewer soldiers remained in the army to write letters home. Franklin and Nashville broke the will of the residents and defenders of the Confederate heartland. Even soldiers who remained in the army and civilians who continued to support the Confederacy found little reason to believe that they would actually win the war. Among those who realized that the end had come were many of the diehard Confederates whose diaries and letters revealed such determined spirits throughout the highs and lows of 1864.

Although western Confederates had suffered many defeats before and their spirits had always rebounded, the severity of the defeats at Franklin and Nashville meant that there would be no recovery this time. The Army of Tennessee, at least as it stood in the immediate aftermath of the Tennessee campaign, could no longer be considered a viable army. Old foe William T. Sherman had already marched through Georgia almost at will, and within a week after the Battle of Nashville had captured Savannah. Soon he would turn his armies north and tear through the Carolinas. Later in the spring, units from what remained of the Army of Tennessee would be called on to face Sherman again, but they could offer limited resistance at best. More important, the people and soldiers knew that they could not stop Sherman and therefore could not prevent his joining Ulysses S. Grant's forces against Robert E. Lee's Richmond defenders. Whether Franklin and Nashville were the decisive battles of the war is debatable, and a recent survey of the historiography of the campaign suggests that historians have (unfortunately) placed less emphasis on the campaign in recent decades. That diminished emphasis apparently stems from the perception that the campaign was unlikely to succeed for the Confederates anyway, though this hardly prevented the campaign from proving decisive in the Federals' favor.[41] What *is* clear is that the bloody defeats in Middle Tennessee crushed the spirit of the people of the western Confederacy.

Considerable evidence suggests that the defeats at Franklin and Nashville also contributed significantly to defeatism in other parts of the Confederacy. Hood's vanquishing certainly played a role in undermining morale in Georgia and the Carolinas and even in Virginia, particularly when placed in context alongside the fall of Savannah and the forceful success of Sherman's March. As one historian has pointed out, even Sherman knew that his march through Georgia would remain incomplete without the destruction of the Army of Tennessee. Furthermore, Jefferson Davis unquestionably sensed increased pressure and heard more than his usual criticism after the dual disasters of Hood's defeat and the fall of Savannah spread unparalleled gloom across the Confederacy. South Carolina diarists Grace Brown Elmore, Catherine Ann Devereux Edmondston, and Emma Holmes understood the bigger picture as well. Holmes carefully tracked Hood's progress the best she could during the campaign and appears to have understood the destructive potential of Sherman's forces without Hood's Confederates to oppose them. One Georgia Confederate explicitly stated in a letter to her mother that the defeat of Hood's army would leave her state at Sherman's mercy. A traveling newspaper correspondent, then in Macon, Georgia, perhaps expressed it best when he asserted that it "became evident to thinking men, as soon as Sherman reached the sea at Savannah, that Hood's army having been badly beaten and broken in Tennessee, that it would soon become impossible for the Confederates to maintain their hold upon Richmond, and difficult, if not impossible, for them to withdraw. The remains of Hood's army . . . could not be relied upon in the desperate emergency. . . ."[42]

Interestingly, recent scholarship suggests that, rather than undercutting Confederate morale, Sherman's March ultimately galvanized many Confederates' dedication to their cause. The suffering experienced during that famous campaign united Rebels around the Confederacy and made real the connection between their fledgling nation and their homes and families. As historian Jacqueline Glass Campbell has argued, many Confederates came to connect the endurance of the Confederacy to the survival of their families. Thus, they could defend one for the sake of both. Suffering at the hands of Federal troops further united Confederates and directed their discontent toward their common enemy—the Federal armies.[43] Certainly none of that mattered to Sherman, who sought to illustrate the Confederates' helplessness in the face of his armies. Once again, this only highlights the importance of Franklin and Nashville. The Confederates in the Carolinas awaiting Sherman's destructive forces were indeed essentially helpless, just as Sherman claimed, but this was true largely because the Army of Tennessee had been severely crippled.

It is impossible to comprehend the collapse of the Confederacy without an appreciation for the importance of Franklin and Nashville. In the end, the defeats meant the end for western Confederates because "their" army had been devastated and their homeland left virtually unprotected from enemy forces. Moreover, it meant probable defeat for Confederates elsewhere because they would likely be next without the services of the Confederacy's major western army.

After the war a Mississippi soldier reflected on the Tennessee campaign and could not explain why Confederates fought at all after Nashville, regardless of their theater of operation. He understood why they had always continued before, after major defeats such as Gettysburg and Vicksburg, but not after Franklin and Nashville. The answer to his question, of course, differed from one man to the next. Indeed, many chose not to fight again after Nashville, while others continued to serve out of a sense of duty to country and family. Confederate soldiers did not forsake such motives easily. That particular veteran admitted that perhaps many men did not want their families to be ashamed of them. Perhaps a relative few even continued to believe that they might somehow achieve victory, or at least gain generous terms of surrender from the Yankees.[44]

Nearly all western Confederates in this study, however, recognized the impending defeat of the Confederacy and would have shared the view of events in late 1864 in Middle Tennessee as expressed in the lengthy poem "Sunset at Franklin." It read in part,

> Red the sky as flame,
>> Red the clouds as blood,
> Red the battle-field
>> Where fought the men of Hood.
> Still the muskets crashed,
>> Still the cannon rolled,
> While now and then a Southern yell
>> Of Southern victory told.
> But oh! too long it seems
>> Since last the yell was heard;
> And save that discord musical
>> From battle not a word.
>
> . . . .
>
> Too well, alas we knew
>> Through all that endless day,
> Five men had come in blue

>   While one had come in gray.
> We knew behind the hill
>   Our boys were dying fast,
> We knew the foe's increasing might
>   Was there for murder massed.
> To think they dared to kneel.
>   To think they dared to pray.
> They asked our God to help them burn,
>   They asked for strength to slay.

. . . .

> Now sharp the orders come,
>   And quicker step the men;
> We knew, though deadly stress before,
>   More deadly stress was then.
> Still toiling up the hill,
>   Till they the summit gain,
> Then plunge into the sea of fire
>   That floods the battle-plain.
> Still they're going in,
>   Still they not come back.
> The lines of gray still melt away
>   In battle's crimson wrack.

> And still I looked in vain
>   For my little brother there,
> Who loved his flowers and kisses sweet
>   To pile upon my hair.
> So swift the soldiers marched,
>   They scarce could turn to look;
> Yet man after man would raise his hat,
>   And we their homage took.
> We knew it was for us,
>   The women of the south,
> They marched and starved, and rushed upon
>   The cannon's hungry mouth.
> Oh! I have thought perchance
>   We served our country's need
> As well as they whom manhood called
>   On battle-field to bleed.

. . . .

The bloody sun went down,
    But battle hid the stars;
Still glared the sky with flame,
      Still shook the earth with jars.
And with each crash I knew
    That many soldiers fell;
I loved them all, although
    Their names I could not tell.
E'en now that tender boy,
    By cannon blown away,
Lies in the shattered, bleeding line
    That charged just now in gray.
No more the yells we heard,
    And in that midnight strife
(I know not how or where)
    My brother gave his life.[45]

7

January–February 1865

"WE CAN CERTAINLY LIVE WITHOUT NEGROS BETTER THAN WITH YANKEES"

MISSISSIPPIAN CORA WATSON began her journal entries for 1865 uncertain of what the year might bring. Not yet aware of the disasters that met the Army of Tennessee only weeks earlier and having heard only rumors, the twenty-one-year-old teacher and diarist recorded a hopeful entry that reflected her appreciation for that calm winter day and her desire for peace. From the war-torn northern Mississippi village of Holly Springs, she wrote, "The new year dawns bright and beautiful; all nature seems glad, and only the voice of man is in discord. Still we hear the clash of arms, and see the glittering bayonets reflected in pools of blood. Oh! may this calm, lovely new year's day be typical of the time here at hand, when 'The drums shall throb no longer,' and 'The kindly earth shall slumber lapt in universal law.' All went to church."[1]

But within days reality set in for Watson and other western Confederates. Indeed, for many of those who even bothered to continue their diaries and correspondence, the cold winter days of January and February 1865 marked the darkest period of the Confederacy's brief history. News of the disaster in Middle Tennessee spread just as westerners learned about the Federal capture of Savannah, Georgia. The Army of Tennessee, described by one civilian observer as "not much better than an armed mob," appeared practically useless, and Union general William T. Sherman marched seemingly unopposed through much of the Confederacy. Lieutenant General Richard Taylor, commander of the Confederate Department of Alabama, Mississippi, and East Louisiana, informed Richmond officials that his department bordered on bankruptcy and could collapse at any time. Without significant improvement, he wrote, "[R]ailroads, steam-boats, citizens, and soldiers will no longer work, sell, or fight." A study of wartime Alabama concluded that after the battles of Franklin and Nashville, the entire state was "alienated" from the Confederacy. Perhaps worst of all for the western Confederates, unlike the previous year, the coming spring seemed to offer little reason to predict victory.[2]

Although the defeats at Franklin and Nashville, more than anything else, crushed the confidence of the western Confederates examined here, their *desire* for southern independence typically remained. In fact, in January and February 1865 western Confederates revealed much about their spirits and their changing perspectives when they looked to things other than southern military prowess for reasons to believe in the possibility of southern independence. Three factors—the reappointment of Joseph E. Johnston to command the Army of Tennessee, the possibility of arming slaves or former slaves to fight for the Confederacy, and the peace conference at Hampton Roads, Virginia—provided what amounted to the last gasps of Confederate morale.

Within one week of her hopeful New Year's Day diary entry, Cora Watson recognized the difficulties that faced the Confederacy by early 1865. She acknowledged that John Bell Hood's failure in Tennessee and the loss of Savannah demoralized many people in the area. Although she continued to consider the Confederate cause "too just and holy" to fail, and her hatred for Yankees only continued to grow, she admitted to her diary her distress about the "feeling of subjugation" that prevailed around her. Fellow Mississippian Amanda Worthington thought little about ultimate victory and could only mourn those killed at Franklin and Nashville, "names I shall ever love and remember as belonging to heroes who died for our country!" Northeastern Alabama resident Sarah Espy battled depression and hoped for peace. Understandably, she worried particularly that Hood's defeat might mean the return of Federal soldiers to her home in the war-ravaged area near the Georgia border.[3]

Even fiery Yankee-hater Ellen Renshaw House, an East Tennessee refugee then in Georgia, acknowledged the gloom that descended over the Confederate heartland, though she continued to hold out hope and could barely contain her disgust for southerners who had given up. House certainly expressed no sympathy for the residents of Savannah. Instead, she deemed the surrender of their city nothing short of disgraceful. However, despite their continued hatred of northerners and persistent desires for independence, western women like Ellen House and Cora Watson recognized and, more important, acknowledged that the Confederacy's prospects for victory and independence had reached a new low.[4]

Defeatism struck western Confederate men as clearly as it did women in early 1865. Civilian men's diaries and letters from the period frequently echoed the sentiments expressed by women. Seventy-four-year-old Tennessean Nimrod Porter, a man with unquestioned Confederate sympathies, by February 1865 longed for peace and stability under any circumstances. He admitted that if only he and his family could escape their current "trouble and misfortune" he would agree to live anywhere under any kind of government. Interestingly, although he expressed little faith in the Confederacy's prospects, he apparently continued to believe that the sacrifice of so many had not been in vain and that perhaps it had all been God's will. Certainly many "widows and orphans" would "mourn the loss of their all," he noted, but if "providence wills it to be so, who should complain?"[5]

Alabaman Robert Mallory expressed his despair in simple, more practical terms, by lamenting the "dark condition" of the Confederate cause, the enemy's ever-increasing numerical advantage on the battlefield, and an alarming scarcity of food. Such circumstances could and eventually did weaken the resolve of even the most hardened and dedicated Confederates. Thomas Watkins, a wealthy Mississippi slaveholder, certainly thought so, particularly in the aftermath of a Federal cavalry raid in early 1865. He wrote to his daughter in Texas that in the once-prosperous community of Carrolton, Mississippi, approximately halfway between Memphis and Jackson, "The population is somewhat changed and most persons look sad, badly dressed, and many look prematurely old. The people visit about on wagons and horseback," apparently unlike the prosperous days of elegant carriages. Years of war had taken an emotional and physical toll on western Confederates of both genders and all social classes. The reality of warfare and defeat transcended such distinctions.[6]

As western Confederate civilians searched for signs of hope, they added their voices to the clamor that demanded the reappointment of Joseph E. Johnston to command the Army of Tennessee. Alabaman Margaret Gillis, for example, considered January 1865 the darkest period of the war, described the entire country as demoralized, and insisted that everything had gone wrong since Jefferson Davis had removed Johnston from command. Tennessean Robert Cartmell also pointed to the dismissal of Johnston the previous July as a source of the current difficult times. Cartmell fumed that Confederate officials listened to "public clamor" rather than respect the "universal opinion" of the army in their choice of leaders. In February, Davis opted for the latter and reappointed the general, creating "universal satisfaction," according to another civilian diarist.[7]

Such frequent sentiments among western Confederate civilians echoed the thoughts and writings of soldiers in the Army of Tennessee. Among both common soldiers and officers studied here, demand for Johnston's return proved virtually universal. Both wartime and postwar sources revealed the widespread demand for the reappointment of the army's most popular commander. That they would desire Johnston's return is hardly surprising. The soldiers' affections for Johnston and their belief in his abilities could not be clearer, particularly in light of their writings regarding his removal in July. The soldiers and, in early 1865, the civilians believed in Johnston, and they could not have made their feelings more apparent. Unlike other questions with regard to Hood and Johnston, Civil War historians generally agree on this point. Johnston's biographer contended that the move, though probably born out of desperation, could only have helped morale. Perhaps more significant, Hood's biographer asserted that after the failed Tennessee campaign, the soldiers would not fully recover as long as Hood remained in command.[8]

A Mississippi Confederate soldier, Charles Roberts, expressed sentiments representative of his comrades' opinions. They certainly wanted Johnston, but the hardened veterans knew better than to assume that they would get him. From Aberdeen, Mississippi, on January 7, Roberts wrote to his wife, "That there should be a change of commanders I think is absolutely necessary, but nothing short of Genl Johnston will satisfy the bulk of the army. It is astonishing with what tenacity they retain implicit faith in Genl Johnston and . . . I never expect to see the wish of the army gratified on this point, for should President Davis so overcome his prejudice [against Johnston] as to tender Genl Johnston the command, I very much doubt if he would accept it under the circumstances."[9]

As Roberts's comrades throughout the western Confederacy expressed their demands for Johnston, certain common themes emerged. First, the soldiers who remained in the army no longer wanted to serve under Hood but still refused to submit. Second, their sentiments must be characterized as clearly both anti-Hood and pro-Johnston, not simply the former. The soldiers' animosity toward Hood and their distrust of his command abilities and their love and respect for Johnston ring clear in diary after diary and letter after letter. Predictably, not a single soldier among those studied here continued to support Hood. Virtually all called for Johnston and insisted that he was the only man for the job. If anyone could repair Hood's damage to the army, Old Joe could. But that "if" points to a telling statement about western Confederate morale in early 1865. True, almost everyone, soldier and civilian, considered Johnston the man for the job. Yet most of those same Confederates now clearly doubted that the job could be done at all.[10]

A daunting task indeed faced Confederate officials, civilians, and soldiers by early 1865. The Army of Tennessee, and therefore the entire western Confederacy, teetered on the verge of ruin. Tennessee was forever lost to the Confederacy, and Mississippi and Alabama boasted a dwindling number of defenders. Hood had entered Tennessee with a formidable army. By February fewer than twenty thousand soldiers remained, and Davis expected as many as possible to move east to assist in the Confederate defense against Sherman's relentless advance through the Carolinas. After some fifteen thousand western troops shifted east, Lieutenant General Richard Taylor, commander of the Department of Alabama, Mississippi, and East Louisiana, found himself with approximately thirty thousand soldiers stretched from Tupelo and Corinth to Mobile.[11]

During January, officers assessed the condition of their troops and cringed at what they found. Even Major General Nathan Bedford Forrest admitted the demoralization of the army, while Taylor described the scene at Tupelo as "my first view of a beaten army." Taylor pointed to the shortage of arms, clothing, and blankets. Many soldiers suffered frostbite, and exposure took the lives of others. Amid such conditions the beleaguered Hood finally asked to be relieved of command. Confederate general P. G. T. Beauregard, essentially Confederate chief officer over the entire western theater, had already made that decision anyway and upon Hood's resignation appointed Taylor commander of the Army of Tennessee. Like virtually everyone else, Taylor instantly insisted that the position should go to Johnston. Only after the Confederate Congress and Robert E. Lee officially joined the chorus of calls for Johnston did Davis relent and appoint his old rival. Johnston assumed command of the remnants of the Army of Tennessee in North Carolina on February 23.[12]

New Year's assessments of the country's predicament were not unique to prominent officers. Common soldiers also recognized the army's plight, and during January and February, as the soldiers scattered from northern Mississippi to southern Alabama to the Carolinas, they recorded their thoughts in private diaries and in letters to loved ones. Demoralization, longing for peace, lack of confidence in the weakened Confederate military, and the ardent desire to see their families dominated the soldiers' early 1865 writings. Generally, they continued to hope for southern independence but no longer predicted it. Those who remained in the military, wherever they were in the western Confederacy, did so out of a sense of honor, duty, and loyalty. Soldiers such as James Montgomery Lanning, William Nugent, and James Orr longed to go home but refused to do so under anything other than honorable circumstances. A few, such as Thomas McGuire, Joseph Branch O'Bryan, and George Phifer Erwin, refused to submit and insisted that independence might yet be won in battle.[13]

Despite some variation of opinion regarding the Confederacy's chances by early 1865, demoralization, dissatisfaction, and an unprecedented lack of discipline proved virtually universal. Even those who continued to call for a fight to the end admitted the gloom and demoralization that surrounded them. William Pitt Chambers, for example, a hardened Confederate veteran who showed little patience for weakness in others, mocked the "fight on" resolutions passed by various groups of soldiers and deemed them mostly talk. He insisted that the majority of the soldiers simply wanted peace on the best possible terms. Some western Confederate soldiers thought that only God could now determine their country's fate, while others continued to hope for some major development that might turn the tide of war. Yet even the most optimistic knew that dreams of independence would slip away without some dramatic turn of events. They were losing the war, and now, for the first time, the vast majority of them admitted it.[14]

Besides the gloomy predictions and declarations of honor and duty to family and country, two other interesting themes emerged that shed light on the western Confederate soldiers' mind-set in early 1865. First, soldiers frequently celebrated when assigned to Mobile. All sources indicated that the city on the bay continued to boast a quasi-normal atmosphere, almost certainly the most cheerful place in the Confederacy east of the Mississippi River. The soldiers typically offered no explanation for their pleasure with the Mobile assignment, though the relative safety that characterized that city throughout the war likely helps explain it. To be fair, some Confederate soldiers there chafed at their inactivity while the Army of Tennessee and other forces fought for the cause elsewhere, but many clearly were perfectly content with the comparative security of Mobile. Although none admitted it, service in Mobile offered soldiers the opportunity to maintain their honor and demonstrate their loyalty to the cause while facing significantly less risk to their lives in a war they appeared increasingly unlikely to win. Even soldiers in Mobile who continued to declare their faith in the cause, by February 1865, clearly thought about what might happen in case of defeat. Tennessee soldier Joseph Branch O'Bryan refused to admit being "whipped," and fumed that the Federals might scatter Rebel armies and issue proclamations of peace, but boasted proudly that it would never be safe for a Yankee to live in the South.[15]

One Confederate in particular poured his emotions and obvious concern for the postwar South into letters to his wife. In a series of February letters John H. Marshall pointed with pride to his service to the cause and insisted that he would never disgrace his wife or children. If he never made it home, he would have left a "good carrecter." In fact, if not for them he would rather die than submit to the Yankee invaders. He admitted that Confederate victory was unlikely, unless more southern men did their duty as he saw it, but he could not bring himself to stomach the image of subjugation by Yankees or the thought of his wife at the "wash tub" or "cook pot." In case of defeat he would rather go to hell and fumed that no "blue villains" would be safe in Mississippi after the war as long as he lived. If any Federals mistreated his wife, he swore that he would have his revenge. Marshall's emotions ranged from intense anger to deep sadness throughout the remainder of the month. Finally, from Montgomery in late February, the Mississippi soldier wrote that, after more than a year's absence from his family, he simply wanted to go home.[16]

Marshall's concerns point to the other revealing theme from soldiers' early 1865 writings. Whether he lamented the Confederacy's plight or continued to believe that independence could be won, the individual soldier frequently insisted that, whatever happened in the coming months, he had done all that he could do. He wanted friends and relatives to know that he had not disappointed them, that he had performed his duty and retained his honor. Even if the Confederacy collapsed, the common soldier wanted it known that he had done his part as a defender of the South and should be remembered as a man who had remained faithful until the end. Joseph Branch O'Bryan assured his sisters in the uncertain days of late February that "I have done my duty and regret no step I have taken." Another soldier admitted that he could not say what the future held and did not know how the war should proceed, but maintained that he would simply do his duty. The wife of a Georgia soldier clearly understood the soldiers' sentiments when she asked her husband to come home in January 1865, assuring him that he had served long enough. In the end, an Alabaman provided perhaps the best illustration of the "did all I could" sentiment when he explained in a letter that he must go to Texas to care for his ailing wife, that he had given all that he could to the cause from the beginning, and that the revolution had left him penniless and without property. To reassure his correspondent, or perhaps to convince himself, he maintained that the cause surely would not suffer without his services.[17]

Those sentiments proved general in the writings of common soldiers and officers alike among those in this study. On New Year's Day an officer from Tennessee lamented that all was "valueless" to him without his country, but insisted that he had done all he could, even if it accomplished nothing. Similarly, department commander Lieutenant General Richard Taylor by early 1865 considered the war lost but proclaimed it a soldier's duty to fight until his government stopped him or until it ceased to exist. In his famous postwar memoirs, like the common soldiers in 1865, Taylor wanted it known that he had performed his duty to the bitter end—even if he saw it coming.[18]

Taylor's former brother-in-law, Confederate president Jefferson Davis, refused to acknowledge the possibility of defeat and successfully manipulated the agenda of a peace conference to provide a fleeting boost to Rebel morale. On February 3, 1865, aboard a steamship at Hampton Roads, Virginia, United States president Abraham Lincoln and Secretary of State William H. Seward met with Confederate representatives Vice President Alexander H. Stephens, Senator Robert M. T. Hunter, and Assistant Secretary of War John A. Campbell. Davis authorized the delegates to accept nothing less than complete Confederate independence. The president also likely selected Stephens, Hunter, and Campbell because they were known advocates of peace and negotiation. Thus, aware all along that Lincoln and Seward would reject Confederate demands, Davis sought to embarrass Confederate officials who sympathized with anything that resembled a peace movement, and at the same time fire the spirits of Confederates around the country who would be insulted by the Federal demands for unconditional submission. For better or worse, so reads the standard interpretation, Davis succeeded in convincing most Confederates of the impossibility of a negotiated peace and aroused the ire of his people.[19]

Historians generally agree on the fundamental results of the conference, that Davis successfully quashed the credibility of negotiations, and that he briefly inspired a significant portion of the Confederate people. Yet no such consensus exists with regard to the Confederate leader's initial thoughts and motives or on the climate in which he acted. Paul D. Escott found more significant peace sentiment among Confederates before the conference than most other historians have and suggested that Davis intentionally misled the Confederate people about Federal demands, but admitted that Davis effectively defeated the idea of a negotiated peace. Charles W. Sanders Jr. rejected the notion that Davis sought to discredit the peace movement and argued that Davis had radically evolved during his four years as Confederate president, to the point that he would embrace almost any measure that might secure Confederate independence. Thus Sanders insisted that Davis truly believed that he might secure a peace settlement. Finally, in one of the most insightful examinations of the Confederate government's late-war activities, Steven E. Woodworth also contended that Davis, at least initially, genuinely believed that he might secure Confederate independence through the conference. Woodworth, however, deemed Davis's expectations "preposterous" and maintained that the Confederate leader might have secured concessions such as gradual emancipation with compensation for slaveholders and greater state government autonomy if he had seriously considered any terms other than Confederate independence. More important to the question of morale, Woodworth further demonstrated that once the meeting had failed, Davis aggressively and expertly shaped public reaction. Woodworth described the president's actions during the early days of February as some of the "most energetic and skillful political activity of his life" and concluded that Davis steeled the morale and nerve of much of the Confederate populace. Even a "disgusted" Vice President Stephens, long a Davis critic, begrudgingly deemed one of Davis's speeches during this episode "brilliant."[20]

The writings of western Confederates in early 1865 support the notion that the failure of the conference temporarily raised a fire in the bellies of at least some Rebels, military and civilian, and suggest that at least some western Confederates believed that the conference might result in Confederate independence. Even a soldier in Mississippi who expected the negotiations to fail admitted that many others around him anticipated success. Historians may disagree whether Davis decided before or after the conference to spin northern rejections of Confederate demands as yet one more insult to southern honor, but regardless of the timing his ploy clearly succeeded, and western Confederates indeed perceived the results exactly as Davis intended. Mississippian Cora Watson blamed Yankee demands, while Confederate artillerist Thomas Key suggested that the Federal terms were so dishonorable that they should unify all true Confederates. Others expressed strikingly similar sentiments and typically blamed the failure of negotiations entirely on Lincoln. Alabama civilian Robert Mallory blamed the leadership of both sides even before he knew the results. Mallory lamented that the bloodshed would likely continue, "God only knows how long, for he cannot be heard so long as the rulers on both sides seem so determined."[21]

Davis could not have found more model Confederates to receive and spread his message than East Tennessee refugee Ellen House and army chaplain, newspaper correspondent, and Confederate propagandist Robert F. Bunting. The fiery young Ellen House wanted nothing less than independence, considered Lincoln "an old fool," and could not understand how anyone could consider reunion. She even hoped that there would be no temporary armistice because that would bring a pause in the fighting, and she believed independence likely could be secured only through fighting. Bunting's correspondence to a Texas newspaper from a military hospital in Auburn, Alabama, read as though Davis himself had scripted it. Bunting deemed the horrors of war preferable to the "deplorable," "degrading," and "enslaving" proposals of Lincoln. He confidently predicted that every true southern patriot would rise in opposition to northern suggestions of reunion. "Breathes there a Southern man so lost to national pride and individual shame, as to stretch out his hand for Northern fetters, and bow his dishonored head for the yoke which abolitionism stands ready to place upon him? Do not these words of unparalleled insolence cause the painted idol of reconstruction to crumble and vanish forever from our midst?" Ultimately, Bunting concluded that the northern demand for reunion, complete with the end of slavery, "brings us back again to the point we started at four years ago."[22]

In the end, western Confederate reaction to the Hampton Roads peace conference proved Jefferson Davis correct only in theory—much of the populace indeed took offense to the northern rejection of Confederate demands for independence and called for continued unity and a rejuvenation of the fighting spirit. But in reality, much like reactions to the reappointment of Johnston to command the Army of Tennessee, the entire episode proved little more than an ephemeral swelling of Confederate pride. True enough, the results angered many western Confederates, but they were already angry. The proceedings certainly reminded some western Confederates why they hated northerners so intensely, but with the carnage and devastation of warfare all around them, they hardly needed reminding. What happened, or rather did not happen, aboard the steamship *River Queen* in the bigger picture changed nothing. Robert E. Lee still faced a stalemate at best with Ulysses S. Grant's large and powerful forces in Virginia; Sherman and his armies yet marched wherever they pleased; and the dead at Franklin and Nashville were not coming back, effectively leaving the Confederacy without the services of its "other" army.

On the heels of the Hampton Roads affair, an idea for how to rebuild the diminishing Confederate armies brought forth the true last gasp of Rebel morale in a far more controversial and fundamentally revealing form— Confederate plans to arm black soldiers. In February 1865 the Confederate House of Representatives passed a bill that authorized the enlistment of blacks, who might or might not receive freedom in exchange for their service, only to see that legislation defeated in the Senate. During the desperate days of mid-March, however, both houses passed the Act to Increase the Military Force of the Confederate States, and the formation of black companies began in Richmond with only days remaining in the life of the Confederacy. (Without the consent of Congress, Davis manipulated enlistment regulations to allow for the promise of emancipation in exchange for enlistment.) Despite enduring myths about thousands of black men in gray, however, the 1865 legislation brought probably fewer than a couple hundred men into Confederate military service. The legislation ultimately hinged on the support of Robert E. Lee, and the administration of the program was left to the state governments rather than the Confederate government.[23]

The concept of arming slaves to fight in defense of the Confederacy was not new in early 1865. Since 1863 some Confederates, including military officers, state governors, and newspaper editors, had endorsed the idea. Major General Patrick Cleburne of the Army of Tennessee authored the most famous written proposal and presented the plan to other officers during the winter of 1863–1864 at Dalton, Georgia. Cleburne pointed to the Confederate manpower shortage and proclaimed the slaves the "common sense" remedy. He advocated arming slaves with the expectation of freedom for themselves and their wives and children within a "reasonable" period of time. More important, the general understood that in the eyes of the outside world, Lincoln's emancipation plans had provided the Union with the higher moral ground and would prevent international intervention. The popular officer maintained that the existence of thousands of black Confederate soldiers would challenge the northern Republican claims that the war was being waged to free the slaves, and it might also attract international support for the southern cause. Cleburne obviously understood at Dalton what most others would not grasp until early 1865—that the Confederates might be forced to choose between southern independence and slavery, and he clearly advocated the former.[24]

Predictably, Cleburne's proposal met primarily with opposition among officers in the Army of Tennessee. Several expressed nothing short of outrage, while army commander Joseph E. Johnston sidestepped the issue when he refused to forward the document to Richmond on the grounds that it was not of a military nature. Someone else made sure that Davis received the treatise, however, and the president proceeded to suppress the topic entirely for almost another year. But in November 1864, only weeks before Cleburne's death at the Battle of Franklin, Davis proposed to Congress legislation that would purchase for the government forty thousand slaves to be employed in noncombat military duties. Not only did Davis suggest the emancipation of those laborers in exchange for their services, but in the same address the increasingly anxious executive hinted at the possible future necessity of enlisting black soldiers.[25]

The defeats of late 1864 and the resultant desperate circumstances of early 1865 certainly opened Davis's mind to the notion of enlisting black troops. The same proved true among some soldiers, civilians, and the press in the western Confederacy. Interestingly, whether they favored or opposed the proposals, virtually all western Confederates examined here acknowledged that black soldiers could help. The Army of Tennessee, after all, had recently faced black Federal soldiers at Nashville. It is unclear how this affected the Confederate soldiers' position on the black troops question, but obviously they knew firsthand that black men were capable of combat service. Thus, for most the question became not could black men serve as soldiers, but should they? Although the fact that Confederates even debated arming slaves reveals their desperation, in the western Confederacy nothing resembling a consensus emerged.

Those who opposed the use of black troops and/or their emancipation conveyed predictable sentiments. Three basic points proved common. First, some soldiers fumed that they simply would not serve next to black soldiers. Second, as one Alabama newspaper editor wrote, if whites could not win southern independence, perhaps they did not deserve it. Finally, and most important, some western Confederates raised the big-picture questions that so many southern leaders had pointed to all along: What would arming slaves mean about the entire Confederate cause? If blacks would make good soldiers, then the traditional southern theory of slavery was all wrong.

Moreover, if the Confederates themselves dismantled slavery, why had there been a war to begin with?[26]

The arguments in favor of arming black troops proved far more interesting and revealing about the state of morale in the Confederate heartland in early 1865. Like Cleburne more than a year earlier, some western Confederates considered slavery the primary impediment to international recognition for their country. Relinquishing slavery might convince England and France to grant the fledgling nation diplomatic recognition, thereby creating conflict between those nations and the United States.

Although many clearly hoped for such recognition and rumors persisted, by 1865 the western Confederates studied here generally knew better than to believe wild rumors and certainly never allowed their spirits to rise too high based on unconfirmed gossip. Some even warned each other not to become too despondent as a result of discouraging reports. Certainly rumors could affect the spirits of a population in a war-ravaged area such as the Confederate heartland, but nearly four years of war had taught those battle-hardened people many lessons, including the fallibility of much gossip. An excellent recent study has demonstrated the potential importance of rumors in shaping the morale of "diehard" Confederates. However, the western Confederates examined here proved capable of discerning between realistic and ridiculous rumors and in either case *consciously* sought to avoid allowing rumors of either a positive or negative nature to shape their morale. After all, throughout much of the previous year, especially the spring and summer of 1864, they genuinely believed that they were winning the war, and those beliefs were based primarily on battlefield results. Whether correct or not, such sentiments were at least realistic. Regardless of the influence of rumors or the likelihood of foreign intervention, all understood the importance of international relations and that the arming of black troops (with emancipation) might change the war entirely.[27]

The hopes of winning over foreign countries proved minimal compared to more immediate, practical concerns. Increasing numbers of western Confederates came to believe that by early 1865 the Confederacy would not win the war if they did not use black soldiers. In defeat, they would lose both slavery and their dreams of independence. Why not enlist black troops and at least conceivably win southern independence? Moreover, as more than one western Confederate wrote, if the Confederates did not use blacks against the North, the North would use the South's own slaves against them. For example, a military chaplain, who defended slavery as "providential," sneered from Alabama that perhaps the Confederates should fight the Yankees with "their favorite hobby." Meanwhile, northern Mississippian Cora Watson agreed that most people in that area supported using black troops, particularly because the Union would eventually employ them against the Confederacy. But unlike the chaplain who hoped to preserve slavery, Watson apparently considered emancipation a condition of their service. That idea hardly bothered her, as indicated by her February 7 diary entry. "We can soon learn to do without them, and, in the end, I have no doubt we will be better off rid of them. It will be harder for the Negroes themselves than for us. Thousands of the worthless, lazy creatures will starve to death. . . ."[28]

Watson's repugnant statement illustrates a fundamentally important development: emancipation served only to galvanize many western Confederates in their quest for independence. Obviously, the emancipation of thousands of slaves eventually weakened the Confederate war effort, but Confederates often did not interpret it that way. Instead, the destruction of slavery and the role of northern whites and slaves themselves in the process made clear what a Federal victory would mean to southern society and reinforced the worrisome notion that the South was being reshaped from the outside. Similar to the reactions of some who witnessed Sherman's March or that general's earlier Meridian campaign, emancipation only fueled Confederate hatred for those they perceived as northern invaders and boosted the pride and resolve of those who survived the war's many trials. Overall, the greater lesson in Watson's comments is not the obvious racist venom, but rather her insistence that southern society would survive just fine without the institution of slavery and that the slaves themselves would not.[29]

James D. Lynch, a captain and former private from Mississippi stationed in Alabama during the war's closing months, articulated the common viewpoint succinctly. He wrote to his wife, "We are all up for putting the negroes in even if it results in the entire amancipation of the whole race. We are willing to give up everything if necessary but our Independence, that we will never think of giving up, if we have to arm every negroe man in the South. I see Congress is about to adopt this policy, and I think the sooner the better, for we want more men, and more men we must have and the question is whether we will allow the Enemy gradually to get possession of all the Negroes and arm them against us, or put them in our own army to fight for our independence. I think the choice can't for a moment be doubted even if it results in the emancipation. . . ."[30]

In perhaps the most telling statement on the issue of arming and eman-cipating blacks and on the status of western Confederate morale overall in the winter of 1865, Tennessee soldier Joseph Branch O'Bryan wrote, "[W]e can certainly live without negros better than with Yankees. . . ." Even by January 20, 1865, O'Bryan told his sisters to expect to see black troops join the Confederate service because public opinion had changed so much on the question. The soldier repeated the familiar refrain that most people now understood that slavery would be lost one way or another, so they might as well use slaves to help secure independence. Simply put, for average Con-federates such as O'Bryan, Lynch, Cora Watson, and others, the question of arming black troops boiled down to one thing—anything for indepen-dence. Of course southern independence had always been one goal, but now that appeared to be the only goal. A soldier from East Texas concurred. He admitted that some favored the proposal and some opposed it, but that "I favor anything over subjugation." A Louisiana diarist in the Army of Tennes-see agreed, finding "anything better than subjugation." For most individuals examined here, they continued to see the war that way—a war to avoid subjugation by a hated group of tormenters.[31]

Surprisingly few historians have engaged the question of Confederate plans to arm black troops. In a recent study, Aaron Sheehan-Dean found considerable support for arming black troops among Virginia soldiers and civilians and argued that the question in Confederate minds had become whether to use slaves in the fight for independence or surrender "with the dignity of never having abandoned the interest that distinguished North from South." Similar to conclusions presented here, Sheehan-Dean argued that the willingness to arm black soldiers reveals desperation among the Confederates but also illustrates their continued commitment to white su-premacy and the fight for southern independence. Similarly, in an excellent essay Philip D. Dillard found mixed reactions to the proposals to arm black troops. Dillard found staunch opposition in Texas, relatively distant from the war's major campaigns, but considerable support for the idea in war-torn Virginia, where "Union threats and harsh sacrifices had made true Confed-erates out of many Virginians." Those western Confederates who supported the idea evinced sentiments and motives similar to those of the Virginians described by Sheehan-Dean and Dillard.[32]

Only one book-length monograph deals exclusively with the subject of Confederates arming black troops. Bruce Levine's intriguing study offered the most detailed analysis of the issue thus far, though it essentially echoed an argument put forth by Paul D. Escott almost thirty years earlier. Both authors maintained that, despite a lack of cooperation from many in the planter class, Confederate leaders attempted to arm black troops because they understood that slavery was doomed one way or another. Therefore, they reasoned that they should take the step not as a radical change but rather in order to *preserve* the Old South as much as possible. They could not sustain slavery, so they would hold on to what Levine called "the next-best state of affairs"—limited freedom for black southern laborers and the preservation of white supremacy.[33]

That thesis makes perfect sense when applied to the Confederate leadership class, but not to the rank and file of southern soldiery and citizenry. Levine demonstrated that, similar to the western Confederate sources cited above, soldiers gradually and increasingly supported the arming of slaves, but not for the same reasons as their leaders. Levine argued plausibly that among soldiers and officers, those men actually risking their lives for southern independence, practical concerns took precedence over long-term socioeconomic visions. Soldiers hoped that arming slaves might help them avoid subjugation, win their independence, and simply stay alive. Too, some soldiers eventually came to believe that they had no other alternatives. Common Confederate support for arming black troops indicated no fundamental shift in their beliefs about race. They continued to consider black men inferior and typically did not support emancipation as a condition of black military service. Moreover, even the ordinary Confederate obviously would have appreciated the preservation of white supremacy as sought by the leadership class.[34]

Manifest Confederate commitment to white supremacy notwithstanding, outside of the leadership class, most Confederates did not think of employing black troops as a means to preserve the racial, social, and economic status quo. They sought independence from the hated North, and they admitted to themselves that black men with guns could help them achieve it. What better evidence of intense hatred of Yankees and the desire for independence than the willingness to fight beside black soldiers? In a war instigated primarily by decades-old differences with regard to slavery, the vast majority of Confederates clearly supported the peculiar institution and the continued subjugation of blacks. Yet, to ask what caused a war, any war, is not the same as to ask why each man fought. The support for the use of black troops further demonstrates that countless Confederates fought foremost for southern independence. Without independence, in the minds of most average Confederates, the rhetoric hardly seemed to matter. As historian Emory Thomas wrote, by late in the war "the Confederacy had become for many Southerners an end in itself."[35]

In early 1865 western Confederates confronted the reality of a probable defeat in their bid for independence, and their writings depict a disheartened, desperate population in search of any sign of hope or reason to believe. The willingness of so many western Confederates to arm black troops, or even seriously consider it, suggests a drowning people grasping at straws. Similarly, the dialogue that surrounded the reappointment of Joseph E. Johnston to command the Army of Tennessee and reactions to that decision reveal a populace with painfully paradoxical sentiments. Western Confederates scrutinized in this study almost unanimously considered Johnston the man for the job but did not appear to believe that the job could be done. These same western Rebels also held out genuine hopes for a peace settlement at the Hampton Roads conference. Yet, when what should have been predictable northern demands for complete surrender, reunion, and the abolition of slavery insulted southern honor, Confederates fumed and ranted to no avail. For the purposes of tracking western Confederate morale, the entire affair resulted in little more than a momentary flicker of Confederate patriotism.

All of those issues demonstrate the theoretical impediments to measuring the morale of a people whose confidence had already been crushed on the killing fields of Middle Tennessee. As the war's final spring loomed, once hardened and proud western Confederates, witnesses to so much bloodshed and devastation, finally looked beyond their belief in southern military prowess in search of salvation. Some endorsed drastic measures, while others gave up entirely. Most continued to hope for independence, but exceedingly few still predicted victory. In the end, nothing during the winter of 1865 could repair the damage done at Franklin and Nashville. A change of commanders, diplomatic wrangling, and fantasies of arming thousands of willing and loyal black troops could not restore the faith crushed by Federal armies. By winter's end most western Confederates expected defeat. There is no better measure of morale.

8

March–April 1865
and Conclusion

WESTERN TENNESSEE CIVILIAN Robert Cartmell opened his March 1865 diary with the lament, "No person now living ought ever to want to live during another civil war. Of a truth, it is the worst of all wars. I could give no adequate conception of its horrors."[1] Such gloomy and reflective sentiments pervaded the writings of western Confederates in spring 1865. Although a scattered few continued to breathe fire and insist on a fight to the end, among the civilians and soldiers examined here, most admitted the Confederacy's impending defeat. Some soldiers left the ranks because they deemed it a greater obligation to return to their families alive than to fight and possibly die in a war already lost. Those soldiers who remained in Confederate armies that spring generally did so out of their own sense of honor and duty to themselves, their comrades, their families, and their country. With an eye toward the postwar South, those soldiers served until the end because of a sincere concern for their families' and friends' perceptions of them. Until the surrender of the Army of Northern Virginia in early April 1865, even soldiers who recognized the impending defeat frequently refused to go home for fear that they might bring shame upon themselves or their families. Although anticipation of their country's downfall proved the prevailing sentiment among those considered in this study, only the final, surreal scenes of the war made defeat a reality. So, when Robert E. Lee finally surrendered to Union forces in Virginia, western Confederate soldiers and civilians reacted with emotions that included disbelief, disgust, defiance, and even relief.

That news arrived amid a string of dismal reports for the Confederates in 1865. In January, Federals captured Fort Fisher in North Carolina and in the process closed the final blockade-running port in the eastern Confederacy.

Later that month William T. Sherman and his Federals began their march north from Savannah, through the Carolinas, brushing aside feeble Confederate resistance. Reenforced by Federal forces from Wilmington, North Carolina, in late March, Sherman and one hundred thousand Union soldiers stood poised to cross into Virginia and unite with Ulysses S. Grant against Lee and Richmond. As it turned out, Grant never needed Sherman's help. Federals broke through Confederate defenses southwest of Petersburg on April 1–2, and the Confederates evacuated Richmond April 2–3. The surrender at Appomattox occurred one week later, followed by Joseph E. Johnston's capitulation to Sherman in North Carolina, finalized on April 26. In the West, Federal raids crossed Mississippi, Alabama, and Georgia. In early April, Selma and Mobile fell into Federal hands, and remaining Confederate forces in the western and trans-Mississippi theaters were surrendered during the next several weeks.[2]

Despite the circumstances in March and early April, before they learned of Lee's surrender, a few western Confederate soldiers continued to insist that victory could be achieved. Mississippi infantryman Evan Shelby Jeffries boasted that the Confederacy would prevail as long as there remained one man with forty rounds of ammunition, while Texan Andrew J. Fogle insisted that only fifty thousand men were necessary to carry on the fight. A Georgia soldier urged his wife to remain hopeful and confident and to maintain her faith in the Confederates' abilities to defeat Sherman's Federal forces in the Carolinas. Meanwhile, an Alabama cavalryman insisted that the Confederates could yet prevail if only some of those "trifling cowards" at home would "shoulder their guns" and join the fight. That soldier clearly resented those southerners who he claimed wanted independence but were unwilling to fight for it. Such conditions unquestionably frustrated him further because he obviously believed that the war could still be won. Yet by that point such confident soldiers constituted a distinct minority, and even they recognized the odds they faced.[3]

In fact, most western Confederate soldiers examined here wrote in realistic terms by spring 1865. They understood the overall situation, believed that most civilians had given up, and many resigned themselves to serve out their terms as honorably as possible. While Confederate armies slowly disintegrated in all theaters of the war, soldiers such as Jeffries and Fogle wanted to go home as badly as anyone but refused to dishonor themselves or their families by leaving the ranks before an official surrender and parole. With conflicted emotions, diminished dreams of independence, images of grave sacrifice, and the probability of looming defeat, Fogle wrote a letter that doubtless expressed the sentiments of thousands of Confederate soldiers that spring. In the broken grammar of a southern yeoman, and yet at times articulate, Fogle pointed to his sense of duty and honor and the sacrifice of thousands of southern men who risked "all and dair all for our independence." In light of that sacrifice, the Texas infantryman expressed his disgust for those who gave up on the Confederacy while soldiers still roamed battlefields. Soldiers bore everything with "cheerfulness," he insisted, but could not live with the "cowerdly ignominious and base spirit of submission on the part of the people. . . ."[4]

Fogle correctly diagnosed the defeated spirit of most western Confederate civilians under consideration here. Although, like the soldiers, a small minority continued to demand a fight to the end, even before Lee's surrender most knew that their defeat was only a matter of time. Alabaman Robert Mallory, for example, considered the eastward movement of western soldiers to help defend against Sherman pointless, and by late March he knew that his home state would soon fall entirely under Federal control. In fact, civilian diarists that spring frequently listed recently captured southern cities and wondered which would fall next. When Richmond finally fell, that removed any doubt in the minds of all but the most hardcore Confederates, including Myra Inman, who admitted subjugation for the first time. At that late date of the war, perhaps their distance from the battlefield allowed some civilians to see the bigger picture.[5]

News of Lee's surrender and the unofficial end of the war brought home the reality of defeat for soldier and civilian alike, though many initially refused to believe the news. They could believe neither that the Federals could have defeated Lee and his army nor that the Confederate experiment had in fact failed. Despair followed that disbelief in many written reactions to the news. While some recorded heartfelt and dramatic commentaries about freedom from northern tyranny and the death of the Confederate dream, others finally admitted Lee's mortality. Perhaps they had placed too much hope in one man, some reasoned. Invoking the out-manned, out-gunned thesis that would endure for generations to come, Alabama diarist Sarah Espy wrote in late April 1865 that she "saw a soldier, who says it is true that Gen Lee has surrendered. His army was thought to be invincible, but numbers can overpower any."[6]

By April many of Espy's contemporaries had already recognized the futility of further resistance, and they reacted to overall Confederate defeat with an unusual mixture of disgust and relief. The thought of submitting to "Yankee tyranny" and the sight of victorious Federal soldiers tramping through southern cities fueled the disgust. From Mobile, for example, William Fulton wrote to his sister to describe the Federal takeover of the city. He expressed revulsion at the raising of the "despicable gridiron" (American flag) and the regiments of "house-burners" who paraded through the streets. Still more sickened, Fulton admitted that some residents were hardly upset and even cheered the Federals. Weeks later, Kate Hopkins Oliver, a southern woman also in Mobile, revealed her horror and anger at the sight of black Federal soldiers when she wrote, "Oh, it is so humiliating to see them march with such a free air. It makes my blood boil." She simply could not tolerate thoughts of living among Yankees and free blacks.[7]

Individuals such as those who so appalled Fulton perhaps typified the second half of the unusual disgust-relief combination expressed around the western Confederacy. No doubt representative of thousands of others, a Tennessee infantry captain remembered, "The news of Lincoln's assassination, Lee's surrender and Johnston's followed each other in such rapid succession that we had hardly breathing time." He described the "mirth and gayety" in the village of Eatonton, Georgia, and admitted that, though they regretted the war's outcome, "With all our sorrow there was a feeling of relief that the war was at last over, that we were at liberty to go home, once more. I am afraid if the truth were known that we were not as sorry as we should have been."[8]

Like so many of his comrades, a lonely former Confederate soldier and army musician spent most of May 1865 on a homeward journey to his wife, at least five children, and his farm. Surrendered by Johnston in North Carolina, Albert Quincy Porter traveled from North Carolina to Mississippi mostly by foot, occasionally by rail and boat, and witnessed the early results of civil war. He traveled through Abbeville, South Carolina, and the tiny Georgia village of Crawfordville before revisiting the Atlanta battlegrounds. His homeward march continued through western Georgia and Opelika in eastern Alabama. On May 22, with blistered feet, Porter walked into Montgomery, where he witnessed a city full of Federals and "some three or four thousand negroes who left their homes and came to the Yanks." In that historic city the former Confederate soldier witnessed the most fundamental transformation brought by four years of brutal war. The ragged veteran had nothing more to say on what he witnessed. Perhaps his silence spoke volumes in that he understood just how revolutionary Confederate defeat might prove to be. Porter's trek continued through the familiar sites of Selma, Demopolis, Meridian, and Jackson. Eventually he turned south again, toward his home and family in Meadville, deep in southwest Mississippi. On May 30, the ragged Rebel "marched 15 miles today which brought me to the end of my journey. I found my family all in good health and doing well. Some of my children had grown so much I scarcely knew them." He wrapped up his diary with "reflections upon our situation as a down-fallen people." Those reflections concluded with thoughts of the "devastation and ruin sweeping over our beloved land. . . ." Predictably and perhaps understandably, the reality of the devastation of his southern homeland and the defeat of his cause affected Porter more than the other revolutionary social effects of the conflict that he had witnessed in action in Montgomery. Re-enacted by thousands of former Confederates all across the South, so ended the western Confederacy.[9]

Little more than one year earlier, Porter and most of his comrades would not have envisioned such a denouement. Western Confederates began 1864 with mixed feelings. The appointment of Joseph E. Johnston to command the Army of Tennessee and the subsequent improvement of the army helped restore confidence after the disastrous loss of Chattanooga in late 1863. True to his reputation, Johnston put the common soldiers first and immediately took steps to improve rations and discipline. Johnston's mere presence at the head of the army and his administrative accomplishments almost immediately improved morale. The increasing confidence also spread to the civilian population, particularly in light of the perceived "failure" of Sherman's Meridian campaign across Mississippi and Forrest's success in the northern phase of that campaign. As spring approached, western Confederates in and out of the military looked with increasing optimism to the coming spring campaigns and the opportunity to earn their independence.

March and April 1864 in fact represented a new beginning of sorts. The conflicted feelings and cautious optimism transformed into a revitalized belief in the Confederate cause. Winter was over, and spring promised new crops, the end of frustrating inactivity, and the chance to take action. Western Confederates knew that the Army of Tennessee would soon take the field improved and reinvigorated by the huge religious revival and Johnston's guidance at Dalton. Soldiers saw themselves as God's soldiers and defenders of their homes and families, touched by a new spiritualism and unafraid to die. The rank and file of the Army of Tennessee now believed in themselves and their commander and assertively, even defiantly, predicted ultimate victory. Soldiers and civilians alike drew inspiration from their belief in the inferiority of Federal commanders, the lack of unity behind the northern war effort, and the sacrifice already endured by the Confederate people. Minor springtime victories in North Carolina, Florida, Louisiana, and Tennessee contributed to the growing sense of unity and self-assurance. When the western Confederates under consideration here looked to the looming summer campaigns in Georgia and Virginia, they genuinely expected to win the war and southern independence.

When the major campaigns of 1864 began in the early summer, western Confederates followed the action in Georgia as much as the more heralded fighting in Virginia. The action in northern Georgia more directly affected their homes and families, but they also understood the importance of the campaign in the greater scope of the war. Moreover, many western Confederates were so confident in Lee that they more or less assumed that he could hold off Grant in Virginia. Confederate confidence, military and civilian, remained high during the first month of the Atlanta campaign. Johnston's retreats did not initially hurt morale because soldiers enjoyed fighting Federals from behind defensive positions and because they soon understood and supported Johnston's tactics and overall strategy. The first dip in morale occurred upon the retreat from Cassville after Johnston's bombastic order that proclaimed his intention to turn and fight. But spirits quickly recovered, particularly after Confederate victories in late May.

Overall morale among soldiers and civilians cited throughout this study only continued to climb throughout June. Forrest scored a strategically minor but tactically spectacular victory at Brice's Cross Roads in northern Mississippi that provided a noteworthy boost to morale. Western Confederates in and out of the army considered that victory another indication of southern military superiority, and Forrest continued to build the image of an invincible Confederate defender. In Georgia, Army of Tennessee soldiers believed in Johnston and supported his strategy that kept them alive and allowed them to inflict casualties upon the enemy. A Confederate victory at Kennesaw Mountain in late June boosted confidence to its highest point for the campaign. In fact, for the individuals examined here from points around the entire western Confederacy, in and out of the armies, late June 1864 marked the peak for morale during the entire final year and a half of the war.

On the heels of that crest in confidence, July and August 1864 witnessed significant blows to the soldiers' spirits. A retreat from Kennesaw Mountain in early July caused another slip in the army's morale, but soldier diaries and letters revealed continued faith in Johnston. His removal from command in mid-July shook the soldiers' spirits. Their initial reactions of disbelief and despondency proved near universal among those examined for this study. During the following days and weeks the sentiments of shock and dismay softened somewhat. Most continued to lament the loss of Johnston and never approved of his removal, but soon resigned themselves to the situation. Postwar writings that described the doomsday reactions of soldiers paralleled the soldiers' wartime writings, except that the postwar accounts rarely acknowledged how quickly most combatants came to terms with the command change. In reality, though the majority of the soldiers never approved of John Bell Hood as an army commander and many worried about his reputation for rash decisions, most soon focused on the positives that the young general brought to the army, namely his reputation as a valiant fighter. Hood's proclivity for aggression, however, led to three especially bloody battles around Atlanta. The idea that the general would stubbornly fight for the besieged city temporarily proved popular among the soldiers, but the results, particularly the casualties, quickly undercut morale. Throughout the August lull in the campaign, the army rested and recuperated. Their confidence gradually returned, and the soldiers continued to believe that they would somehow win the campaign.

Meanwhile, in the bigger picture of the western theater, civilian morale remained relatively high, though civilian diarists and correspondents displayed less confidence than did the soldiers. The loss of Mobile Bay proved rather insignificant to morale because the city itself remained in southern hands, and western Confederates viewed their continued control of the city as a sign of strength and considered the entire campaign a secondary matter. Of course, Union commanders also considered the city more valuable to them in Confederate possession. Sherman insisted that maintaining Federal possession of Mobile would essentially waste a Union force on garrison duty while keeping importation open through the city, only to see those goods end up in Confederate hands anyway. Instead, from the northern perspective, Union possession of Mobile Bay and Confederate possession of the city itself would maintain the effectiveness of the Federal blockade without denying Union commanders the services of would-be occupation troops for their impending campaigns. Besides, again from the northern perspective, Confederate possession of Mobile essentially tied down valuable Confederate forces that the Federals would not have to deal with elsewhere.[10] Overall, when the Federals launched what would be the decisive blow for Atlanta in late August and defeated a rare lackluster Confederate effort at Jonesboro, considerable doubt crept into western Confederate minds, and general morale drifted back toward the mixed feelings and uncertainty of winter 1864.

The actual loss of Atlanta in early September 1864 upset western Confederate morale among both civilians and soldiers. In both cases, however, individuals typically considered the loss a major—but hardly fatal—blow to the Confederate cause. Civilians tended to take the loss harder than did the soldiers, who recovered relatively quickly because they believed that they had no other alternative, because they still defended their homes and families, and because the soldiers of the Army of Tennessee had suffered significant defeats before but had always returned to fight another day. Fair or not, most western Confederates examined for this study, military and civilian, immediately blamed Hood for the loss of Atlanta.

Attention then shifted, albeit temporarily, to the northern presidential election of 1864. But even that event proved anticlimactic for western Confederates because Sherman's victory in the Atlanta campaign undercut northern Democratic plans for a peace platform. The election once had seemed to offer at least the possibility of a peaceful solution should Republican incumbent Abraham Lincoln lose, but the battlefield results in Georgia forced the Democratic nominee, George McClellan, to promise to fight the war to ultimate victory if elected. (McClellan also pointed to his loyalty to his fellow soldiers to explain why he would continue the war effort.) So in the end, the election essentially offered western Confederates nothing with regard to a possible peace settlement because both candidates pledged to continue the war. The Confederates would have to keep fighting either way.

By late September and early October, most western Confederates examined in these pages intended to do just that. Morale once again gradually recovered in the Army of Tennessee with rest, improved rations, pay, speeches from prominent Confederates, and the return to the offensive in the form of a campaign in northern Georgia. That relatively minor campaign in Sherman's rear and preparations for a major invasion of Tennessee clearly improved the soldiers' spirits, and their writings reflected a sort of cautious optimism as winter approached. Civilians exhibited lower morale and more apparent war weariness. The loss of Atlanta, a devastated landscape, and their inability to affect the war's outcome help explain the lower spirits among civilians by October 1864. Still, most western Confederates examined in this study had not yet given up on their cause. They maintained what they considered a realistic hope for independence and watched cautiously as the Army of Tennessee prepared for a major offensive that would resolve the conflict for better or worse.

When the Army of Tennessee marched north to begin its fateful campaign, it did so with high spirits. The chance to return to the aggressors' role and to "liberate" the Volunteer State lifted morale. Civilian morale, however, reached a new low for 1864. Most civilians examined as part of this study continued to desire southern independence, and Hood's invasion seemed to offer an opportunity to strike a major blow. But their confidence and expectations could not match their desires. Simply put, those western Confederate civilians by late 1864 still wanted independence but they no longer expected it. What happened in Middle Tennessee in November and December 1864 crushed the hopes of most western Confederate soldiers and civilians whose names appear in these pages. At Franklin and Nashville the Federals effectively crippled the Army of Tennessee. The retreat from Tennessee further demoralized even the most hard-bitten Confederate soldiers, and the spectacle of the ragged remnants of a once-proud army disheartened all civilians who witnessed it. Historians in search of the crushing blow to western Confederate spirits, the death knell of the western Confederate heart, must look beyond Gettysburg and Vicksburg, past Atlanta and the reelection of Lincoln. At least in the minds of westerners, the Confederacy all but died in Middle Tennessee.

In the aftermath of Hood's crushing defeats, the winter of 1865 proved the darkest period of the war for western Confederates. Most learned of the disasters at Franklin and Nashville just as they learned of the fall of Savannah, Georgia. For the first time, the coming spring seemed to offer little reason for optimism. The reappointment of Johnston to command the Army of Tennessee proved almost universally satisfactory, but in the end made little difference. The failed peace negotiations at Hampton Roads, Virginia, temporarily raised the ire of Confederates, who blamed northern impudence for the breakdown, but ultimately the entire affair produced only a late flash of Confederate pride.

Finally, the debate with regard to arming black troops to fight for the Confederacy proved the last gasp for western Confederate morale. Most agreed that blacks could be effective soldiers, so the question became not could they help the Confederate cause, but should they? Most who advocated the move considered it necessary to Confederate victory and believed that independence might be saved, but only by sacrificing slavery. For those western

Confederates, their reasoning boiled down to "anything for independence," and soldiers in particular proved increasingly likely to support the plan. Soldiers and civilians who opposed the idea did so because they refused to serve next to blacks, because they believed that if whites could not win their independence they did not deserve it, or because arming black troops would reveal the flaws in the entire belief system of race-based slavery. A Confederate dismantling of slavery from the inside also would raise anew the question of why the war had been fought in the first place. Of course, one might ask: If white southerners believed that they deserved to benefit from the exploitation of black labor before the war, why should they conclude that southern whites did not deserve independence if they were forced to employ black soldiers in the fight? Two things likely explain this. First, most white southerners would hardly consider the use of slave labor "exploitation," particularly when so many found biblical justification for their peculiar institution. Second, and perhaps more important, white southern men and women clearly found a particular honor in military service for white men and would not have considered it "labor" to be equated with that performed by slaves. In other words, at least in the minds of those who opposed the concept of arming black soldiers, to do so would have dishonored the cherished notion of white military prowess and would have meant that independence would have been secured by less than honorable means. The thought of independence without honor, no doubt, motivated those Confederates who insisted that their country would not deserve independence if it were secured in part through the enlistment of black soldiers.

On the question of morale, regardless of the Confederate people's stance on the black troops question, the entire issue revealed their desperation by the winter of 1865. More important in the bigger picture, by the war's last winter the vast majority of the western Confederates cited in this study clearly recognized and frequently admitted their impending defeat. All that remained during the awkward and desperate weeks of March and early April were questions of honor, duty, and the news from Appomattox.

That news, of course, brought an end to four years of combat and sacrifice. For those four years, western Confederate men and women, military and civilian, struggled for their ultimate goal of southern independence until Federal armies crushed those aspirations on the battlefield. Until the crippling of the Army of Tennessee at Franklin and Nashville, most western Confederates still hoped for victory and believed it at least possible. Until the end, western Confederates drew inspiration from battlefield developments, but also from their families, communities, comrades in arms, the sacrifices already endured, and frequently from anxiety for what a Federal victory might mean to their lives. The condition of loved ones at home, overall chances for success of the cause, and even their confidence—or lack thereof—in certain officers helped shape morale among soldiers specifically. Soldiers and civilians alike more often than not put their faith in prominent military commanders and believed wholeheartedly in southern military prowess until near the war's end.

As important as any of those motivations, after decades of sectional animosity and years of warfare, most western Confederates under consideration here genuinely hated northerners and considered Federal soldiers armed invaders bent on the destruction of southern homes and families. It is hardly surprising that soldiers who envisioned themselves as defenders of hearth and home maintained high morale until the end of 1864.

Like their northern counterparts, western Confederates presented less than a perfectly united front, but significant numbers of Mississippians, Alabamans, and Tennesseans from all social classes and both genders remained supportive of the Confederate cause until very late in the war. In their diaries and letters they wrote about loved ones, religion, the war, politics, and sometimes even basic survival. Western Confederates infrequently mentioned social classes in their writings, and as a group certainly displayed no crippling conflict between classes. The poor knew that they were poor, but class awareness does not constitute class conflict, particularly not discord enough to undermine the Confederate war effort. The content of letters and diaries suggests that western Confederates routinely wrote whatever they pleased, so there is no reason to believe that they intentionally omitted discussions of class. Soldiers and their families frequently exchanged letters that included graphic details from the battlefield (sometimes even when soldiers wrote to their wives and mothers), admissions of defeatism late in the war, and any number of personal topics between husbands and wives. If class conflict had played a significant role in the lives of a majority of western Confederates, they would have written about it.

Other "internal" factors also proved relatively insignificant to morale in the Confederate heartland when compared to the effects of battlefield results. Western Confederates' writings occasionally reflected predictable, yet rather negligible resentment toward military impressment and heavy tax burdens. Conscription legislation in early 1864 met with little meaningful resistance because those in the army (and their families) welcomed the help and most others at least understood the necessity of the act. Until late in the war, Confederate desertion rates remained similar to Union rates, and, as diaries and letters make clear, western Confederates frequently considered desertion one of the worst offenses a southern man could commit. The cumulative effect of all such internal factors over the course of the entire war obviously weakened the Confederate war effort to some degree, but in shaping morale, those factors paled in importance to battlefield developments.

All of those factors and the shared Civil War experience helped shape a Confederate identity. Although most historians disagree on the extent, strength, or basic characteristics of Confederate nationalism, they now recognize at least its existence.[11] Yet the lack of a clear, universal definition of nationalism presents the principal obstacle to a more meaningful historiographical consensus on the subject. Similar to historians' debates about whether the Civil War constituted a "total war," or the question of how "revolutionary" was the American Revolution, the nationalism dialogue typically devolves into a disagreement regarding elusive definitions of the key terms. One historian's evidence of a discernable national identity, or total war, or a revolution, falls short of another's standards. In the end, until scholars can agree upon more meaningful and useful definitions of essential terminology, the debate with regard to the *relative strength* of Confederate nationalism threatens to become little more than an academic exercise.

Nevertheless, the words of western Confederates presented throughout this study demonstrate that those men and women, soldiers and civilians, considered themselves Confederates, not members of local and state communities only. Like morale, individuals' sense of nationalism defies exact quantification, but residents and defenders of the Confederate heartland found a common identity in a sense of shared sacrifice, a common view of Federal soldiers as armed invaders, a genuine hatred for those invaders, and the belief that southerners represented the true legacy of 1776. Though simple hatred could not constitute nationalism, widespread hatred of an "aggressor" population on the part of hundreds of thousands of southerners certainly contributed to a sense of identity, particularly after decades of sectional conflict and in light of the fact that Confederates typically blamed the North for the war and the carnage and destruction that it brought. Considering how much punishment Confederates endured, and for that matter how much they meted out, the notion that they believed in their cause seems much more plausible than the idea that they fought, died, and killed for a cause they never really supported.

Perhaps this examination of the experiences of western Confederates and their determined fight for independence will also shed light on a related and relatively overlooked question in Civil War historiography. For all of the volumes dedicated to explaining the causes of the war, far too few books teach us something about how the war ended. A handful of relatively recent volumes are especially strong on this subject and should inspire other studies of the war's conclusion.[12] In the case of this book, a year and a half in the lives of western Confederates during the crucible of war demonstrates just how far one group of nineteenth-century Americans had to be pushed before they submitted and illustrates how a population only slowly and reluctantly learned to accept failure, defeat, and, in their minds, disaster. Even in the Confederate heartland, where the residents witnessed repeated defeat throughout the war, only a series of bloody and catastrophic defeats in Middle Tennessee convinced the majority of these Confederates that they had in fact lost their cause. Their willingness to discuss enlisting black soldiers, almost certainly at the cost of losing slavery, rather than succumb to northern foes and lose their bid for independence illustrates not only considerable dedication to the cause, but that independence had become the ultimate goal, exclusive of issues such as states' rights or slavery. Moreover, the physical extremes and ideological reexaminations to which these soldiers and civilians were willing to resort for their independence reinforce not only the importance of antebellum sectional politics, but also the genuine vitriol characteristic of that era and should contribute to the discussion of why so many white southerners resisted Federal reconstruction efforts after the war. After these Confederates fought to a bitter, bloody end in an effort to preserve an old world, it is hardly surprising that many continued that resistance after the war. Such extreme effort, willingness to revise their ideological agenda in search of independence, the impassioned language of the Rebels examined here, and those individuals' willingness to endure so much sacrifice and inflict so much punishment on their enemies collectively reinforce the notion that these people genuinely considered themselves different from their northern countrymen. If that common bond had not existed between southerners before the war, the war itself made the Confederates "confederates." Therefore, more so than a study of the public rhetoric at the beginning of the secession crisis and before the carnage of war, the examination of the conflict's desperate closing scenes persuasively illustrates the widespread dedication among these nineteenth-century southerners to that concept of a separate southern identity.

Finally, the wartime experiences and writings of western Confederates demonstrate plainly the fundamental relationship between home front and battlefield. In addition to the predictable concerns for hearth and home, a civilian with a brother, husband, father, or son in a Confederate army quite naturally took great interest in military developments. In fact, military news frequently dominated the writings of male and female civilian diarists and correspondents. Sometimes violent, occasionally hateful, and frequently intense in their writings, western Confederate women especially proved genuinely dedicated to Confederate armies, the Confederate war effort, and to the idea of the Confederacy. Denied the opportunity to contribute to the war effort on the battlefield, women found in diaries and letters an outlet for the expression of their pro-Confederate passions. At the same time, rough and tough Rebel soldiers thought about much more than just army life and combat. Soldiers habitually wrote about social, political, and family issues. They agonized about their children and pined for their wives. They worried about money and crops and contemplated their own mortality. In the end, that dogged pursuit of southern independence on two "fronts" and the stubborn fight to a bloody end on the killing fields of Middle Tennessee demonstratee dedication to a cause and reflect the perseverance of the Confederate heartland.

Notes

INTRODUCTION

1. Thomas Lawrence Connelly, *Army of the Heartland: The Army of Tennessee, 1861–1862* (Baton Rouge: Louisiana State Univ. Press, 1967), 3–22; Stephen D. Engle, *Struggle for the Heartland: The Campaigns from Fort Henry to Corinth* (Lincoln: Univ. of Nebraska Press, 2001), xv–xxi.

2. United States Department of the Army, *Field Manual 22–100; Army Leadership: Be, Know, Do* (Washington, D.C.: Headquarters, Department of the Army, 1999), section 3–15; William A. Knowlton, "Morale: Crucial, But What Is It?" *Army* 33 (June 1983): 34–40; *The Compact Edition of the Oxford English Dictionary* (New York: Oxford Univ. Press, 1971).

3. Joseph T. Glatthaar, *The March to the Sea and Beyond: Sherman's Troops in the Georgia and Carolina Campaigns* (New York: New York Univ. Press, 1985), 13–14; Gary W. Gallagher, "Home Front and Battlefield: Some Recent Literature Relating to Virginia and the Confederacy," *Virginia Magazine of History and Biography* 98 (April 1990), 161; James M. McPherson, *What They Fought For, 1861–1865* (Baton Rouge: Louisiana State Univ. Press, 1994), 1–25; Conrad Crane, "Mad Elephants, Slow Deer, and Baseball on the Brain: The Writings and Character of Civil War Soldiers," *Mid-America* 68 (October 1986): 121–140; Reid Mitchell, "'Not the General but the Soldier': The Study of Civil War Soldiers," in *Writing the Civil War: The Quest to Understand*, ed. James M. McPherson and William L. Cooper Jr., 88–89 (Columbia: Univ. of South Carolina Press, 1998).

4. Peter Maslowski, "A Study of Morale in Civil War Soldiers" (Master's thesis, Ohio State University, 1968); Pete Maslowski, "A Study of Morale in Civil War Soldiers," *Military Affairs* 34 (December 1970): 122–126; Samuel A. Stouffer et al., *Studies in Social Psychology in World War II*, 4 vols. (Princeton: Princeton Univ. Press, 1949); Bell I. Wiley, *The Life of Johnny Reb: The Common Soldier of the Confederacy* (1943; reprint, Baton Rouge: Louisiana State Univ. Press, 1978); Bell I. Wiley, *The Life of Billy Yank: The Common Soldier of the Union* (Baton Rouge: Louisiana State Univ. Press, 1952); Joseph T. Glatthaar, "The 'New' Civil War History: An Overview," *Pennsylvania Magazine of History and Biography* 115 (July 1991), 355–356; Mitchell, "Not the General but the Soldier," 88–89; Michael Barton and Larry M. Logue, eds., *The Civil War Soldier: A Historical Reader* (New York: New York Univ. Press, 2002), 3–4.

5. James M. McPherson, *Battle Cry of Freedom: The Civil War Era* (New York: Oxford Univ. Press, 1988); Gary W. Gallagher, *The Confederate War: How Popular Will, Nationalism, and Military Strategy Could Not Stave Off Defeat* (Cambridge: Harvard Univ. Press, 1997); James M.

McPherson, *For Cause and Comrades: Why Men Fought in the Civil War* (New York: Oxford Univ. Press, 1997); James M. McPherson, "American Victory, American Defeat," in *Why the Confederacy Lost,* ed. Gabor S. Boritt, 17–42 (New York: Oxford Univ. Press, 1992); Daniel E. Sutherland, "Getting the 'Real War' into the Books," *Virginia Magazine of History and Biography* 98 (April 1990), 193–220. Stephen V. Ash called persistent faith in the armies the cornerstone of Confederate morale. See Ash, *When the Yankees Came: Conflict and Chaos in the Occupied South, 1861–1865* (Chapel Hill: Univ. of North Carolina Press, 1995), 74–75. For the best-known studies that examine or emphasize internal divisions, see David Williams, *A Rich Man's War: Class, Caste, and Confederate Defeat in the Lower Chattahoochee Valley* (Athens: Univ. of Georgia Press, 1998); Paul D. Escott, *After Secession: Jefferson Davis and the Failure of Confederate Nationalism* (Baton Rouge: Louisiana State Univ. Press, 1978); Richard E. Beringer, Herman Hattaway, Archer Jones, and William N. Still Jr., *Why the South Lost the Civil War* (Athens: Univ. of Georgia Press, 1986); Drew Gilpin Faust, "Altars of Sacrifice: Confederate Women and the Narratives of War," *Journal of American History* 76 (March 1990): 1200–1228; Drew Gilpin Faust, *Mothers of Invention: Women of the Slaveholding South in the American Civil War* (Chapel Hill: Univ. of North Carolina Press, 1996); Bell I. Wiley, *The Plain People of the Confederacy* (Baton Rouge: Louisiana State Univ. Press, 1943); Bell I. Wiley, *The Road to Appomattox* (Memphis, Tenn.: Memphis State College Press, 1956); Charles W. Ramsdell, *Behind the Lines of the Southern Confederacy* (Baton Rouge: Louisiana State Univ. Press, 1944).

6. Aaron Sheehan-Dean, *Why Confederates Fought: Family and Nation in Civil War Virginia* (Chapel Hill: Univ. of North Carolina Press, 2007); Jason Phillips, *Diehard Rebels: The Confederate Culture of Invincibility* (Athens: Univ. of Georgia Press, 2007). For more on the ability of modern scholars to recognize Confederate sacrifice without being labeled Lost Cause apologists, see James L. Roark, "Behind the Lines: Confederate Economy and Society," in McPherson and Cooper, eds., *Writing the Civil War*, 226–227; Gallagher, *The Confederate War*, 13; and Drew Gilpin Faust, *The Creation of Confederate Nationalism: Ideology and Identity in the Civil War South* (Baton Rouge: Louisiana State Univ. Press, 1988), 2–3.

7. Beringer et al., *Why the South Lost the Civil War*; Paul D. Escott, "The Failure of Confederate Nationalism: The Old South's Class System in the Crucible of War," in *The Old South in the Crucible of War*, ed. Harry P. Owens and James J. Cooke, 15–28 (Jackson: Univ. Press of Mississippi, 1983); Escott, *After Secession*; Lawrence N. Powell and Michael S. Wayne, "Self-Interest and the Decline of Confederate Nationalism," in Owens and Cooke, eds., *The Old South in the Crucible of War*, 29–45.

8. McPherson, "American Victory, American Defeat," in Boritt, ed, *Why the Confederacy Lost*, 30–32; Faust, *The Creation of Confederate Nationalism*, 2–21; Emory M. Thomas, "Reckoning with Rebels," in Owens and Cooke, eds., *The Old South in the Crucible of War*, 3–14; Gallagher, "Home Front and Battlefield," 136–145. For yet another study that finds considerable Confederate nationalism, see Sheehan-Dean, *Why Confederates Fought*.

9. William Blair, *Virginia's Private War: Feeding Body and Soul in the Confederacy, 1861–1865* (New York: Oxford Univ. Press, 1998).

10. Escott, "The Failure of Confederate Nationalism," 20–21. Two recent studies of Sherman's campaigns through Georgia and the Carolinas, 1864–1865, found that Federal destruction of southern property actually strengthened the resolve of some Confederate civilians. See Jacqueline Glass Campbell, *When Sherman Marched North from the Sea: Resistance on the*

Confederate Home Front (Chapel Hill: Univ. of North Carolina Press, 2003), especially 91–92; Lisa Tendrich Frank, "To 'Cure Her of Her Pride and Boasting': The Gendered Implications of Sherman's March" (Ph.D. diss., University of Florida, 2001), especially chapters 3 and 4.

11. In addition to the material presented throughout this study, see the essay by Jason Phillips, "A Brothers' War?: Exploring Confederate Perceptions of the Enemy," in *The View from the Ground: Experiences of Civil War Soldiers*, ed. Aaron Sheehan-Dean, 67–90 (Lexington: Univ. Press of Kentucky, 2007).

12. Gallagher, *The Confederate War*, 17–28; Wiley, *The Road to Appomattox*; Clement Eaton, *A History of the Southern Confederacy* (New York: MacMillan, 1954); Escott, *After Secession*; Charles H. Wesley, *The Collapse of the Confederacy* (Chapel Hill: Univ. of North Carolina Press, 1934).

13. Gallagher, *The Confederate War*; Blair, *Virginia's Private War*; Mark Grimsley and Brooks D. Simpson, eds., *The Collapse of the Confederacy* (Lincoln: Univ. of Nebraska Press, 2001); Phillips, *Diehard Rebels*; Sheehan-Dean, *Why Confederates Fought*; Beringer et al., *Why the South Lost the Civil War*, especially 434–435.

14. For a discussion of these themes, see Grimsley and Simpson, eds., *Collapse of the Confederacy*, 1–11.

15. For discussions of the value of narrative in historical writing and/or continued attention to blending military and civilian topics, see Sutherland, "Getting the 'Real War' into the Books," 198–199; James M. McPherson, "What's the Matter with History?" *Drawn with the Sword: Reflections on the American Civil War* (New York: Oxford Univ. Press, 1996), 231–253; Frank J. Wetta, "Battle Histories: Reflections on Civil War Military Studies," *Civil War History* 53 (September 2007): 229–235; George Rable, "The Battlefield and Beyond," *Civil War History* 53 (September 2007): 244–251.

16. Benjamin B. Williams, ed., "Two Uncollected Civil War Poems of Alexander Beaufort Meek," *Alabama Historical Quarterly* 25 (spring 1963): 114–119.

1. JANUARY–FEBRUARY 1864: HOPE AND DESPAIR

1. Robert H. Cartmell Diary, January 1 (first quotation), 11 (second quotation), 1864, Robert H. Cartmell Papers, Tennessee State Library and Archives, Nashville (hereafter cited as TSLA).

2. William R. Snell, ed., *Myra Inman: A Diary of the Civil War in East Tennessee* (Macon, Ga.: Mercer Univ. Press, 2000), 239–250 (quotations 246); George C. Rable, *Civil Wars: Women and the Crisis of Southern Nationalism* (Urbana: Univ. of Illinois Press, 1989), 57–58, 202–203.

3. Stephen V. Ash, *When the Yankees Came: Conflict and Chaos in the Occupied South, 1861–1865* (Chapel Hill: Univ. of North Carolina Press, 1995), 73–75; Stephen V. Ash, *Middle Tennessee Society Transformed, 1860–1870* (Baton Rouge: Louisiana State Univ. Press, 1988), 167; Walter T. Durham, *Reluctant Partners: Nashville and the Union, July 1, 1863 to June 30, 1865* (Nashville: Tennessee Historical Society, 1987), 80–90.

4. Daniel E. Sutherland, ed., *A Very Violent Rebel: The Civil War Diary of Ellen Renshaw House* (Knoxville: Univ. of Tennessee Press, 1996), 78–91, 91 (first quotation), 86 (second quotation), 89 (third and fourth quotations).

5. Ibid., 96–108, 105 (first quotation), 108 (second quotation). For examples of historians arguing that there was a lack of nationalism on the part of Confederates, see Richard E. Beringer, Herman Hattaway, Archer Jones, and William N. Still Jr., *Why the South Lost the Civil War* (Athens: Univ. of Georgia Press, 1986), especially 64–65; Paul D. Escott, *After Secession: Jefferson Davis and the Failure of Confederate Nationalism* (Baton Rouge: Louisiana State Univ. Press, 1978).

6. Vernon H. Crow, ed., "The Justness of Our Cause: The Civil War Diaries of William W. Stringfield," *East Tennessee Historical Quarterly* 57 (1985): 83 (first quotation); Mary Wyche Burgess, ed., "Civil War Letters of Abram Hayne Young," *South Carolina Historical Magazine* 78 (January 1977), 59–60 (second quotation).

7. James H. Wilkes to Cousin Mary, January 9, 1864 (first quotation), Mary E. Wilkes Shell Papers, Mississippi Department of Archives and History, Jackson (hereafter cited as MDAH); H.J.H. Rugeley, ed., *Batchelor-Turner Letters, 1861–1864: Written by Two of Terry's Texas Rangers* (Austin, Tex.: Steck, 1961), 75–76 (second quotation); J. Gary Laine and Morris M. Penny, *Law's Alabama Brigade in the War Between the Union and the Confederacy* (Shippensburg, Pa.: White Mane Publishing, 1996), 215–217; Ray Mathis, ed., *In the Land of the Living: Wartime Letters by Confederates from the Chattahoochee Valley of Alabama and Georgia* (Troy, Ala.: Troy State Univ. Press, 1981), 83–84; John E. Fisher, *They Rode with Forrest and Wheeler: A Chronicle of Five Tennessee Brothers' Service in the Confederate Western Cavalry* (Jefferson, N.C.: McFarland, 1995), 68–72; Elvis E. Fleming, ed., "Some Hard Fighting: Letters of Private Robert T. Wilson, 5th Texas Infantry, Hood's Brigade, 1862–1864," *Military History of Texas and the Southwest* 9, no. 4 (1971): 293–294; William J. Mims, "Letters of Major W. J. Mims, C. S. A.," *Alabama Historical Quarterly* 3 (1941): 203–231; Stanley F. Horn, ed., *Tennessee's War, 1861–1865* (Nashville: Tennessee Civil War Centennial Commission, 1965), 245–246.

8. W. Stanley Hoole, ed., "The Letters of Captain Joab Goodson, 1862–1864," *Alabama Review* 10 (July 1957): 215 (first quotation); Wilkes to Cousin Mary, January 9, 1864, Shell Papers, MDAH; Benjamin Rountree, ed., "Letters of a Confederate Soldier," *Georgia Review* 18 (fall 1964): 282 (second quotation); Katherine S. Holland, ed., *Keep All My Letters: The Civil War Letters of Richard Henry Brooks, 51st Georgia Infantry* (Macon, Ga.: Mercer Univ. Press, 2003), 111–113; Thomas W. Cutrer, ed., *Longstreet's Aide: The Civil War Letters of Major Thomas J. Goree* (Charlottesville: Univ. Press of Virginia, 1995), 116; Mathis, ed., *In the Land of the Living*, 84.

9. Richard Lewis, *Camp Life of a Confederate Boy, of Bratton's Brigade, Longstreet's Corps, C.S.A.: Letters Written by Lieut. Richard Lewis, of Walker's Regiment, to His Mother, during the War* (Charleston, S.C.: News and Courier Book Press, 1883), 81–82.

10. Malcolm Cook McMillan, *The Disintegration of a Confederate State: Three Governors and Alabama's Wartime Home Front, 1861–1865* (Macon, Ga.: Mercer Univ. Press, 1986), 1–2; Bessie Martin, *A Rich Man's War, a Poor Man's Fight: Desertion of Alabama Troops from the Confederate Army* (Tuscaloosa: Univ. of Alabama Press, 2003), 33–57; John Rather and J.W.S. Donnell to Robert Jemison, February 7, 1864, in United States War Department, *The War of the Rebellion: A Compilation of the Official Records of the Union and Confederate Armies*, 128 vols. (hereafter cited as *Official Records*) (Washington, D.C.: Government Printing Office, 1880–1901), ser. 1, vol. 52, pt. 2, 609–611; James E. Saunders to Jemison, January 30, 1864, *Official Records*, ser. 1, vol. 52, pt. 2, 611–614; Paul Horton, "Submitting to the 'Shadow of Slavery': The Secession Crisis and Civil War in Alabama's Lawrence County," *Civil War History* 44 (June 1998): 134;

Margaret M. Storey, *Loyalty and Loss: Alabama's Unionists in the Civil War and Reconstruction* (Baton Rouge: Louisiana State Univ. Press, 2004), 2–17 (quotations 16 and 5).

11. Sarah Rousseau Espy Diary, January 14, 19 (quotations), February 25, 1864, Alabama Department of Archives and History, Montgomery (hereafter cited as ADAH); United States Bureau of the Census, Eighth Census of the United States, 1860, Schedule 1 (Free Inhabitants); Margaret Josephine Miles Gillis Diary, February 9, 14, 1864, ADAH.

12. Major General Dabney Maury to Secretary of War James A. Seddon, December 28, 1863, and enclosures, *Official Records*, ser. 1, vol. 26, pt. 2, 548–551; Maury to Seddon, January 11, 1864, and enclosures, *Official Records*, ser. 1, vol. 26, pt. 2, 551–553; William H. Davidson, ed., *Word from Camp Pollard, C. S. A.* (West Point, Ga.: Davidson, 1978), 152 (first quotation), 154 (second quotation); Chattahoochee Valley Historical Society, ed., *War Was the Place: A Centennial Collection of Confederate Soldier Letters*, Bulletin 5 (Chambers County, Ala.: Chattahoochee Valley Historical Society, 1961), 97–99.

13. Rebecca Grant Sexton, ed., *A Southern Woman of Letters: The Correspondence of Augusta Jane Evans Wilson* (Columbia: Univ. of South Carolina Press, 2002), 92.

14. William Warren Rogers Jr., *Confederate Home Front: Montgomery during the Civil War* (Tuscaloosa: Univ. of Alabama Press, 1999), 152; Mary K. Haynes and James Wilkins, comps., "The Stanley Letters," *Papers of the Pike County Historical Society* 4 (April 1965): 8–9; Edward Noyes, ed., "Excerpts from the Civil War Diary of E. T. Eggleston," *Tennessee Historical Quarterly* 17 (December 1958): 338; Martin, *A Rich Man's War, a Poor Man's Fight*, 33–57; Arthur W. Bergeron Jr., *Confederate Mobile* (Baton Rouge: Louisiana State Univ. Press, 2000), 92–101; Fitzgerald Ross, "Gaiety as Usual in Mobile," in *The Confederate Reader*, ed. Richard Barksdale Harwell, 253–261 (New York: Longmans, Green, 1957); Richard Barksdale Harwell, ed., *Kate: The Journal of a Confederate Nurse* (Baton Rouge: Louisiana State Univ. Press, 1959), 189 (quotation); Harriet E. Amos, "'All-Absorbing Topics': Food and Clothing in Confederate Mobile," *Atlanta Historical Journal* 22 (fall–winter 1978): 17–28.

15. A. L. McGowen to brother, January 17, 1864, McGowen Family Letters, Civil War Soldiers' Letters, ADAH; William N. Still, ed., "The Civil War Letters of Robert Tarleton," *Alabama Historical Quarterly* 32 (spring and summer 1970): 51–53; F. Jay Taylor, ed., *Reluctant Rebel: The Secret Diary of Robert Patrick, 1861–1865* (Baton Rouge: Louisiana State Univ. Press, 1959), 138; John Kent Folmar, ed., *From That Terrible Field: Civil War Letters of James M. Williams, Twenty-First Alabama Infantry Volunteers* (University: Univ. of Alabama Press, 1981), 126–128; Lewis N. Wynne and Robert A. Taylor, eds., *This War So Horrible: The Civil War Letters of Hiram Smith Williams* (Tuscaloosa: Univ. of Alabama Press, 1993), 23–25; M. S. Hunter to sister and Frank, February [?], 1864, Horn Collection, Special Collections Department, Mitchell Memorial Library, Mississippi State University, Starkville (hereafter cited as MSU Special Collections).

16. *Mobile Daily Advertiser and Register*, January 3, 5, 6, 7, 8, 15, 16, February 3, 6, 16 (quotation), 1864. See also *Troy (Alabama) Southern Advertiser*, February 12, 1864.

17. William Galbraith and Loretta Galbraith, eds., *A Lost Heroine of the Confederacy: The Diaries and Letters of Belle Edmondson* (Jackson: Univ. Press of Mississippi, 1990), 81 (quotation), 82–87.

18. Drew Gilpin Faust, *Mothers of Invention: Women of the Slaveholding South in the American Civil War* (Chapel Hill: Univ. of North Carolina Press, 1996), (especially 234–238); Drew Gilpin Faust, "Altars of Sacrifice: Confederate Women and the Narratives of War," *Journal of*

American History 76 (March 1990): 1200–1228. Two interesting studies have found continued commitment to the Confederate cause among women in Georgia and the Carolinas in the path of William T. Sherman's armies in 1864–1865. See Jacqueline Glass Campbell, *When Sherman Marched North from the Sea: Resistance on the Confederate Home Front* (Chapel Hill: Univ. of North Carolina Press, 2003); Lisa Tendrich Frank, "To 'Cure Her of Her Pride and Boasting': The Gendered Implications of Sherman's March" (Ph.D. diss., University of Florida, 2001).

19. Thomas Smyrl to Mary Jane Smyrl, January 1, 1864 (first quotation), Thomas Smyrl Letters, ADAH; Gordon A. Cotton, ed., *From the Pen of a She-Rebel: The Civil War Diary of Emilie Riley McKinley* (Columbia: Univ. of South Carolina Press, 2001), 58–68, 61 (second and fourth quotations), 64 (third quotation), 63 (fifth quotation).

20. James W. Silver, ed., "The Breakdown of Morale in Central Mississippi in 1864: Letters of Judge Robert S. Hudson," *Journal of Mississippi History* 16 (spring 1954): 99–120; Robert Hudson to Jefferson Davis, March 14, 1864, *Official Records*, ser. 1, vol. 32, pt. 3, 625–627; David A. Welker, ed., *A Keystone Rebel: The Civil War Diary of Joseph Garey, Hudson's Battery, Mississippi Volunteers.* (Gettysburg, Pa.: Thomas Publications, 1996), 102 (first quotation); Thomas McGuire, *McGuire Papers, Containing Major Thomas McGuire's Civil War Letters; and Patriotic Documents and Other Letters from 1854 to the Turn of the Twentieth Century* (Tusquahoma, La.: Daughters of the American Revolution, 1966), 8 (second quotation); Vicki Betts, ed., "The Civil War Letters of Elbridge Littlejohn," *Chronicles of Smith County, Texas* 18 (summer 1979): 18–22.

21. Albert Castel, *Decision in the West: The Atlanta Campaign of 1864* (Lawrence: Univ. Press of Kansas, 1992), 19 (first quotation), 44 (second quotation), 43–56; Mark M. Boatner, *The Civil War Dictionary* (New York: McKay, 1959), 543–544; Margie Riddle Bearss, *Sherman's Forgotten Campaign: The Meridian Expedition* (Baltimore: Gateway Press, 1987), 9.

22. Castel, *Decision in the West*, 43–56; Boatner, *Civil War Dictionary*, 543–544; Herman Hattaway, *General Stephen D. Lee* (Jackson: Univ. Press of Mississippi, 1976), 108–110; Andrew J. Fogle Civil War Letters, March 7, 1864, 9th Texas Infantry File, Simpson History Complex, Hill College, Hillsboro, Texas (hereafter cited as Hill College).

23. Galbraith and Galbraith, eds., *A Lost Heroine*, 86–87 (first and second quotations); Eliza Lucy Irion Neilson Journal, Irion-Neilson Family Papers, MDAH; Castel, *Decision in the West*, 53–54; Brian Steel Wills, *A Battle from the Start: The Life of Nathan Bedford Forrest* (New York: HarperCollins, 1992), 158–168; *Mobile Daily Advertiser and Register*, March 5, 1864.

24. Buck T. Foster, *Sherman's Mississippi Campaign* (Tuscaloosa: Univ. of Alabama Press, 2006), 168–175.

25. Castel, *Decision in the West*, 55–56; William M. Cash and Lucy Somerville Howorth, eds., *My Dear Nellie: The Civil War Letters of William L. Nugent to Eleanor Smith Nugent* (Jackson: Univ. Press of Mississippi, 1977), 157. The fleeting effects of Sherman's Meridian campaign on the morale of western Confederates in his path proved similar to the effects noted by Jacqueline Glass Campbell in her study of Sherman's Carolina campaign in 1865. Campbell, *When Sherman Marched North from the Sea*, see especially 6, 70–72.

26. Anne Shannon Martin Diary, March 9, 1864 (first quotation), MDAH; Daniel R. Hundley Diary, February 27, 1864, Hoole Special Collections Library, University of Alabama, Tuscaloosa (hereafter cited as Hoole Collections); Cotton, ed., *From the Pen of a She-Rebel*, 69–70; Samuel Andrew Agnew Diary, February 11–24, 1864, MSU Special Collections; Johnston to

Polk, February 3, 1864, *Official Records*, ser. 1, vol. 26, pt. 2, 662; *Mobile Daily Advertiser and Register*, March 11, 1864; Joseph Howard Parks, *General Leonidas Polk, C. S. A.: The Fighting Bishop* (Baton Rouge: Louisiana State Univ. Press, 1962), 362–363, (second, third, and fourth quotations); John A. Cato to wife, February 9, March 9, 1864, John A. Cato Letters, Civil War Miscellaneous Collection, United States Army Military History Institute, Carlisle, Pennsylvania (hereafter cited as USAMHI).

27. Thomas Warrick to Martha Warrick, January 3, 1864, and Martha Warrick to Thomas Warrick, January 20, 1864 (quotation), Thomas Warrick Papers, ADAH.

28. Daniel R. Hundley Diary, January 1, 1864 (first quotation), Hoole Collections; Isaiah Harlan to Ma, January 18, 1864 (second quotation), Isaiah Harlan Civil War Letters, 10th Texas Infantry File, Hill College; Robert H. Ferrell, ed., *Holding the Line: The Third Tennessee Infantry, 1861–1864* (Kent, Ohio: Kent State Univ. Press, 1996), 151 (third quotation).

29. Charles T. Jones, ed., "Five Confederates: The Sons of Bolling Hall in the Civil War," *Alabama Historical Quarterly* 24 (winter 1962): 191 (first quotation); Ferrell, ed., *Holding the Line,* 152 (second and third quotations); United States Bureau of the Census, Eighth U. S. Census, 1860, Schedule 1 (Free Inhabitants); Andrew Haughton, *Training, Tactics, and Leadership in the Confederate Army of Tennessee: Seeds of Failure* (Brookfield, Vt.: Frank Cass, 2000), 137–139; Louis P. Towles, "Dalton and the Rebirth of the Army of Tennessee," *Proceedings of the South Carolina Historical Association* (2002): 87–88; Ann K. Blomquist and Robert A. Taylor, eds., *This Cruel War: The Civil War Letters of Grant and Malinda Taylor, 1862–1865* (Macon, Ga.: Mercer Univ. Press, 2000), 207–210.

30. Craig L. Symonds, *Joseph E. Johnston: A Civil War Biography* (New York: Norton, 1992), 249, 250 (quotation); Sam Watkins, *"Co. Aytch," Maury Grays, First Tennessee Regiment; or, a Side Show of the Big Show* (1882; reprint, Wilmington, N.C.: Broadfoot, 1987), 101–102; Albert D. Kirwan, ed., *Johnny Green of the Orphan Brigade: Journal of a Confederate Soldier* (Lexington: Univ. of Kentucky Press, 1956), 118; Haughton, *Training, Tactics, and Leadership,* 140–141; Jones, "Five Confederates," 190–191; Douglas John Cater, *As It Was: Reminiscences of a Soldier of the Third Texas Cavalry and the Nineteenth Louisiana Infantry* (Austin, Tex.: State House Press, 1990), 167–169.

31. Symonds, *Joseph E. Johnston,* 249–257; Haughton, *Training, Tactics, and Leadership,* 139–144; General Orders No. 5, Headquarters of the Army of Tennessee, January 8, 1864, *Official Records*, ser. 1, vol. 32, pt. 2, 530–535; Joseph E. Brown to Johnston, January 16, 1864, *Official Records*, ser. 1, vol. 32, pt. 2, 564–565.

32. Edward Norphlet Brown to Fannie, January 23, 25, 28 (first quotation), February 12, 1864, Edward Norphlet Brown Letters, ADAH; Isaiah Harlan to Ma, January 28, 1864, and Isaiah Harlan to Margaret, February 10, 1864 (second quotation), Isaiah Harlan Civil War Letters, 10th Texas Infantry File, Hill College; William T. Alderson, ed., "The Civil War Diary of Captain James Litton Cooper, September 30, 1861, to January 1865," *Tennessee Historical Quarterly* 15 (June 1956): 162; Hezekiah Rabb to wife, January 16, 1864, Michael P. Musick Collection, USAMHI.

33. John Crittenden to Bettie, February 21, 1864, John Crittenden Letters, Center for American History, University of Texas, Austin (hereafter cited as CAH); Ferrell, ed., *Holding the Line,* 154, 156; Blomquist and Taylor, eds., *This Cruel War,* 221–222; Enoch L. Mitchell, ed., "The Civil War Letters of Thomas Jefferson Newberry," *Journal of Mississippi History* 10 (Janu-

ary 1948): 76; George Peddy Cuttino, ed., *Saddle Bag and Spinning Wheel: Being the Civil War Letters of George W. Peddy, M. D., Surgeon, 56th Volunteers Regiment, C. S. A. and His Wife Kate Featherston Peddy* (Macon, Ga.: Mercer University Press, 1981), 205, 209.

34. Albert Burton Moore, *Conscription and Conflict in the Confederacy* (New York: Macmillan, 1924), 308; Larry J. Daniel, *Soldiering in the Army of Tennessee: A Portrait of Life in a Confederate Army* (Chapel Hill: Univ. of North Carolina Press, 1991), 127–128; Escott, *After Secession*, 116.

35. Moore, *Conscription and Conflict*, 354; Cuttino, ed., *Saddle Bag and Spinning Wheel*, 205, 209.

36. Sam Settle to David Settle, January 25, 1864 (first quotation), and Sam Settle to Mollie Settle, February 7, 1864, Settle Family Letters, Department of Archives and Special Collections, University of Mississippi, Oxford, (hereafter cited as University of Mississippi Archives); United States Bureau of the Census, Eighth U. S. Census, 1860, Schedule 1 (Free Inhabitants); Edward Norphlet Brown to Fannie, February 5, 1864, Edward Norphlet Brown Letters, ADAH; John Crittenden to Bettie, February 21, 1864, John Crittenden Letters, CAH; Ferrel, ed., *Holding the Line*, 154, 156; Taylor, *This Cruel War*, 221–222; Mitchell, ed., "The Civil War Letters of Thomas Jefferson Newberry," 76; James A. Hall to father, January 24, 1864, Hall Letters, Civil War Miscellaneous Collection, USAMHI.

37. Jim R. Cabaniss, ed., *Civil War Journal and Letters of Washington Ives, 4th Fla., C. S. A.* (Tallahassee, Fla.: Jim Cabaniss, 1987), 60 (first quotation); Mark K. Christ, ed., *Getting Used to Being Shot At: The Spence Family Civil War Letters* (Fayetteville: Univ. of Arkansas Press, 2002), 77 (second quotation), 91 (third quotation); Daniel R. Hundley Diary, February 26, 1864 (fourth quotation), Hoole Collections; James T. Searcy to father, January 31, 1864, James T. Searcy Letters, Civil War Soldiers' Letters, ADAH; Jones, "Five Confederates," 192; Ann York Franklin, ed., *The Civil War Diaries of Captain Alfred Tyler Fielder, 12th Tennessee Regiment Infantry, Company B, 1861–1865* (Louisville, Ky.: A. Y. Franklin, 1996), 162–163; Watkins, "Co. Aytch," 101–115; Ferrell, ed., *Holding the Line*, 156–160.

38. Isaiah Harlan to Margaret, February 10, 1864 (first quotation), 10th Texas Infantry File, Hill College; William C. Davis, ed., *Diary of a Confederate Soldier: John S. Jackman of the Orphan Brigade* (Columbia: Univ. of South Carolina Press, 1990), 104 (second quotation); Cash and Howorth, eds., *My Dear Nellie*, 155 (third quotation); Jill K. Garrett, ed., *Confederate Diary of Robert D. Smith* (Columbia, Tenn.: Tennessee Division, United Daughters of the Confederacy, 1975), 55 (fourth quotation); Edward Norphlet Brown to Fannie, February 5, 1864, (fifth and sixth quotations), Edward Norphlet Brown Letters, ADAH; Daniel R. Hundley Diary, February 24, 1864, Hoole Collections.

39. Escott, *After Secession*, 102–104.

40. These predictions of success among western Confederates are discussed in detail in chapter 2 of this study. A recent book by Jason Phillips finds high morale and expectations of military success among Confederates in all theaters of the war looking toward spring 1864. Phillips also contends that the "culture of invincibility" existed among Confederates across class lines. See Jason Phillips, *Diehard Rebels: The Confederate Culture of Invincibility* (Athens: Univ. of Georgia Press, 2007), 5–6, 95–101.

Other historians have questioned the strength of Confederate morale as of 1864. For example, see Escott, *After Secession*; David Williams, *A Rich Man's War: Class, Caste, and Confeder-*

ate Defeat in the Lower Chattahoochee Valley (Athens: Univ. of Georgia Press, 1998), 168–169, especially chapter 7 and notes on pages 242–245. In a study of the Chattahoochee River Valley area, Williams concluded that "by 1864" most Confederates there had in fact submitted, resented the Confederate government, and even looked forward to the Confederacy's demise. In one instance Williams offered another "by 1864" assessment yet cited one Georgia newspaper entry from *October* of that year. Later, he asserted that "by 1864, conditions were so bad that most soldiers had long since deserted" and contended that soldiers at the front operated under a "perpetual depression." Where had "most" Confederate soldiers deserted by 1864? To support that assertion Williams provides two secondary sources and no desertion statistics. The dubious notion that most soldiers on the western front lines operated under a state of depression is simply not borne out by the evidence. Referring to events later in 1864 around Atlanta and relying on Lieutenant General John Bell Hood's self-aggrandizing postwar memoirs, Williams asserts that "most" Confederate soldiers under the general's command would not fight at all. In reality, only the final battle for Atlanta, Jonesboro, witnessed unusually low soldier morale. Until that point, the determined defense of that city and the staggering casualty rates of the campaign belie any contention that the western Confederate soldiers would not fight. Although western Confederate morale was not as high as it had once been, or indeed as high it would soon be again, it also was nowhere close to the gloomy, class-conflict ridden diagnosis offered by Williams. Although some class conflict certainly existed, as more capably argued by Paul D. Escott, both historians frequently appear to find more class consciousness than conflict. At any rate, by 1864 the western Confederate will to fight and win their war for independence remained formidable and would only grow stronger that spring.

Fred A. Bailey also pointed to class conflict within the Confederacy, but employed postwar questionnaires completed decades after the war. Postwar sources that reveal division should be handled as carefully as those that illustrate unity or high morale. Fred A. Bailey, *Class and Tennessee's Confederate Generation* (Chapel Hill: Univ. of North Carolina Press, 1987).

2. MARCH–APRIL 1864: A NEW BEGINNING

1. John D. Floyd to Mary, March 18, 1864, John D. Floyd Letters, Civil War Collection, Tennessee State Library and Archives, Nashville (hereafter cited as TSLA).

2. William M. Cash and Lucy Somerville Howorth, eds., *My Dear Nellie: The Civil War Letters of William L. Nugent to Eleanor Smith Nugent* (Jackson: Univ. Press of Mississippi, 1977), 172 (quotation).

3. *Selma Morning Reporter,* April 22, 1864 (quotation); Thomas McGuire, *McGuire Papers, Containing Major Thomas McGuire's Civil War Letters; and Patriotic Documents and Other Letters from 1854 to the Turn of the Twentieth Century* (Tusquahoma, La.: Daughters of the American Revolution, 1966), 14–16; *Mobile Daily Advertiser and Register,* March 11, April 16, 24, 1864; *Montgomery Daily Advertiser,* April 28, 1864; *Troy (Alabama) Southern Advertiser,* April 1, 1864; *Chattanooga Daily Rebel* (Marietta, Georgia), March 22, 1864; *Tuskegee South Western Baptist,* April 14, 1864; George C. Osborn, ed., "Stephen Washington Holladay's Civil War Letters," *Tennessee Historical Quarterly* 4 (September 1945): 260–263; John Kent Folmar, ed., *From That Terrible Field: Civil War Letters of James M. Williams, Twenty-First Alabama Infantry Volunteers*

(University: Univ. of Alabama Press, 1981), 129; Mary K. Haynes and James Wilkins, comps., "The Stanley Letters," *Papers of the Pike County Historical Society* 4 (April 1965): 11–12; F. Jay Taylor, ed., *Reluctant Rebel: The Secret Diary of Robert Patrick, 1861–1865* (Baton Rouge: Louisiana State Univ. Press, 1959), 154; William Pitt Chambers, *Blood and Sacrifice: The Civil War Journal of a Confederate Soldier* (Huntington, W.Va.: Blue Acorn Press, 1994), 129–133; Richard Lowe, ed., *A Texas Cavalry Officer's Civil War: The Diary and Letters of James C. Bates* (Baton Rouge: Louisiana State Univ. Press, 1999), 284–287.

4. *Mobile Daily Advertiser and Register,* March 11, 1864; *Tuskegee South Western Baptist,* April 14, 1864; *Monticello (Mississippi) Southern Journal,* April 30, 1864; Lowe, ed., *A Texas Cavalry Officer's Civil War,* 284–287; Andrew J. Fogle to Miss Loo, March 7, 1864, Andrew J. Fogle Civil War Letters, 9th Texas Infantry File, Simpson History Complex, Hill College, Hillsboro, Texas (hereafter cited as Hill College); Albert Quincy Porter Diary, March 10–April 25, 1864, Mississippi Department of Archives and History, Jackson (hereafter cited as MDAH); Cash and Howorth, eds., *My Dear Nellie,* 160–167.

5. Mary Fitzpatrick to Phillips Fitzpatrick, April 14, 24 (quotation), May 9, 1864, Fitzpatrick to Mary, April 13, 14, 28, 1864, Thomas Y. Nutam to Fitzpatrick, March 30, 1864, Phillips Fitzpatrick Letters, ADAH.

6. John N. Fain, ed., *Sanctified Trial: The Diary of Eliza Rhea Anderson Fain, a Confederate Woman in East Tennessee* (Knoxville: Univ. of Tennessee Press, 2004), ix–xlii, 161–171.

7. Ibid., 172.

8. William R. Snell, ed., *Myra Inman: A Diary of the Civil War in East Tennessee* (Macon, Ga.: Mercer Univ. Press, 2000), 259–260; Daniel E. Sutherland, ed., *A Very Violent Rebel: The Civil War Diary of Ellen Renshaw House* (Knoxville: Univ. of Tennessee Press, 1996), 110–131 (poem 123–124).

9. Robert Partin, ed., "The Civil War in East Tennessee as Reported by a Confederate Railroad Bridge Builder," *Tennessee Historical Quarterly* 22 (September 1963): 248 (first quotation); Ray Mathis, ed., *In the Land of the Living: Wartime Letters by Confederates from the Chattahoochee Valley of Alabama and Georgia* (Troy, Ala.: Troy State Univ. Press, 1981), 85 (second quotation); M. S. Hunter to sister, April 7, 1864 (third quotation), Horn Collection, Special Collections, Mitchell Memorial Library, Mississippi State University, Starkville (hereafter cited as MSU Special Collections); William J. Mims, "Letters of Major W. J. Mims, C. S. A.," *Alabama Historical Quarterly* 3 (1941), 219; Mary Wyche Burgess, ed., "Civil War Letters of Abram Hayne Young," *South Carolina Historical Magazine* 78 (January 1977), 62–63.

10. Robert W. Fort to father, April 1, 1864 (first quotation), Craft-Fort Papers, Department of Archives and Special Collections, University of Mississippi, Oxford (hereafter cited as University of Mississippi Archives); William Galbraith and Loretta Galbraith, eds., *A Lost Heroine of the Confederacy: The Diaries and Letters of Belle Edmondson* (Jackson: Univ. Press of Mississippi, 1990), 101–102, 103 (second quotation), 104–105, 113.

11. Gary Gallagher, *The Confederate War: How Popular Will, Nationalism, and Military Strategy Could Not Stave Off Defeat* (Cambridge: Harvard Univ. Press, 1997), 36–37; Mark M. Boatner, *The Civil War Dictionary* (New York: McKay, 1959), 655; Stephen E. Woodworth and Kenneth J. Winkle, eds., *Atlas of the Civil War* (New York: Oxford Univ. Press, 2004), 218–223; Arthur W. Bergeron Jr., "The Battle of Olustee," in *Black Soldiers in Blue: African American Troops in the Civil War Era,* ed. John David Smith, 136–149 (Chapel Hill: Univ. of North Carolina

Press, 2002); Gordon A. Cotton, ed., *From the Pen of a She-Rebel: The Civil War Diary of Emilie Riley McKinley* (Columbia: Univ. of South Carolina Press, 2001), 69.

12. Gallagher, *The Confederate War,* 36–37; Boatner, *Civil War Dictionary,* 608, 656, 685–689, 715; Woodworth and Winkle, *Atlas of the Civil War,* 218–223; Edward Norphlet Brown to Fannie, April 17, 1864, Edward Norphlet Brown Letters, ADAH; Thomas Warrick to Martha Warrick, April 18, 1864, Thomas Warrick Papers, ADAH; Galbraith and Galbraith, eds., *Lost Heroine of the Confederacy,* 90, 119–120; Sutherland, ed., *A Very Violent Rebel,* 130–131; Perry Wayne Shelton, comp., and Shelly Morrison, ed., *Personal Letters of General Lawrence Sullivan Ross, with Other Letters* (Austin, Tex.: Shelly and Richard Morrison, 1994), 61–63; Cash and Howorth, eds., *My Dear Nellie,* 172; Jill K. Garrett, ed., *Confederate Diary of Robert D. Smith* (Columbia, Tenn.: Tennessee Division, United Daughters of the Confederacy, 1975), 60–61; Harold B. Simpson, ed., *The Bugle Softly Blows: The Confederate Diary of Benjamin M. Seaton* (Waco, Tex.: Texian Press, 1965), 49; *Montgomery Daily Advertiser,* April 30, 1864.

13. Brian Steel Wills, *A Battle from the Start: The Life of Nathan Bedford Forrest* (New York: HarperCollins, 1992), 171–196, 247 (first quotation), 217 (second quotation); Robert W. Fort to Father, April 1, 1864 (third quotation), Craft-Fort Papers, University of Mississippi Archives; Daniel R. Hundley Diary, April 5, 1864 (fourth quotation), Hoole Special Collections Library, University of Alabama, Tuscaloosa (hereafter cited as Hoole Collections).

14. John Cimprich, "The Fort Pillow Massacre: Assessing the Evidence," in John David Smith, ed., *Black Soldiers in Blue,* 150–168; Wills, *Battle from the Start,* 178–196.

15. Sutherland, ed., *A Very Violent Rebel,* 130 (first quotation); Robert H. Cartmell Diary, April 18, 1864 (second and third quotations), Robert H. Cartmell Papers, TSLA; Galbraith and Galbraith, eds., *Lost Heroine of the Confederacy,* 112–114; W. R. Dyer Diary, April 21 (fourth quotation), 28, 1864, TSLA; Wills, *Battle from the Start,* 201.

16. *Chattanooga Daily Rebel* (Marietta, Georgia), April 21, 1864, taken from the *Meridian (Mississippi) Daily Clarion,* no date.

17. Jason Phillips, *Diehard Rebels: The Confederate Culture of Invincibility* (Athens: Univ. of Georgia Press, 2007), 127.

18. Richard Lewis, *Camp Life of a Confederate Boy, of Bratton's Brigade, Longstreet's Corps, C.S.A.: Letters Written by Lieut. Richard Lewis, of Walker's Regiment, to His Mother, during the War* (Charleston, S.C.: News and Courier Book Press, 1883), 84–92, 92 (quotation).

19. Sarah Rousseau Espy Diary, April 2, 1864, ADAH; Edward Norphlet Brown to Fannie, March 13, 1864, Edward Norphlet Brown Letters, ADAH; John Crittenden to Bettie, March 12, 1864, John Crittenden Letters, Center for American History, University of Texas at Austin (hereafter cited as CAH); Isaiah Harlan letters, March 3 (to E.), 3 (to Alpheus), 23 (to Ma), April 9 (to Ma), 25 (to Alpheus), 1864, Isaiah Harlan Civil War Letters, 10th Texas Infantry File, Hill College; Thomas Hopkins Deavenport Diary, March 31, April 5, 26, 1864, Civil War Collection, TSLA; Daniel R. Hundley Diary, March 21, April 3, 21, 26, 1864, Hoole Collections; B. F. Gentry to Ma, March 16, 1864, B. F. Gentry Letters, University of Mississippi Archives; Thomas Warrick to Martha, March 28, 1864, Thomas Warrick Papers, ADAH; James T. Searcy to brother, March 15, 1864, James T. Searcy Letters, Civil War Soldiers' Letters, ADAH. To prevent a footnote of unnecessarily awkward length, these citations are for only the unpublished sources used here. Most of the published sources cited throughout this study reflect analogous sentiments.

20. Robert H. Ferrell, ed., *Holding the Line: The Third Tennessee Infantry, 1861–1864* (Kent, Ohio: Kent State Univ. Press, 1996), 166–167, 179; Isaiah Harlan to Ma, March 23, 1864, Isaiah Harlan Civil War Letters, 10th Texas Infantry File, Hill College; Joseph Branch O'Bryan to sister, March 6, 1864, Joseph Branch O'Bryan Letters, TSLA; Henry D. Jamison and Marguerite J. McTigue, eds., *Letters and Recollections of a Confederate Soldier, 1860–1865* (Nashville, Tenn.: H. D. Jamison, 1964), 90–91; Douglas John Cater, *As It Was: Reminiscences of a Soldier of the Third Texas Cavalry and the Nineteenth Louisiana Infantry* (Austin, Tex.: State House Press, 1990), 169; Sam Watkins, *"Co. Aytch," Maury Grays, First Tennessee Regiment; or, a Side Show of the Big Show* (1882; reprint, Wilmington, N.C.: Broadfoot, 1987), 104–105; H.J.H. Rugeley, ed., *Batchelor-Turner Letters, 1861–1864, Written by Two of Terry's Texas Rangers* (Austin, Tex.: Steck, 1961), 79–81; William T. Alderson, ed., "The Civil War Diary of Captain James Litton Cooper, September 30, 1861, to January 1865," *Tennessee Historical Quarterly* 15 (June 1956): 162; George Phifer Erwin to sister, March 25, 27, April 13, 1864, George Phifer Erwin Papers, Southern Historical Collection, University of North Carolina, Chapel Hill (hereafter cited as SHC).

21. R. W. Colville to father, April 29, 1864, R. W. Colville Letters, Civil War Collection, TSLA; John H. Marshall to wife, April 25, 31, 1864, John H. Marshall Letters, MSU Special Collections; Isaiah Harlan to Brother E., March 3, 1864, Isaiah Harlan Civil War Letters, 10th Texas Infantry File, Hill College; Daniel R. Hundley Diary, March 13, April 19, 1864, Hoole Collections; Ferrell, ed., *Holding the Line*, 179.

22. Thomas Warrick to Martha, April 1, 1864 (first quotation), Thomas Warrick Papers, ADAH; Edward Norphlet Brown to Fannie, March 27 (second quotation), April 12 (third quotation), 17, 23, 27, 1864, Edward Norphlet Brown Letters, ADAH; John Crittenden to Bettie, March 18, 1864 (fourth quotation), John Crittenden Letters, CAH; James A. Hall to father, April 29, 1864, James A. Hall Letters, Civil War Miscellaneous Collection, United States Army Military History Institute, Carlisle, Pennsylvania (hereafter cited as USAMHI).

23. Thomas Warrick to Martha, April 9, 1864 (quotation), Thomas Warrick Papers, ADAH; Edward Norphlet Brown to Fannie, March 13, 20, 1864, Edward Norphlet Brown Letters, ADAH; Enoch L. Mitchell, ed., "Letters of a Confederate Surgeon in the Army of Tennessee to His Wife," *Tennessee Historical Quarterly* 5 (June 1946): 153–163; Wirt Armistead Cate, ed., *Two Soldiers: The Campaign Diaries of Thomas J. Key, C. S. A., and Robert J. Campbell, U. S. A.* (Chapel Hill: Univ. of North Carolina Press, 1938), 52–53; John Crittenden to Bettie, March 5, 1864, John Crittenden Letters, CAH; Lewis N. Wynne and Robert A. Taylor, eds., *This War So Horrible: The Civil War Letters of Hiram Smith Williams* (Tuscaloosa: Univ. of Alabama Press, 1993), 48; Alton L. Jackson, ed., *So Mourns the Dove: Letters of a Confederate Infantryman and His Family* (New York: Exposition Press, 1965), 80; Daniel R. Hundley Diary, March 1, 1864, Hoole Collections; Jamison and McTigue, eds., *Letters and Recollections of a Confederate Soldier*, 85–86; Lucille Griffith, ed., *Yours Till Death: Civil War Letters of John W. Cotton* (Tuscaloosa: Univ. of Alabama Press, 1951), 104; Ann K. Blomquist and Robert A. Taylor, eds., *This Cruel War: The Civil War Letters of Grant and Malinda Taylor, 1862–1865* (Macon, Ga.: Mercer Univ. Press, 2000), 231–232, 238–239; D. Coleman Diary, February 2, 1864, SHC.

24. Cate, ed., *Two Soldiers*, 70.

25. Mark A. Weitz, *A Higher Duty: Desertion among Georgia Troops during the Civil War* (Lincoln: Univ. of Nebraska Press, 2000), 1–9, 61–120, 171–179; Mark A. Weitz, *More Damning than Slaughter: Desertion in the Confederate Army* (Lincoln: Univ. of Nebraska Press, 2005),

254–255, 278–293; Larry J. Daniel, *Soldiering in the Army of Tennessee: A Portrait of Life in a Confederate Army* (Chapel Hill: Univ. of North Carolina Press, 1991), 137–138; Ella Lonn, *Desertion during the Civil War* (1928; reprint, Lincoln: Univ. of Nebraska Press, 1998), 21–37; Ferrell, ed., *Holding the Line*, 165; Jackson, ed., *So Mourns the Dove*, 80.

Many factors, of course, explain desertion, but class conflict was not chief among them. In the Georgia study, Weitz demonstrated that soldiers from the state's wealthier counties deserted at significantly lower rates and showed that the northern Georgia deserters were not necessarily poor folk. Next, he admitted that significant desertion did not characterize the Georgia troops he studied before this period of the war, nor more surprisingly, even afterward. In other words, most of the Georgia deserters identified by Weitz hailed from northern counties and deserted when Sherman's Federal armies passed through their homelands. On the one hand, this makes perfect sense, because they quite naturally feared for their families or in some cases probably simply saw an irresistible opportunity to go home. On the other hand, if class-based resentment played such a significant role in these soldiers' decisions to leave their posts, why did they do so in such a clear geographical pattern only in this brief window of months?

The basic "higher duty" thesis is generally convincing and probably fundamentally correct for many soldiers. If so, obviously soldiers from nonelite classes would be less able to remain away from their families and therefore were more likely to face the question of which duty to answer, family or country. A soldier of yeoman stock, of course, knew that he was not a planter and was therefore by definition class conscious, and he might very well desert in order to take care of his family. But none of that suggests that he consciously decided that the planter class and his government had failed to hold up their end of the bargain, so he was going home. It seems more likely that some soldiers believed that their families needed them and home they went. Weitz's evidence also challenges his tendency to place the nonmilitary causes for desertion ahead of military events in shaping morale and desertion patterns. Many factors beyond the battlefield help explain Confederate desertion, as Weitz skillfully demonstrates, but if Sherman's armies had not been where they were when they were, Georgia troops obviously would not have deserted in such a clear pattern. In the larger study of Confederate desertion overall, the patterns of desertion in 1864 appeared less uniform, but the only discernible pattern, pointed to by Weitz himself, generally related to the movements of the armies. Desertion frequently corresponded to the movement of Union armies into a soldier's home region or to the retreat of a Confederate army out of his home area, thus potentially exposing it to the enemy and leaving a soldier's family undefended. Weitz also pointed to the encirclement of Atlanta in July 1864 as possibly the period of highest desertion rates for the western Confederate states overall and found another increase in desertion among western soldiers after their catastrophic defeat at the battles of Franklin and Nashville in late 1864. None of this is surprising, and in each case, military events appear to have dictated desertion patterns at least as much, and probably more, than anything else.

The larger contention that desertion proved "more damning than slaughter" is difficult to accept. Two million Federal soldiers and nearly 1 million Confederates probably would have disagreed with the notion that desertion did more to decide the war than did their actions on the battlefield. Desertion mattered, to be sure, but not more than the battlefield.

26. Weitz, *A Higher Duty*, 1 (quotation); Gallagher, *The Confederate War*, 31–32.

27. Jamison and McTigue, eds., *Letters and Recollections of a Confederate Soldier,* 85–86; Mitchell, ed., "Letters of a Confederate Surgeon," 161 (quotation); Cater, *As It Was,* 177; Watkins, *"Co. Aytch,"* 106; Daniel, *Soldiering in the Army of Tennessee,* 137–138.

28. *Mobile Daily Advertiser and Register,* April 17, 1864.

29. Daniel, *Soldiering in the Army of Tennessee,* 116–117; Drew Gilpin Faust, "Christian Soldiers: The Meaning of Revivalism in the Confederate Army," *Journal of Southern History* 52 (February 1987): 67–68, 72–73; Bell I. Wiley, *The Life of Johnny Reb: The Common Soldier of the Confederacy* (1943; reprint, Baton Rouge: Louisiana State Univ. Press, 1978), 182–184; Herman Norton, "Revivalism in the Confederate Armies," *Civil War History* 6 (1960): 410–411; G. Clinton Prim Jr., "Born Again in the Trenches: Revivals in the Army of Tennessee," *Tennessee Historical Quarterly* 43 (fall 1984): 255–258; James M. McPherson, *For Cause and Comrades: Why Men Fought in the Civil War* (New York: Oxford Univ. Press, 1997), 67–75; Steven E. Woodworth, *While God Is Marching On: The Religious World of Civil War Soldiers* (Lawrence: Univ. Press of Kansas, 2001), 236–253; Albert D. Kirwan, ed., *Johnny Green of the Orphan Brigade: Journal of a Confederate Soldier* (Lexington: Univ. of Kentucky Press, 1956), 122 (quotation).

30. John Crittenden to Bettie, March 29, 1864 (quotation), John Crittenden Letters, CAH; Thomas Hopkins Deavenport Diary, March 31, April 26, 1864, Civil War Collection, TSLA; Edward Norphlet Brown to Fannie, April 25, 1864, Edward Norphlet Brown Letters, ADAH; B. F. Gentry to Ma, March 16, 1864, B. F. Gentry Letters, University of Mississippi Archives; Thomas Smyrl to Mary Jane Smyrl, April 15, 1864, Thomas Smyrl Letters, ADAH; Thomas Warrick to Martha, April 8, 1864, Thomas Warrick Papers, ADAH; Daniel, *Soldiering in the Army of Tennessee,* 120–121; Prim, "Born Again in the Trenches," 250–272; Kirwan, ed., *Johnny Green of the Orphan Brigade,* 120; William C. Davis, ed., *Diary of a Confederate Soldier: John S. Jackman of the Orphan Brigade* (Columbia: Univ. of South Carolina Press, 1990), 109–115; Garrett, ed., *Confederate Diary of Robert D. Smith,* 56; Jim R. Cabaniss, ed., *Civil War Journal and Letters of Washington Ives, 4th Fla. C. S. A.* (Tallahassee, Fla.: Jim Cabaniss, 1987), 63.

31. John Crittenden to Bettie, April 4, 1864, John Crittenden Letters, CAH.

32. Edward Norphlet Brown to Fannie, March 13 (first quotation), April 8, 1864, Edward Norphlet Brown Letters, ADAH; Ferrell, ed., *Holding the Line,* 175 (second quotation); A. Wideman to sister, April 26, 1864, Thomas Warrick Papers, ADAH; Cate, ed., *Two Soldiers,* 76–77 (third quotation).

33. B. F. Gentry to Ma, March 16, 1864, B. F. Gentry Letters, University of Mississippi Archives; Ferrell, ed., *Holding the Line,* 173–174; Thomas Hopkins Deavenport Diary, April 5, 1864 (quotation), Civil War Collection, TSLA.

34. Holy Bible, New International Version (first quotation); Edward Norphlet Brown to Fannie, March 27, April 17 (second quotation), 1864, Edward Norphlet Brown Letters, ADAH; Cate, ed., *Two Soldiers,* 75 (third quotation).

35. *Tuskegee South Western Baptist,* March 3, 1864.

36. Edward Norphlet Brown to Fannie, May 1, 1864, Edward Norphlet Brown Letters, ADAH.

37. Cater, *As It Was,* 170 (first quotation), 177 (third quotation); William W. Bennett, *A Narrative of the Great Revival Which Prevailed in the Southern Armies* (Philadelphia: Claxton, Remsen, and Haffelfinger, 1877), 377 (second quotation); Prim, "Born Again in the Trenches," 277; Faust, "Christian Soldiers," 75, 81–88; Woodworth, *While God Is Marching On,* 231–249;

McPherson, *For Cause and Comrades,* 75; Samuel J. Watson, "Religion and Combat Motivation in the Confederate Armies," *Journal of Military History* 58 (January 1994), 29–55.

38. For the status of morale in the Army of Northern Virginia and of Confederates in other theaters, February to May 1864, see Gary W. Gallagher, "Our Hearts Filled with Hope," in *The Wilderness Campaign,* ed. Gary W. Gallagher, 36–65 (Chapel Hill: Univ. of North Carolina Press, 1997); Phillips, *Diehard Rebels,* 95–101.

3. MAY–JUNE 1864: WINNING THE WAR

1. William M. Cash and Lucy Somerville Howorth, eds., *My Dear Nellie: The Civil War Letters of William L. Nugent to Eleanor Smith Nugent* (Jackson: Univ. Press of Mississippi, 1977), 191, 193. For general histories of the war during this period, see James M. McPherson, *Battle Cry of Freedom: The Civil War Era* (New York: Oxford Univ. Press, 1988), 718–750, and Herman Hattaway and Archer Jones, *How the North Won: A Military History of the Civil War* (Urbana: Univ. of Illinois Press, 1991), 538–628.

2. M. Patton to Lizzie, June 10, 1864 (first quotation), Lizzie McFarland Blakemore Collection, Mississippi Department of Archives and History, Jackson (hereafter cited as MDAH); Richard Lowe, ed., *A Texas Cavalry Officer's Civil War: The Diary and Letters of James C. Bates* (Baton Rouge: Louisiana State Univ. Press, 1999), 290–292; Charles Dubuisson to Sallie, May 18, 1864 (second quotation), Charles L. Dubuisson and Family Papers, MDAH; William Galbraith and Loretta Galbraith, eds., *A Lost Heroine of the Confederacy: The Diaries and Letters of Belle Edmondson* (Jackson: Univ. Press of Mississippi, 1990), 122 (third quotation); John A. Cato to wife, May 19, June 15, 1864, John A. Cato Letters, Civil War Miscellaneous Collection, United States Army Military History Institute, Carlisle, Pennsylvania (hereafter cited as USAMHI).

3. Phillips Fitzpatrick letters for May and June, Phillips Fitzpatrick Letters, Alabama Department of Archives and History, Montgomery (hereafter cited as ADAH); Mark Lyons to Amelia, May 11, June 10, 13 (quotation), 15, 17, 1864, Mark Lyons Letters, ADAH; Mary K. Haynes and James Wilkins, comps., "The Stanley Letters," *Papers of the Pike County Historical Society* 4 (April 1965): 18–20; Vicki Betts, ed., "The Civil War Letters of Elbridge Littlejohn," *Chronicles of Smith County, Texas* 18 (summer 1979): 25; Cash and Howorth, eds., *My Dear Nellie,* 174–177.

4. *Meridian (Mississippi) Daily Clarion,* June 6, 1864; *Greensboro (Mississippi) Southern Motive,* May 7, 1864.

5. *Selma Morning Reporter,* June 4, 1864; *Jackson Daily Mississippian* (published in Selma, Alabama), June 16, 1864; *Montgomery Daily Advertiser,* May 5 (first quotation), June 4 (second quotation), 1864. For additional patriotic songs, tributes to soldiers, and predictions of ultimate victory in Alabama newspapers see, *Mobile Daily Advertiser and Register,* May 1, 7, 14, 22, 1864.

6. William R. Snell, ed., *Myra Inman: A Diary of the Civil War in East Tennessee* (Macon, Ga.: Mercer Univ. Press, 2000), 261–263; Stephen V. Ash, *Middle Tennessee Society Transformed, 1860–1870* (Baton Rouge: Louisiana State Univ. Press, 1988), 167.

7. Sarah Rousseau Espy Diary, May 19, 22, 28, June 3, 30 (quotations) 1864, ADAH.

8. Grady McWhiney, Warner O. Moore Jr., and Robert F. Pace, eds., *Fear God and Walk Humbly: The Agricultural Journal of James Mallory, 1843–1877* (Tuscaloosa: Univ. of Alabama Press, 1997), xiii–xix, 335 (quotation).

9. James Palmer Civil War Diary, 22–23, MDAH; United States Census Bureau, Eighth Census of the United State, 1860, Schedule 1 (Free Inhabitants).

10. I. B. Cadenhead to Leusa F. Cadenhead, May 22, 26 (quotation), 1864, James T. Moore to Leusa F. Cadenhead, July 23, 1864, I. G. Patten to Leusa F. Cadenhead, August 5, 1864, all in I. B. Cadenhead Letters, Civil War Soldiers' Letters, ADAH.

11. Thomas McGuire, *McGuire Papers, Containing Major Thomas McGuire's Civil War Letters; and Patriotic Documents and Other Letters from 1854 to the Turn of the Twentieth Century* (Tusquahoma, La.: Daughters of the American Revolution, 1966), 19.

12. John Daniel Cooper Civil War Diary, May 1, 1864, 7th Texas Infantry File, Simpson History Complex, Hill College, Hillsboro, Texas (hereafter cited as Hill College).

13. Thomas Warrick to Martha Warrick, May 1, 1864, Thomas Warrick Papers, ADAH; Albert Castel, *Decision in the West: The Atlanta Campaign of 1864* (Lawrence: Univ. Press of Kansas, 1992), 121–128; Robert H. Ferrell, ed., *Holding the Line: The Third Tennessee Infantry, 1861–1864* (Kent, Ohio: Kent State Univ. Press, 1996), 185.

14. Edward Norphlet Brown to Fannie, May 1, 1864, Edward Norphlet Brown Letters, ADAH; Ray Mathis, ed., *In the Land of the Living: Wartime Letters by Confederates from the Chattahoochee Valley of Alabama and Georgia* (Troy, Ala.: Troy State Univ. Press, 1981), 94; Donald W. Lewis, "A Confederate Officer's Letters on Sherman's March to Atlanta," *Georgia Historical Quarterly* 51 (December 1967): 492 (quotation); Henry Rodney Raymond to wife, May 5, 6, 7, 1864, Henry Rodney Raymond Papers, Special Collections, Mitchell Memorial Library, Mississippi State University, Starkville (hereafter cited as Special Collections, MSU).

15. Thomas Jefferson Burnett to wife, May 9, 1864 (first quotation), Thomas Jefferson Burnett Papers, Pearce Civil War Collection, Navarro College, Corsicana, Texas (hereafter cited as Pearce Collection); Mathis, ed., *In the Land of the Living*, 94 (second quotation); Edward Norphlet Brown to Fannie, May 5, 1864 (third quotation), Edward Norphlet Brown Letters, ADAH; H. E. Sterkx, ed., "Autobiography and Letters of Joel Dyer Murphree of Troy, Alabama, 1864–1865," *Alabama Historical Quarterly* 19 (spring 1957): 176 (fourth quotation); Thomas Smyrl to Mary Jane Smyrl, May 10, 1864, Thomas Smyrl Letters, ADAH; McGuire, *McGuire Papers*, 18–20.

16. M. S. Hunter to sister, May 10, 1864, Horn Collection, Special Collections, MSU; George Phifer Erwin to mother, May 5, 1864, George Phifer Erwin Papers, Southern Historical Collection, University of North Carolina, Chapel Hill (hereafter cited as SHC); Wirt Armistead Cate, ed., *Two Soldiers: The Campaign Diaries of Thomas J. Key, C. S. A., and Robert J. Campbell, U. S. A.* (Chapel Hill: Univ. of North Carolina Press, 1938), 80, 82; Harold B. Simpson, ed., *The Bugle Softly Blows: The Confederate Diary of Benjamin M. Seaton* (Waco, Tex.: Texian Press, 1965), 50–51.

17. Jill K. Garrett, ed., *Confederate Diary of Robert D. Smith* (Columbia, Tenn.: Tennessee Division, United Daughters of the Confederacy, 1975), 62 (first quotation); F. Jay Taylor, ed., *Reluctant Rebel: The Secret Diary of Robert Patrick, 1861–1865* (Baton Rouge: Louisiana State Univ. Press, 1959), 163–164; Benjamin Rountree, ed., "Letters of a Confederate Soldier," *Georgia Review* 18 (fall 1964): 285 (second quotation); Edward Noyes, ed., "Excerpts from the Civil War Diary of E. T. Eggleston," *Tennessee Historical Quarterly* 17 (December 1958): 340; Cate,

ed., *Two Soldiers,* 82 (third quotation); M. S. Hunter to sister, May 10, 12, 1864, Horn Collection, Special Collections, MSU; George Anderson Mercer Diary, May 7, 1864, SHC.

18. Craig L. Symonds, *Joseph E. Johnston: A Civil War Biography* (New York: Norton, 1992), 280; Castel, *Decision in the West,* 148–154, 185–186; Steven E. Woodworth and Kenneth J. Winkle, eds., *Atlas of the Civil War* (New York: Oxford Univ. Press, 2004), 230–231.

19. Symonds, *Joseph E. Johnston,* 280–281; Castel, *Decision in the West,* 150–154; Woodworth and Winkle, eds., *Atlas of the Civil War,* 230–231; Richard M. McMurry, *Atlanta 1864: Last Chance for the Confederacy* (Lincoln: Univ. of Nebraska Press, 2000), 69–72.

20. Garrett, ed., *Diary of Robert D. Smith,* 63 (first and second quotations); William C. Davis, ed., *Diary of a Confederate Soldier: John S. Jackman of the Orphan Brigade* (Columbia: Univ. of South Carolina Press, 1990), 122, 123 (third quotation); J. P. Cannon, *Bloody Banners and Barefoot Boys: A History of the 27th Alabama Infantry C. S. A.; The Civil War Memoirs and Diary Entries of J. P. Cannon M.D.,* comp. and ed. Noel Crowson and John V. Brogden (Shippensburg, Pa.: Burd Street Press, 1997), 66 (fourth quotation).

21. Castel, *Decision in the West,* 186–195; McMurry, *Atlanta 1864,* 72–74.

22. Lewis N. Wynne and Robert A. Taylor, eds., *This War So Horrible: The Civil War Diary of Hiram Smith Williams* (Tuscaloosa: Univ. of Alabama Press, 1993), 70–71.

23. A. Snodgrass to Mary, May 16, 1864 (first quotation), A. Snodgrass Letters, Civil War Soldiers' Letters, ADAH; Edward Norphlet Brown to Fannie, May 16, 1864 (second quotation), Edward Norphlet Brown Letters, ADAH; Mary M. Jones and Leslie J. Martin, eds., *The Gentle Rebel: The Civil War Letters of William Harvey Berryhill, Co. D., 43rd Regiment, Mississippi Volunteers* (Yazoo City, Miss.: Sassafras Press, 1982), 26–28; Jim R. Cabaniss, ed., *Civil War Journal and Letters of Washington Ives, 4th Fla. C. S. A.* (Tallahassee, Fla.: Jim Cabaniss, 1987), 8; Lewis, ed., "A Confederate Officer's Letters," 493.

24. Cannon, *Bloody Banners and Barefoot Boys,* 66–67.

25. George Peddy Cuttino, ed., *Saddle Bag and Spinning Wheel: Being the Civil War Letters of George W. Peddy, M. D., Surgeon, 56th Georgia Volunteers Regiment, C. S. A. and His Wife Kate Featherston Peddy* (Macon, Ga.: Mercer Univ. Press, 1981), 242; Albert Quincy Porter Diary, May 17–18, MDAH; Garrett, ed., *Confederate Diary of Robert D. Smith,* 64 (first quotation); Taylor, ed., *Reluctant Rebel,* 165–167 (second quotation 167).

26. Symonds, *Joseph E. Johnston,* 291–292; General Orders No. 5, May 19, 1864, in United States War Department, *The War of the Rebellion: A Compilation of the Official Records of the Union and Confederate Armies,* 128 vols. (hereafter cited as *Official Records*) (Washington: Government Printing Office, 1880–1901), ser. 1, vol. 38, pt. 4, 728 (quotation).

27. A. Wideman to sister, May 19, 1864, Thomas Warrick Papers, ADAH; Albert D. Kirwan, ed., *Johnny Green of the Orphan Brigade: The Journal of a Confederate Soldier* (Lexington: Univ. of Kentucky Press, 1956), 130; Davis, ed., *Diary of a Confederate Soldier,* 127–128; Simpson, ed., *The Bugle Softly Blows,* 52; *Mobile Daily Advertiser and Register,* May 19, 1864.

28. Symonds, *Joseph E. Johnston,* 291–295; Thomas Lawrence Connelly, *Autumn of Glory: The Army of Tennessee, 1862–1865* (Baton Rouge: Louisiana State Univ. Press, 1971), 371–372.

29. Symonds, *Joseph E. Johnston,* 295; Castel, *Decision in the West,* 206; McMurry, *Atlanta 1864,* 83.

30. Thomas Jefferson Burnett to wife, May 21, 1864 (quotation), Thomas Jefferson Burnett Papers, Pearce Civil War Collection; James T. Searcy Letters, May 19, 22, 27, 28, 1864, James T.

Searcy Letters, Civil War Soldiers' Letters, ADAH; Symonds, *Joseph E. Johnston*, 295; William D. Cole to wife, May 21, 1864, William D. Cole Letters, Civil War Miscellaneous Collection, USAMHI; William E. Sykes to wife, May 29, 1864, William E. Sykes Letters, Special Collections, MSU; Edward Norphlet Brown to Fannie, May 22, 1864, Edward Norphlet Brown Letters, ADAH; Noyes, ed., "Excerpts from the Civil War Diary of E. T. Eggleston," 342; Nathaniel Cheairs Hughes Jr., *The Pride of the Confederate Artillery: The Washington Artillery in the Army of Tennessee* (Baton Rouge: Louisiana State Univ. Press, 1997), 184; Garrett, ed., *Confederate Diary of Robert D. Smith*, 65; Castel, *Decision in the West*, 217.

31. Castel, *Decision in the West*, 209–264; Avington Wayne Simpson Diary, May 28, 1864, SHC; Simpson, ed., *The Bugle Softly Blows*, 25–31; Davis, ed., *Diary of a Confederate Soldier*, 129–136; Edward Norphlet Brown to Fannie, May 29, 1864, Edward Norphlet Brown Letters, ADAH; Albert Quincy Porter Diary, June 2, 1864, MDAH; James R. Fleming, *Band of Brothers: Company C, 9th Tennessee Infantry* (Shippensburg, Pa.: White Mane Publishing, 1996), 102.

32. M. H. Dixon Diary, May 27, 1864 (first quotation), Civil War Collection, Tennessee State Library and Archives, Nashville (hereafter cited as TSLA); William E. Sloan Diary, May 27, 31(second quotation), 1864, Civil War Collection, TSLA; C. T. Hardman to wife, May 25, 1864 (third quotation), Hardman Family Letters, Civil War Soldiers' Letters, ADAH; Albert Quincy Porter Diary, May 29, 1864, MDAH.

33. John Crittenden to Bettie, May 29, 1864 (quotations), John Crittenden Letters, Center for American History, University of Texas at Austin (hereafter cited as CAH); Thomas Hopkins Deavenport Diary, May 23, 30, June 5, 1864, Civil War Collection, TSLA. Another Alabama soldier twice told his family that he considered the Union soldiers' letters "vulgar" and "obscene," though he chose some of the less offensive to send home. See James T. Searcy to Evie, May 27, 1864, and James T. Searcy to Stella, May 31, 1864, James T. Searcy Letters, Civil War Soldiers' Letters, ADAH.

34. William E. Sykes to wife, June 9, 1864 (first quotation), William E. Sykes Letters, Special Collections, MSU; John Crittenden to Bettie, May 31, 1864 (second quotation), John Crittenden Letters, CAH; Cuttino, ed., *Saddle Bag and Spinning Wheel*, 247–248; Cannon, *Bloody Banners and Barefoot Boys*, 69–72 (third quotation 72); David E. Maxwell, "Some Letters to His Parents by a Floridian in the Confederate Army," trans. Gilbert Wright, *Florida Historical Quarterly* 36 (April 1958): 369; Shepherd Spencer Neville Brown, ed., *War Years, C. S. A.: 12th Mississippi Regiment, Major S. H. Giles, Q. M., Original Letters, 1860–1865* (Hillsboro, Texas: Hill College Press, 1998), 271; George C. Osborn, ed., "Civil War Letters of Robert W. Banks: The Atlanta Campaign," *Georgia Historical Quarterly* 27 (June 1943): 211–213; Enoch L. Mitchell, ed., "Letters of a Confederate Surgeon in the Army of Tennessee to His Wife," *Tennessee Historical Quarterly* 5 (June 1946), 167–169; Thomas Warrick to Martha Warrick, May 12, 1864, Thomas Warrick Papers, ADAH.

35. John Daniel Cooper Civil War Diary, 7th Mississippi Infantry File, Hill College.

36. McMurry, *Atlanta 1864*, 100–101. In addition to the sources cited above, for evidence of high morale in early June see other sources cited by Castel in *Decision in the West*, 594 n. 13. For further discussion of morale during the campaign and afterward, see William J. McNeill, "A Survey of Confederate Soldier Morale during Sherman's Campaigns Through Georgia and the Carolinas," *Georgia Historical Quarterly* 55 (spring 1971): 1–25.

37. Cuttino, ed., *Saddle Bag and Spinning Wheel,* 251; John Crittenden to Bettie, June 7, 1864, John Crittenden Letters, CAH; Mark K. Christ, ed., *Getting Used to Being Shot At: The Spence Family Civil War Letters* (Fayetteville: Univ. of Arkansas Press, 2002), 94–97; William Milner Kelly, "A History of the Thirtieth Alabama Volunteers (Infantry) Confederate States Army," *Alabama Historical Quarterly* 9 (spring 1947): 154–155. For more comments pointing to especially high morale, support of Johnston and his strategy, and blaming the Federals for refusing to fight, see William Martin to father, June 7, 1864, Martin Family Letters, Pearce Collection; Lucille Griffith, ed., *Yours Til Death: Civil War Letters of John W. Cotton* (University: Univ. of Alabama Press, 1951), 111–112; Phillip Bond, "The Alabama State Artillery," *Alabama Historical Quarterly* 20 (summer 1958): 335; Brown, ed., *War Years, C. S. A.,* 292; Taylor, ed., *Reluctant Rebel,* 179–182; Leona T. Aiken, ed., "Letters of the Offield Brothers, Confederate Soldiers from Upper East Tennessee," *East Tennessee Historical Society Publications* 46 (1974): 123; Rountree, ed., "Letters of a Confederate Soldier," 285–289; McGuire, *McGuire Papers,* 22–23.

38. Jesse P. Bates Civil War Letters, 9th Texas Infantry File, Hill College; John Daniel Cooper Civil War Diary, June 24, 1864, 7th Mississippi Infantry File, Hill College.

39. Cash and Howorth, eds., *My Dear Nellie,* 179–181 (first and second quotation 179); Christ, ed., *Getting Used to Being Shot At,* 96 (third quotation).

40. Woodworth and Winkle, *Atlas of the Civil War,* 224–226; Brian Steel Wills, *A Battle from the Start: The Life of Nathan Bedford Forrest* (New York: HarperCollins, 1992), 202–215; Herman Hattaway, *General Stephen D. Lee* (Jackson: Univ. Press of Mississippi, 1976), 114–115; Nathan Bedford Forrest Report on Brice's Cross Roads, July 1, 1864, *Official Records,* ser. 1, vol. 39, pt. 1, 221–226.

41. *Jackson Daily Mississippian* (Selma, Alabama), June 15, 1864; *Meridian Daily Clarion,* June 14, 1864; *Montgomery Daily Advertiser,* June 19, 1864.

42. James A. Carpenter, ed., "James D. Lynch in War and Peace," *Alabama Historical Quarterly* 20 (spring 1958): 77 (first quotation); Jennie Pendleton Journal, June 10 (second quotation), 14 (third quotation), 1864, Mary E. Wilkes Shell Papers, MDAH; Richard Barksdale Harwell, ed., *Kate: The Journal of a Confederate Nurse* (Baton Rouge: Louisiana State Univ. Press, 1959), 206.

43. Samuel Andrew Agnew Diary, June 11, 1864, Special Collections, MSU.

44. Ibid., June 11–16, 1864.

45. Castel, *Decision in the West,* 274.

46. Ibid., 275–276; Edward Norphlet Brown to Fannie, June 16, 1864 (quotation), Edward Norphlet Brown Letters, ADAH; William E. Sloan Diary, June 14, 1864, Civil War Collection, TSLA; Cannon, *Bloody Banners and Barefoot Boys,* 73–74; Albert Quincy Porter Diary, June 14, 1864, MDAH; Thomas Jefferson Burnett to wife, June 15, 1864, Thomas Jefferson Burnett Papers, Pearce Collection; H. Grady Howell Jr., *Going to Meet the Yankees: A History of the "Bloody Sixth" Mississippi Infantry, C. S. A.* (Jackson, Mississippi: Chickasaw Bayou Press, 1981), 222; Sam Davis Elliott, ed., *Doctor Quintard, Chaplain C. S. A. and Second Bishop of Tennessee* (Baton Rouge: Louisiana State Univ. Press, 2003), 86.

47. R. W. Colville to father, June 26, 1864, Civil War Collection, TSLA; W. K. Martin to brother, June 25, 1864, Martin Family Letters, Pearce Collection; Edward Norphlet Brown to Fannie, June 20, 26, 1864, Edward Norphlet Brown Letters, ADAH; John Crittenden to

Bettie, June 20, 22, 24, 28, 1864, John Crittenden Letters, CAH; M. H. Dixon Diary, June 13, 1864, Civil War Collection, TSLA; Thomas Warrick to Martha, June 11, 1864, Thomas Warrick Papers, ADAH; Cuttino, ed., *Saddle Bag and Spinning Wheel*, 255–256; Cash and Howorth, eds., *My Dear Nellie*, 184; *Montgomery Daily Advertiser*, June 19, 1864.

48. Castel, *Decision in the West*, 285–322.

49. William E. Sloan Diary, June 27, 1864 (first quotation), Civil War Collection, TSLA; Garrett, ed., *Confederate Diary of Robert D. Smith*, 71 (second quotation); McPherson, *Battle Cry of Freedom*, 750; Howell, *Going to Meet the Yankees*, 224; H.H.H. Rugeley, ed., *Batchelor-Turner Letters, 1861–1864, Written by Two of Terry's Texas Rangers* (Austin, Tex.: Steck Company, 1961), 81; William E. Sykes to wife, June 27–28 (third quotation), 1864, William E. Sykes Letters, Special Collections, MSU.

50. Richard M. McMurry, "Confederate Morale in the Atlanta Campaign of 1864," *Georgia Historical Quarterly* 54, no. 2 (1970): 226–243. For the excellent biography of Hood referred to in the text, see McMurry, *John Bell Hood and the War for Southern Independence* (Lincoln: Univ. of Nebraska Press, 1982).

51. Charles Dubuisson to father, June 26, 1864 (first quotation), Dubuisson Family Papers, MDAH; John Crittenden to Bettie, June 19, 1864 second quotation), John Crittenden Letters, CAH.

4. JULY–AUGUST 1864: RETREAT, REMOVAL, AND DOUBT

1. Richard Lowe, ed., *A Texas Cavalry Officer's Civil War: The Diary and Letters of James C. Bates* (Baton Rouge: Louisiana State Univ. Press, 1999), 301–306 (quotations 303–304); William Galbraith and Loretta Galbraith, eds., *A Lost Heroine of the Confederacy: The Diaries and Letters of Belle Edmondson* (Jackson: Univ. Press of Mississippi, 1990), 152.

2. Margaret Josephine Miles Gillis Diary, July 3, 1864, Alabama Department of Archives and History, Montgomery (hereafter cited as ADAH); Sarah Rousseau Espy Diary, July 3–15, 1864, ADAH; Grady McWhiney, Warner O. Moore Jr., and Robert F. Pace, eds., *Fear God and Walk Humbly: The Agricultural Journal of James Mallory, 1843–1877* (Tuscaloosa: Univ. of Alabama Press, 1997), 337; Nannie E. Haskins Diary, July 14, 1864 (quotation), Nannie E. Haskins Papers, Tennessee State Library and Archives, Nashville (hereafter cited as TSLA).

3. Steven E. Woodworth and Kenneth J. Winkle, eds., *Atlas of the Civil War* (New York: Oxford Univ. Press, 2004), 233–234; Albert Castel, *Decision in the West: The Atlanta Campaign of 1864* (Lawrence: Univ. Press of Kansas, 1992), 319–320.

4. For examples of soldiers beginning to express mixed feelings or observing others doing so, see Bell Irvin Wiley, ed., "The Confederate Letters of John W. Hagan," *Georgia Historical Quarterly* 38 (September 1954): 281–283; F. Jay Taylor, ed., *Reluctant Rebel: The Secret Diary of Robert Patrick, 1861–1865* (Baton Rouge: Louisiana State Univ. Press, 1959), 186–191; Andrew Haughton, *Training, Tactics, and Leadership in the Confederate Army of Tennessee: Seeds of Failure* (Brookfield, Vt.: Frank Cass, 2000), 161; H. E. Sterkx, ed., "Autobiography and Letters of Joel Dyer Murphree of Troy, Alabama, 1864–1865," *Alabama Historical Quarterly* 19 (spring 1957): 181–183; Lewis N. Wynne and Robert A. Taylor, eds., *This War So Horrible: The Civil War Diary of Hiram Smith Williams* (Tuscaloosa: Univ. of Alabama Press, 1993), 100–101.

5. John Crittenden to Bettie, July 1, 1864, John Crittenden Letters, Center for American History, University of Texas, Austin (hereafter cited as CAH); Edward Norphlet Brown to Fannie, July 2, 8, 1864, Edward Norphlet Brown Letters, ADAH; J. P. Cannon, *Bloody Banners and Barefoot Boys: A History of the 27th Regiment Alabama Infantry, C. S. A.: The Civil War Memoirs and Diaries of J. P. Cannon, M.D.*, comp. and ed. Noel Crowson and John V. Brogden (Shippensburg, Pa.: Burd Street Press, 1997), 80 (quotation); William M. Cash and Lucy Somerville Howorth, eds., *My Dear Nellie: The Civil War Letters of William L. Nugent to Eleanor Smith Nugent* (Jackson: Univ. Press of Mississippi, 1977), 186; Mathew Andrew Dunn to wife, July 6, 1864, Mathew Andrew Dunn Letters, MDAH; Ray Mathis, ed., *In the Land of the Living: Wartime Letters by Confederates from the Chattahoochee Valley of Alabama and Georgia* (Troy, Ala.: Troy State Univ. Press, 1981), 101; Craig L. Symonds, *Stonewall of the West: Patrick Cleburne and the Civil War* (Lawrence: Univ. Press of Kansas, 1997), 208; Craig L. Symonds, *Joseph E. Johnston: A Civil War Biography* (New York: Norton, 1992), 317; Lucia R. Douglas, ed., *Douglas's Texas Battery, C. S. A.* (Tyler, Tex.: Smith County Historical Society, 1966), 109; Vicki Betts, ed., "The Civil War Letters of Elbridge Littlejohn," *Chronicles of Smith County, Texas* 18 (summer 1979): 26; Mary K. Haynes and James Wilkins, comps., "The Stanley Letters," *Papers of the Pike County Historical Society* 4 (April 1965): 24–28; Lowell H. Harrison, ed., "The Diary of an 'Average' Confederate Soldier," *Tennessee Historical Quarterly* 29 (fall 1970): 267.

6. Thomas Warrick to Martha, July 2, 1864, Thomas Warrick Papers, ADAH; M. H. Dixon Diary, July 2, 3, 1864, Civil War Collection, TSLA.

7. Mathew Andrew Dunn to wife, July 6–7, 1864, Mathew Andrew Dunn Letters, MDAH. For other examples of soldiers endorsing the strategy, supporting Johnston, or understanding the reasons for retreat, see Thomas Warrick to Martha, July 2, 1864, Thomas Warrick Papers, ADAH; M. H. Dixon Diary, July 2, 3, 1864, Civil War Collection, TSLA; William E. Sloan Diary, July 3, 1864, Civil War Collection, TSLA; Norman D. Brown, ed., *One of Cleburne's Command: The Civil War Reminiscences and Diary of Captain Samuel T. Foster, Granbury's Texas Brigade, CSA* (Austin: Univ. of Texas Press, 1980), 100; Ann K. Blomquist and Robert A. Taylor, eds., *This Cruel War: The Civil War Letters of Grant and Malinda Taylor, 1862–1865* (Macon, Ga.: Mercer Univ. Press, 2000), 265–266; Taylor, ed., *Reluctant Rebel,* 187; Wiley, ed., "The Confederate Letters of John W. Hagan," 281–282.

8. John Daniel Cooper Civil War Diary, July 8, 1864, 7th Mississippi Infantry File, Simpson History Complex, Hill College, Hillsboro, Texas (hereafter cited as Hill College). Cooper probably referred to the Pearl River of Mississippi.

9. Symonds, *Joseph E. Johnston,* 317–319; Woodworth and Winkle, eds., *Atlas of the Civil War,* 234; Castel, *Decision in the West,* 357–365. For an exceptional examination of the Davis-Johnston relationship, see Craig L. Symonds, "A Fatal Relationship: Davis and Johnston at War," in *Jefferson Davis's Generals,* ed. Gabor S. Boritt, 3–26 (New York: Oxford Univ. Press, 1999).

10. Harold B. Simpson, ed., *The Bugle Softly Blows: The Confederate Diary of Benjamin M. Seaton* (Waco, Tex.: Texian Press, 1965), 56; John Crittenden to Bettie, July 9, 12 (quotation), 1864, John Crittenden Letters, CAH; Mathis, ed., *In the Land of the Living,* 103; Taylor, ed., *Reluctant Rebel,* 192–195.

11. Joseph Branch O'Bryan to sisters, July 13, 1864 (first quotation), Joseph Branch O'Bryan Letters, TSLA; D.R.C. Martin to sister, July 9, 1864 (second and third quotations), Martin Family Papers, Pearce Civil War Collection, Navarro College, Corsicana, Texas (hereafter cited

as Pearce Collection). For more examples of continued high morale during the period within a week after the Chattahoochee River crossing (July 9, 1864), see William E. Sloan Diary, July 15, 1864, Civil War Collection, TSLA; George Peddy Cuttino, ed., *Saddle Bag and Spinning Wheel: Being the Civil War Letters of George W. Peddy, M. D., Surgeon, 56th Georgia Volunteers Regiment, C. S. A. and His Wife Kate Featherston Peddy* (Macon, Ga.: Mercer Univ. Press, 1981), 264; Cannon, *Bloody Banners and Barefoot Boys*, 81–83; Douglas, ed., *Douglas's Texas Battery*, 111; Enoch L. Mitchell, ed., "Letters of a Confederate Surgeon in the Army of Tennessee to His Wife," *Tennessee Historical Quarterly* 5 (June 1946): 170–172; Wiley, ed., "The Confederate Letters of John W. Hagan," 285; James R. Fleming, *Band of Brothers: Company C, 9th Tennessee Infantry* (Shippensburg, Pa.: White Mane Publishing, 1996); Mary M. Jones and Leslie J. Martin, eds., *The Gentle Rebel: The Civil War Letters of William Harvey Berryhill, Co. D., 43rd Regiment, Mississippi Volunteers* (Yazoo City, Miss.: Sassafras Press, 1982), 45–54; R. Lockwood Tower, ed., *A Carolinian Goes to War: The Civil War Narrative of Arthur Middleton Manigault* (Columbia: Univ. of South Carolina Press, 1983), 199–200; Brown, ed., *One of Cleburne's Command*, 104.

12. Symonds, *Joseph E. Johnston*, 318–331; Castel, *Decision in the West*, 360–365, 561; Craig Symonds, "General Joseph E. Johnston's Civil War: A Conversation with Historian Craig Symonds," interview by Mark Snell, *Civil War Regiments* 6, no. 1 (1998): 107–120; Thomas Lawrence Connelly, *Autumn of Glory: The Army of Tennessee, 1862–1865* (Baton Rouge: Louisiana State Univ. Press, 1971), 391–426; Richard M. McMurry, *John Bell Hood and the War for Southern Independence* (Lexington: Univ. Press of Kentucky, 1982), 116–123. Castel, Symonds, and Connelly judged the removal of Johnston harmful to the Confederate cause. McMurry considered Johnston's replacement necessary.

13. James Marsh Morey Diary, July 18, 1864, James Marsh Morey Papers, TSLA.

14. Cannon, *Bloody Banners and Barefoot Boys*, 83.

15. Brown, ed., *One of Cleburne's Command*, 105–107. For more comments decrying Johnston's removal immediately upon hearing the news, see M. H. Dixon Diary, July 17, 1864, Civil War Collection, TSLA; Joseph Miller Rand Diary, July 18, 1864, MDAH; Avington Wayne Simpson Diary, July 18, 1864, Southern Historical Collection, Wilson Library, University of North Carolina, Chapel Hill (hereafter cited as SHC); Taylor, ed., *Reluctant Rebel*, 197; Wynne and Taylor, eds., *This Was So Horrible*, 104; Alfred Tyler Fielder Diary, July 18, 1864, TSLA; Wiley, ed., "The Confederate Letters of John W. Hagan," 286; Thomas McGuire, *McGuire Papers, Containing Major Thomas McGuire's Civil War Letters; and Patriotic Documents and Other Letters from 1854 to the Turn of the Twentieth Century* (Tusquahoma, La.: Daughters of the American Revolution, 1966), 25–26; Jones and Martin, eds., *Gentle Rebel*, 57–58; Sterkx, ed., "Autobiography and Letters of Joel Murphree," 184–185; Wirt Armistead Cate, ed., *Two Soldiers: The Campaign Diaries of Thomas J. Key, C. S. A., and Robert J. Campbell, U. S. A* (Chapel Hill: Univ. of North Carolina Press, 1938), 89–90.

For still more support for the contention that soldiers overwhelmingly opposed the removal of Johnston and for other historians' conclusions, see Castel, *Decision in the West*, 363–365, 604 n. 46; Symonds, *Joseph E. Johnston*, 330–331; Christopher Losson, *Tennessee's Forgotten Warriors: Frank Cheatham and His Confederate Division* (Knoxville: Univ. of Tennessee Press, 1989), 169–172.

16. Douglas, ed., *Douglas's Texas Battery*, 114 (quotation); Richard M. McMurry, *Atlanta 1864: Last Chance for the Confederacy* (Lincoln: Univ. of Nebraska Press, 2000); Stephen Davis,

Atlanta Will Fall: Sherman, Joe Johnston, and the Yankee Heavy Battalions (Wilmington, Del.: Scholarly Resources, 2001).

17. Edward Norphlet Brown to Fannie, July 23, 1864, Edward Norphlet Brown Letters, ADAH; Robert A. Croxton to brother, July 24, 1864, Robert A. Croxton Letters, Civil War Soldiers' Letters, ADAH. For indications of continued gloom over Johnston's removal, see William E. Sloan Diary, July 23, 1864, Civil War Collection, TSLA; Benjamin Rountree, ed., "Letters of a Confederate Soldier," *Georgia Review* 18 (fall 1964): 290; Jim R. Cabaniss, ed., *Civil War Journal and Letters of Washington Ives, 4th Fla. C. S. A.* (Tallahassee, Fla.: Jim Cabaniss, 1987), 69.

18. W. E. Smith to mother, July 31, 1864 (quotation), W. E. Smith Civil War Letters, 7th Texas Infantry File, Hill College.

19. Joseph Branch O'Bryan to sisters, July 24, 1864 (quotation), Joseph Branch O'Bryan Letters, TSLA; Cuttino, ed., *Saddle Bag and Spinning Wheel,* 268; See also George C. Osborn, ed., "Civil War Letters of Robert W. Banks: The Atlanta Campaign," *Georgia Historical Quarterly* 27 (June 1943): 215–216.

20. For only a sample of the many postwar versions of soldier reactions to Johnston's removal from command, see Sam Watkins, *"Co. Aytch," Maury Grays, First Tennessee Regiment; or a Side Show of the Big Show* (1882; reprint, Wilmington, N.C.: Broadfoot, 1987), 143–144; Daniel E. Sutherland, ed., *Reminiscences of a Private: William E. Bevens of the First Arkansas Infantry, C. S. A.* (Fayetteville: Univ. of Arkansas Press, 1992), 167; Albert D. Kirwan, ed., *Johnny Green of the Orphan Brigade: Journal of a Confederate Soldier* (Lexington: Univ. of Kentucky Press, 1956), 142; Douglas John Cater, *As It Was: Reminiscences of a Soldier of the Third Texas Cavalry and the Nineteenth Louisiana Infantry* (Austin, Tex.: State House Press, 1990), 183–184; William Pitt Chambers, *Blood and Sacrifice: The Civil War Journal of a Confederate Soldier* (Huntington, W.Va.: Blue Acorn Press, 1994), 156–158; Irving Buck, *Cleburne and His Command* (Jackson, Tenn.: McCowat-Mercer Press, 1959), 227–229; Sam Davis Elliott, *Soldier of Tennessee: General Alexander P. Stewart and the Civil War in the West* (Baton Rouge: Louisiana State Univ. Press, 1999), 201; Royce Shingleton, ed., "With Loyalty and Honor as a Patriot: Recollections of a Confederate Soldier," *Alabama Historical Quarterly* 33 (fall and winter 1971): 255–256.

21. J. Cutler Andrews, *The South Reports the Civil War* (Princeton: Princeton Univ. Press, 1970), 454–455; *Montgomery Daily Advertiser,* July 21, 1864; William N. Still, ed., "The Civil War Letters of Robert Tarleton," *Alabama Historical Quarterly* 32 (spring and summer 1970): 74–75; Lowe, ed., *A Texas Cavalry Officer's Civil War,* 313 (quotation).

22. Frances Woolfolk Wallace Diary, July 23, 1864, SHC; Robert H. Cartmell Diary, July 26, 1864, Robert H. Cartmell Papers, TSLA; Richard Barksdale Harwell, ed., *Kate: The Journal of a Confederate Nurse* (Baton Rouge: Louisiana State Univ. Press, 1959), 223; Jane Bonner Peacock, ed., "A Wartime Story: The Davidson Letters, 1862–1865," *Atlanta Historical Bulletin* 20, no. 1 (1975): 91.

23. McMurry, *Atlanta 1864,* 129–130; Richard M. McMurry, "Confederate Morale in the Atlanta Campaign of 1864," *Georgia Historical Quarterly* 54, no. 2 (1970): 226–243. For further discussion of morale during the campaign and afterward, see William J. McNeill, "A Survey of Confederate Soldier Morale during Sherman's Campaigns through Georgia and the Carolinas," *Georgia Historical Quarterly* 55 (spring 1971): 1–25.

24. Woodworth and Winkle, eds., *Atlas of the Civil War,* 258–259; McMurry, *John Bell Hood,* 123–134; Castel, *Decision in the West,* 450. For casualty figures in the three battles, see Castel,

Decision in the West, 381, 412, 434. For more on differing interpretations of casualties during the campaign, see McMurry, *Atlanta 1864,* 194–197.

25. Thomas Smyrl to Mary Jane Smyrl, July 25, 1864 (first quotation), Thomas Smyrl Letters, ADAH; Robert A. Croxton to mother, father, brother, sister, July 21 (second quotation), 23, 24, 1864, Robert A. Croxton Letters, Civil War Soldiers' Letters , ADAH.

26. John Bell Hood, *Advance and Retreat: Personal Experiences in the United States and Confederate States Armies* (Bloomington: Indiana Univ. Press, 1959), 181–185; Braxton Bragg to Jefferson Davis, July 25, 1864, in United States War Department, *The War of the Rebellion: A Compilation of the Official Records of the Union and Confederate Armies,* 128 vols. (hereafter cited as *Official Records*) (Washington, D.C.: Government Printing Office, 1880–1901), ser. 1, vol. 38, pt. 5, 908; Robert A. Croxton to brother, July 23, 1864, and Robert A. Croxton to sister, July 23, 1864, Robert A. Croxton Letters, Civil War Soldiers' Letters, ADAH; W. E. Smith to mother, July 31, 1864, W. E. Smith Civil War Letters, 7th Texas Infantry File, Hill College; Jones and Martin, eds., *Gentle Rebel,* 66, 70 (quotation). See also Edward Norphlet Brown to Fannie, July 27, 1864, Edward Norphlet Brown Letters, ADAH; Cuttino, ed., *Saddle Bag and Spinning Wheel,* 268; Cate, ed., *Two Soldiers,* 101–105.

27. Cash and Howorth, eds., *My Dear Nellie,* 193 (quotation); Taylor, ed., *Reluctant Rebel,* 199–202; Wynne and Taylor, eds., *This War So Horrible,* 106–107.

See also Cash and Howorth, eds., *My Dear Nellie,* 189; Blomquist and Taylor, eds., *This Cruel War,* 269; Chambers, *Blood and Sacrifice,* 158; McGuire, *McGuire Papers,* 26–27; Mathis, ed., *In the Land of the Living,* 104–106; Losson, *Tennessee's Forgotten Warriors,* 188; Nathaniel Cheairs Hughes Jr., *General William J. Hardee: Old Reliable* (Baton Rouge: Louisiana State Univ. Press, 1965), 233; Castel, *Decision in the West,* 450–452, 614 n 7.

28. James O. Breeden, "A Medical History of the Later Stages of the Atlanta Campaign," *Journal of Southern History* 35 (February 1969): 53–54; Cannon, *Bloody Banners and Barefoot Boys,* 84–88.

29. Woodworth and Winkle, eds., *Atlas of the Civil War,* 262–263; Castel, *Decision in the West,* 450–452; McMurry, *Atlanta 1864,* 160–161; A. J. Fogle to Miss, August 25, 1864 (first quotation), Andrew J. Fogle Civil War Letters, 9th Texas Infantry File, Hill College; Edward Noyes, ed., "Excerpts from the Civil War Diary of E. T. Eggleston," *Tennessee Historical Quarterly* 17 (December 1958): 348 (second quotation).

30. Jones and Martin, eds., *Gentle Rebel,* 70–72; Cabaniss, ed., *Civil War Journal and Letters of Washington Ives,* 69; Blomquist and Taylor, eds., *This Cruel War,* 271; Breeden, "A Medical History," 56; Haughton, *Training, Tactics, and Leadership,* 170–172; M. S. Hunter to brother, August 3, 1864, Horn Collection, Special Collections Department, Mitchell Memorial Library, Mississippi State University (hereafter cited as Special Collections, MSU).

31. Edward Norphlet Brown to Fannie, August 10 (first quotation), 25 (second quotation) 1864, Edward Norphlet Brown Letters, ADAH; Joseph Branch O'Bryan to sisters, August 7, 1864, Joseph Branch O'Bryan Letters, TSLA; Linson Montgomery Keener to brother, August 29, 1864, Linson Montgomery Keener Civil War Letters, 7th Texas Infantry File, Hill College; Jesse P. Bates to wife, August 7, 1864, Jesse P. Bates Civil War Letters, 9th Texas Infantry File, Hill College; Thomas Warrick Papers, August 16, 19, 25, 30, 1864, Thomas Warrick Papers, ADAH; Cuttino, ed., *Saddle Bag and Spinning Wheel,* 270–276; Cate, ed., *Two Soldiers,* 109, 119; Mark K. Christ, ed., *Getting Used to Being Shot At: The Spence Family Civil War Letters*

(Fayetteville: Univ. of Arkansas Press, 2002), 98–102; Douglas, ed., *Douglas's Texas Battery,* 123–125; Herman Hattaway, *General Stephen D. Lee* (Jackson: Univ. Press of Mississippi, 1976), 130; Douglas Hale, *The Third Texas Cavalry in the Civil War* (Norman: Univ. of Oklahoma Press, 1993), 245; Rountree, ed., "Letters of a Confederate Soldier," 291; Samuel King Vann, *"Most Lovely Lizzie": Love Letters of a Young Confederate* (Birmingham, Ala.: Privately Published, 1958), 44–45. For an example of a soldier who was clearly wearing down from the trench warfare and the Federal onslaught, see John H. Marshall to wife, August 11, 19, 1864, John H. Marshall Letters, Special Collections, MSU.

32. Cuttino, ed., *Saddle Bag and Spinning Wheel,* 270; Sterkx, ed., "Autobiography and Letters of Joel Murphree," 191–193; Thomas Smyrl to Mary J. Smyrl, August 25, 1864 (first quotation), Thomas Smyrl Letters, ADAH; Cash and Howorth, eds., *My Dear Nellie,* 196 (second quotation). See also Mathew Andrew Dunn to Nora, August 22, 1864, Mathew Andrew Dunn Letters, MDAH.

33. Edward Norphlet Brown to Fannie, August 10, 25(quotation), 1864, Edward Norphlet Brown Letters, ADAH.

34. Thomas Warrick to wife and father, August 4, 1864, Thomas Warrick Papers, ADAH; Vera Dockery Elkins, ed., *Letters from a Civil War Soldier* (New York: Vantage Press, 1969), 53–54; Blomquist and Taylor, eds., *This Cruel War,* vii–xiii, 270–271 (quotation).

35. Frances Woolfolk Wallace Diary, August 5, 13 (first quotation) 1864, SHC; R. F. Bunting Papers, August 20, 1864, CAH; Thomas W. Cutrer, ed., *'Our Trust is in the God of Battles': The Civil War Letters of Robert Franklin Bunting, Chaplain, Terry's Texas Rangers, C. S. A.* (Knoxville: Univ. of Tennessee Press, 2006); Galbraith and Galbraith, eds. *A Lost Heroine of the Confederacy,* 166 (second quotation).

36. Sarah Rousseau Espy Diary, August entries, ADAH; Belle Strickland Diary, August 6, 1864, MDAH; William R. Snell, ed., *Myra Inman: A Diary of the Civil War in East Tennessee*) Macon, Ga.: Mercer Univ. Press, 2000(, 276–282.

37. Woodworth and Winkle, *Atlas of the Civil War,* 224–226; Elizabeth Jane Beach Letter, July 29, 1864 (first quotation), MDAH; Jason Niles Diary, July 29, 1864 (second quotation), SHC.

38. Betts, ed., "The Civil War Letters of Elbridge Littlejohn," 27; Mathis, ed., *In the Land of the Living,* 107; Arthur W. Bergeron Jr., *Confederate Mobile* (Baton Rouge: Louisiana State Univ. Press, 2000), 138–151; Woodworth and Winkle, eds., *Atlas of the Civil War,* 264–265; William N. Still, ed., "The Civil War Letters of Robert Tarleton," *Alabama Historical Quarterly* 32 (spring and summer 1970): 73–77; Mark Lyons to Amelia, July 28, August 18, 19, 20, 1864, Mark Lyons Letters, ADAH; W. V. Fleming to wife, August 22, 1864, W. V. Fleming Letters, Civil War Soldiers' Letters, ADAH; John Kent Folmar, ed., *From That Terrible Field: Civil War Letters of James M. Williams, Twenty-First Alabama Infantry Volunteers* (University: Univ. of Alabama Press, 1981), 135–137.

39. Bergeron, *Confederate Mobile,* 151; Woodworth and Winkle, *Atlas of the Civil War,* 264–265; Galbraith and Galbraith, eds., *A Lost Heroine of the Confederacy,* 168–174.

40. Cash and Howorth, eds., *My Dear Nellie,* 191, 193; Edward Norphlet Brown to Fannie, August 25, 1864, Edward Norphlet Brown Letters, ADAH; Cate, ed., *Two Soldiers,* 120, 123; Douglas, ed., *Douglas's Texas Battery,* 125, 128.

41. Edward Norphlet Brown to Fannie, August 25, 1864, Edward Norphlet Brown Letters, ADAH.

42. Wynne and Taylor, eds., *This War So Horrible*, 110 (quotation); Woodworth and Winkle, *Atlas of the Civil War*, 262–263; Herman Hattaway and Archer Jones, *How the North Won: A Military History of the Civil War* (Urbana: Univ. of Illinois Press, 1991), 622–623; Symonds, *Stonewall of the West*, 239; Hughes, *General William J. Hardee*, 242; Tower, ed., *A Carolinian Goes to War*, 245–248; Homer L. Kerr, ed. *Fighting with Ross' Texas Cavalry Brigade, C. S. A.: Diary of Lieut. George L. Griscom, Adjutant, 9th Texas Cavalry Regiment* (Hillsboro, Tex.: Hill Junior College Press, 1976), 167.

43. Snell, ed., *Myra Inman*, 282 (quotation).

44. Galbraith and Galbraith, eds., *A Lost Heroine of the Confederacy*, 166 (first quotation), 172 (second quotation).

5. SEPTEMBER–OCTOBER 1864: UNCERTAINTY AGAIN

1. James H. Finch Diary, September 4, 1864, Civil War Soldiers' Letters, Alabama Department of Archives and History, Montgomery, Alabama (hereafter cited as ADAH).

2. Albert Castel, *Decision in the West: The Atlanta Campaign of 1864* (Lawrence: Univ. Press of Kansas, 1992), 509–542; Thomas Lawrence Connelly, *Autumn of Glory: The Army of Tennessee, 1862–1865* (Baton Rouge: Louisiana State Univ. Press, 1971), 466–469.

3. Castel, *Decision in the West*, 543–547.

4. James H. Finch Diary, September 4, 1864, Civil War Soldiers' Letters, ADAH; Mark A. Weitz, *More Damning than Slaughter: Desertion in the Confederate Army* (Lincoln: Univ. of Nebraska Press, 2005), 254–255.

5. Letter between unnamed sisters, September 8, 1864, Phillips Fitzpatrick Letters, ADAH; Sarah Rousseau Espy Diary, September 7, 1864, ADAH; William R. Snell, ed., *Myra Inman: A Diary of the Civil War in East Tennessee* (Macon, Ga.: Mercer Univ. Press, 2000), 283; Carrie Berry Diary, September 10, 1864, http://www.americancivilwar.com/women/carrie_berry.html (accessed February 19, 2011).

6. Belle F. Strickland Diary, September 11, 1864, Mississippi Department of Archives and History, Jackson, Mississippi (hereafter cited as MDAH); John N. Fain, ed., *Sanctified Trial: The Diary of Eliza Rhea Anderson Fain, a Confederate Woman in East Tennessee* (Knoxville: Univ. of Tennessee Press, 2004), 234; Ben Kremenak, ed., "Escape from Atlanta: The Huntingdon Memoir," *Civil War History* 11 (June 1965): 167–170; T. Conn Bryan, ed., "A Georgia Woman's Civil War Diary: The Journal of Minerva Leah Rowles McClatchey, 1864–1865," *Georgia Historical Quarterly* 51 (summer 1967): 206–207; Richard Barksdale Harwell, ed., *Kate: The Journal of a Confederate Nurse* (Baton Rouge: Louisiana State Univ. Press, 1959), 231.

7. Ann K. Blomquist and Robert A. Taylor, eds., *This Cruel War: The Civil War Letters of Grant and Malinda Taylor, 1862–1865* (Macon, Ga.: Mercer Univ. Press, 2000), 280–282.

8. Grady McWhiney, Warner O. Moore Jr., and Robert F. Pace, eds., *Fear God and Walk Humbly: The Agricultural Journal of James Mallory, 1843–1877* (Tuscaloosa: Univ. of Alabama Press, 1997), 340; T. Michael Parrish, *Richard Taylor: Soldier Prince of Dixie* (Chapel Hill: Univ. of North Carolina Press, 1992), 405–412.

9. H. W. Bullen to brother, September 4, 1864 (first three quotations), Civil War Papers (Miscellaneous), MDAH; Henry D. Jamison and Marguerite J. McTigue, eds., *Letters and*

Recollections of a Confederate Soldier, 1860–1865 (Nashville, Tenn.: H. D. Jamison, 1964), 95–96; Fain, ed., *Sanctified Trial*, 225–226, 237, 238 (fourth quotation).

10. Harwell, ed., *Kate*, 232; Fain, ed., *Sanctified Trial*, 227–228 (first quotation); Alice Williamson Diary, September 12, 1864, The Digital Scriptorium, Duke University, http://scripto rium.lib.duke.edu/williamson (accessed February 4, 2006); Snell, ed., *Myra Inman*, 285.

11. Charles T. Jones, ed., "Five Confederates: The Sons of Bolling Hall in the Civil War," *Alabama Historical Quarterly* 24 (winter 1962): 213; C. T. Hardman to wife, September 2, 1864, Hardman Family Letters, Civil War Soldiers' Letters, ADAH; John Q. Anderson, ed., *Campaigning with Parson's Texas Cavalry Brigade, C. S. A.* (Hillsboro, Tex.: Hill Junior College Press, 1967), 146; Richard Lowe, ed., *A Texas Cavalry Officer's Civil War: The Diary and Letters of James C. Bates* (Baton Rouge: Louisiana State Univ. Press, 1999), 316.

12. F. Jay Taylor, ed., *Reluctant Rebel: The Secret Diary of Robert Patrick, 1861–1865* (Baton Rouge: Louisiana State Univ. Press, 1959), 223–230; Jamison and McTigue, eds., *Letters and Recollections of a Confederate Soldier*, 130–131; Edward Noyes, ed., "Excerpts from the Civil War Diary of E. T. Eggleston," *Tennessee Historical Quarterly* 17 (December 1958): 349 (quotation). For other examples of soldiers who were much demoralized by the fall of Atlanta but continued to serve without giving up on the cause, see Lewis N. Wynne and Robert A. Taylor, eds., *This War So Horrible: The Civil War Diary of Hiram Smith Williams* (Tuscaloosa: Univ. of Alabama Press, 1993), 110–121; Ray Mathis, ed., *In the Land of the Living: Wartime Letters by Confederates from the Chattahoochee Valley of Alabama and Georgia* (Troy, Ala.: Troy State Univ. Press, 1981), 109.

13. On the concept of the Army of Tennessee soldiers drawing motivation, discipline, and spirit from each other throughout the war, see Larry J. Daniel, *Soldiering in the Army of Tennessee: A Portrait of Life in a Confederate Army* (Chapel Hill: Univ. of North Carolina Press, 1991), 11–22.

14. Richard M. McMurry, *Atlanta 1864: Last Chance for the Confederacy* (Lincoln: Univ. of Nebraska Press, 2000), 186–187; William E. Sykes to wife, September 4, 11, 1864, William E. Sykes Letters, Special Collections, Mitchell Memorial Library, Mississippi State University (hereafter cited as Special Collections, MSU); Mathis, ed., *In the Land of the Living*, 109; Norman D. Brown, ed., *One of Cleburne's Command: The Civil War Reminiscences and Diary of Captain Samuel T. Foster, Granbury's Texas Brigade, CSA.* (Austin: Univ. of Texas Press, 1980), 128–129.

15. John Bell Hood, *Advance and Retreat: Personal Experiences in the United States and Confederate States Armies* (Bloomington: Indiana Univ. Press, 1959), 181–228 (quotation 181); Joseph Branch O'Bryan to sisters, September 12, 1864, Joseph Branch O'Bryan Letters, Tennessee State Library and Archives, Nashville (hereafter cited as TSLA).

16. G. W. Athey to father, September 5, 1864, Athey Family Civil War Letters, ADAH; John H. Marshall to wife, September 5, 16, 1864, John H. Marshall Letters, Special Collections, MSU; William M. Cash and Lucy Somerville Howorth, eds., *My Dear Nellie: The Civil War Letters of William L. Nugent to Eleanor Smith Nugent* (Jackson: Univ. Press of Mississippi, 1977), 202–203; Mark K. Christ, ed., *Getting Used to Being Shot At: The Spence Family Civil War Letters* (Fayetteville: Univ. of Arkansas Press, 2002), 102–103; Wirt Armistead Cate, ed., *Two Soldiers: The Campaign Diaries of Thomas J. Key, C. S. A., and Robert J. Campbell, U. S. A.* (Chapel Hill: Univ. of North Carolina Press, 1938), 129; J. P. Cannon, *Bloody Banners and Barefoot Boys:*

A History of the 27th Regiment Alabama Infantry, C. S. A.: The Civil War Memoirs and Diaries of J. P. Cannon, M.D., comp. and ed. Noel Crowson and John V. Brogden (Shippensburg, Pa.: Burd Street Press, 1997), 94; Vicki Betts, ed., "The Civil War Letters of Elbridge Littlejohn," *Chronicles of Smith County, Texas* 18 (summer 1979): 29; Brown, ed., *One of Cleburne's Command*, 128–129; Mathis, ed., *In the Land of the Living*, 110.

17. Edward Norphlet Brown to Fannie, September 3, 1864, Edward Norphlet Brown Letters, ADAH; Thomas Warrick to Martha, September 5, 8, 1864, Thomas Warrick Papers, ADAH.

18. Castel, *Decision in the West*, 543–547; McMurry, *Atlanta 1864*, 190; Steven E. Woodworth, *Jefferson Davis and His Generals: The Failure of Confederate Command in the West* (Lawrence: Univ. Press of Kansas, 1990), 313. In his excellent study of the campaign Albert Castel argued that the fall of the city effectively crushed Confederate hopes. Richard McMurry offered a fundamentally similar thesis, particularly by connecting the Union capture of Atlanta to the northern reelection of Lincoln. Steven E. Woodworth stopped short of that but made a similar argument in different terms when he contended that the Atlanta campaign represented the Confederacy's last opportunity to demoralize the Union into giving up their war effort.

19. Connelly, *Autumn of Glory*, 469; Herman Hattaway and Archer Jones, *How the North Won: A Military History of the Civil War* (Urbana: Univ. of Illinois Press, 1991), 623–625; *Tuskegee South Western Baptist*, September 1, 1864.

20. E. H. Rennolds Diary, September–October entries, Special Collections, Hoskins Library, University of Tennessee, Knoxville (hereafter cited as Special Collections, University of Tennessee, Knoxville). See also Thomas Hopkins Deavenport Diary, September entries, Civil War Collection, TSLA; Mathis, ed., *In the Land of the Living*, 111; Thomas McGuire, *McGuire Papers, Containing Major Thomas McGuire's Civil War Letters; and Patriotic Documents and Other Letters from 1854 to the Turn of the Twentieth Century* (Tusquahoma, La.: Daughters of the American Revolution, 1966), 28–30; *Troy (Alabama) Southern Advertiser*, September 30, 1864.

21. Historian Richard McMurry estimated the Federal numbers advantage at approximately 1.35 to 1. See McMurry, *Atlanta 1864*, 181–182, 194–197.

22. Cash and Howorth, eds., *My Dear Nellie*, 203; Mathis, ed., *In the Land of the Living*, 110–111.

23. Castel, *Decision in the West*, 268–269, 477–479, 543–544; James M. McPherson, *Battle Cry of Freedom: The Civil War Era* (New York: Oxford Univ. Press, 1988), 716–721, 771–776; Larry E. Nelson, *Bullets, Ballots, and Rhetoric: Confederate Policy for the United States Presidential Contest of 1864* (University: Univ. of Alabama Press, 1980), 117–154.

24. Castel, *Decision in the West*, 268–269, 477–479, 543–544; McPherson, *Battle Cry of Freedom*, 716–721, 771–776; Nelson, *Bullets, Ballots, and Rhetoric*, 117–154.

25. George Peddy Cuttino, ed., *Saddle Bag and Spinning Wheel: Being the Civil War Letters of George W. Peddy, M. D., Surgeon, 56th Georgia Volunteers Regiment, C. S. A. and His Wife Kate Featherston Peddy* (Macon, Ga.: Mercer Univ. Press, 1981), 282; Taylor, ed., *Reluctant Rebel*, 223; Lucia R. Douglas, ed., *Douglas's Texas Battery, C. S. A.* (Tyler, Tex.: Smith County Historical Society, 1966), 128.

26. Cash and Howorth, eds., *My Dear Nellie*, 203–212; Cate, ed., *Two Soldiers*, 123, 133, 136; Mathis, ed., *In the Land of the Living*, 109–110; Wiliam E. Sykes to wife, September 27, 1864,

William E. Sykes Letters, Special Collections, MSU; *Troy (Alabama) Southern Advertiser,* October 14, 1864; George Phifer Erwin to sister, November 5, 1864, George Phifer Erwin Papers, SHC.

27. Lowe, ed., *A Texas Cavalry Officer's Civil War,* 325–326.

28. *Mobile Daily Advertiser and Register,* April 6, 1864.

29. Mathis, ed., *In the Land of the Living,* 109, 110 (first quotation); Douglas, ed., *Douglas's Texas Battery,* 142–143 (second quotation); Taylor, ed., *Reluctant Rebel,* 242 (third quotation).

30. John H. Marshall to wife, September 23, 1864, John H. Marshall Letters, Special Collections, MSU; Connelly, *Autumn of Glory,* 467–469; Castel, *Decision in the West,* 550–551.

31. For examples of these themes and evidence of mixed but improving morale, see Jesse P. Bates to wife, September 17, 1864, Jesse P. Bates Civil War Letters, 9th Texas Infantry File, Simpson History Complex, Hill College, Hillsboro, Texas (hereafter cited as Hill College); C. T. Hardman to wife, September 2, 1864, Hardman Family Letters, Civil War Soldiers' Letters, ADAH; Edward Norphlet Brown to Fannie, September 10, 1864, Edward Norphlet Brown Letters, ADAH; Mary M. Jones and Leslie J. Martin, eds., *The Gentle Rebel: The Civil War Letters of William Harvey Berryhill, Co. D, 43rd Regiment, Mississippi Volunteers* (Yazoo City, Miss.: Sassafras Press, 1982), 91–105; Daniel, *Soldiering in the Army of Tennessee,* 146; Cash and Howorth, eds., *My Dear Nellie,* 202–207; Cate, ed., *Two Soldiers,* 128–137; Mathis, ed., *In the Land of the Living,* 111; Jim R. Cabaniss, ed., *Civil War Journal and Letters of Washington Ives, 4th Fla. C. S. A.* (Tallahassee, Fla.: Jim Cabaniss, 1987), 73–74; Larry Wells Kennedy, "The Fighting Preacher of the Army of Tennessee: General Mark Perrin Lowrey" (Ph.D. diss., Mississippi State University, 1976), 83–97; Perry Wayne Shelton, comp., and Shelly Morrison, ed., *Personal Letters of General Lawrence Sullivan Ross, with Other Letters* (Austin, Tex.: Shelly and Richard Morrison, 1994), 66–68; Nathan Bedford Forrest to Richard Taylor, September 20, 1864, in United States War Department, *The War of the Rebellion: A Compilation of the Official Records of the Union and Confederate Armies,* 128 vols. (hereafter cited as *Official Records*) (Washington, D.C.: Government Printing Office, 1880–1901), ser. 1, vol. 39, pt. 2, 859; Hood to Braxton Bragg, September 21, 1864, *Official Records,* ser. 1, vol. 39, pt. 2, 860.

32. Robert A. Croxton to father, September 8, 1864, Croxton Letters, Civil War Soldiers' Letters, ADAH; Edward Norphlet Brown to Fannie, September 10, 1864, Edward Norphlet Brown Letters, ADAH; Cannon, *Bloody Banners and Barefoot Boys,* 94–95; Cuttino, ed., *Saddle Bag and Spinning Wheel,* 284.

33. Daniel, *Soldiering in the Army of Tennessee,* 20; Sam Watkins, *"Co. Aytch," Maury Grays, First Tennessee Regiment; or, a Side Show of the Big Show* (1882; reprint, Wilmington, N.C.: Broadfoot, 1987), 184–185; James M. Lanning Diary, September 26, 1864, ADAH; William Mebane Pollard Diary, page 7, Civil War Collection, TSLA; Craig L. Symonds, *Stonewall of the West: Patrick Cleburne and the Civil War* (Lawrence: Univ. Press of Kansas, 1997), 244; Woodworth, *Jefferson Davis and His Generals,* 290–294; James Marsh Morey Diary, September 26, 1864, TSLA; Mark K. Christ, ed., *Getting Used to Being Shot At: The Spence Family Civil War Letters* (Fayetteville: Univ. of Arkansas Press, 2002), 104 (quotation). See also note 34 below.

34. Thomas Warrick to Martha, September 25, 1864 (first quotation), Thomas Warrick Papers, ADAH; James Montgomery Lanning Diary, September 26–October 31, 1864, ADAH; Henry Watson to father and mother, September 23, 1864 (second quotation), Henry Watson Civil War Letters, 10th Texas Cavalry File, Hill College; Daniel, *Soldiering in the Army of*

Tennessee, 11–22; Taylor, ed., *Reluctant Rebel*, 228–230; Cannon, *Bloody Banners and Barefoot Boys*, 95–97; William Pitt Chambers, *Blood and Sacrifice: The Civil War Journal of a Confederate Soldier* (Huntington, W.Va.: Blue Acorn Press, 1994), 170; Cabaniss, ed., *Civil War Journal and Letters of Washington Ives*, 74; Douglas, ed., *Douglas's Texas Battery*, 136–137; Kennedy, "Fighting Preacher of the Army of Tennessee," 97.

35. Connelly, *Autumn of Glory*, 476–485; Hattaway and Jones, *How the North Won*, 629–634.

36. Jill K. Garrett, ed., *Confederate Diary of Robert D. Smith* (Columbia, Tenn.: Tennessee Division, United Daughters of the Confederacy, 1975), 74–76; William E. Sloan Diary, October 9, 1864, Civil War Collection, TSLA; Cuttino, ed., *Saddle Bag and Spinning Wheel*, 292; James Montgomery Lanning Diary, October 1, 3, 10, 20, 1864, ADAH; William C. Cross letter, October 3, 1864, Civil War Soldiers' Letters, ADAH; Douglas, ed., *Douglas's Texas Battery*, 140; Wynne and Taylor, eds., *This War So Horrible*, 114; Cabaniss, ed., *Civil War Journal and Letters of Washington Ives*, 74; McGuire, *McGuire Papers*, 30–33; Cash and Howorth, eds., *My Dear Nellie*, 213–216; Brown, ed., *One of Cleburne's Command*, 135–140.

37. Edward Norphlet Brown to Fannie, October 5, 6, 8, 1864, Edward Norphlet Brown Letters, ADAH.

38. Taylor, ed., *Reluctant Rebel*, 230–238.

39. Connelly, *Autumn of Glory*, 484–493; Daniel, *Soldiering in the Army of Tennessee*, 146–147; Hood, *Advance and Retreat*, 264–270; Andrew Haughton, *Training, Tactics, and Leadership in the Confederate Army of Tennessee: Seeds of Failure* (Brookfield, Vt.: Frank Cass, 2000), 173; James M. McPherson, *For Cause and Comrades: Why Men Fought in the Civil War* (New York: Oxford Univ. Press, 1997), 97; Nathaniel Cheairs Hughes Jr., *The Pride of the Confederate Artillery: The Washington Artillery in the Army of Tennessee* (Baton Rouge: Louisiana State Univ. Press, 1997), 223; Wiley Sword, *The Confederacy's Last Hurrah: Spring Hill, Franklin, and Nashville* (Lawrence: Univ. Press of Kansas, 1992), 1–5; Symonds, *Stonewall of the West*, 248–249; John R. Lundberg, *The Finishing Stroke: Texans in the 1864 Tennessee Campaign* (Abilene, Tex.: McWhiney Foundation Press, 2002), 68.

40. Daniel, *Soldiering in the Army of Tennessee*, 146–147; J. A. Bigger Diary, October 24, 1864, MDAH; John Crittenden to Bettie, October 22, 1864, John Crittenden Letters, Center for American History, University of Texas, Austin; D. G. Godwin to Miss Bettie, October 21, 1864, Civil War Collection, TSLA; Edward Norphlet Brown to Fannie, October 19, 21, 1864, Edward Norphlet Brown Letters, ADAH; E. H. Rennolds Diary, October 17, 20, 21, 1864, Special Collections, University of Tennessee, Knoxville; Shelton, comp., and Morrison, ed., *Personal Letters of General Lawrence Sullivan Ross*, 68–69; Watkins, "Co. Aytch," 196; Sam Davis Elliott, ed., *Doctor Quintard, Chaplain C. S. A. and Second Bishop of Tennessee* (Baton Rouge: Louisiana State Univ. Press, 2003), 161–166; Douglas, ed., *Douglas's Texas Battery*, 143–146.

41. Fain, ed., *Sanctified Trial*, 242 (quotation); Sarah Rousseau Espy Diary, October 1864 entries, ADAH; Robert H. Cartmell Diary, October 28, 1864, TSLA; Jason Niles Diary, October 21, 1864, SHC. See also Bryan, ed., "A Georgia Woman's Civil War Diary," 208–210; McWhiney, Moore, and Pace, eds., *Fear God and Walk Humbly*, 340–341.

42. Richard Taylor to James A. Seddon, October 28, 1864, *Official Records*, ser. 1, vol. 39, pt. 3, 860–863; Parrish, *Richard Taylor*, 418–421; Sam Harris to Braxton Bragg, September 7, 1864, *Official Records*, ser. 4, vol. 3, 645–648; Jefferson Davis to Charles Clark, October 17, 1864, *Official Records*, ser. 1, vol. 52, pt. 2, 762–763. See also note 41 above.

6. NOVEMBER–DECEMBER 1864: SUNSET AT FRANKLIN

1. Sarah Rousseau Espy Diary, November 1864 entries, Alabama Department of Archives and History, Montgomery (hereafter cited as ADAH); Grady McWhiney, Warner O. Moore Jr., and Robert F. Pace, eds., *Fear God and Walk Humbly: The Agricultural Journal of James Mallory, 1843–1877* (Tuscaloosa: Univ. of Alabama Press, 1997), 341–342; Richard Barksdale Harwell, ed., *Kate: The Journal of a Confederate Nurse* (Baton Rouge: Louisiana State Univ. Press, 1959), 235–237.

2. Nannie E. Haskins Diary, November 3, 1864, Nannie E. Haskins Papers, Tennessee State Library and Archives, Nashville (hereafter cited as TSLA).

3. Martha Tipton Diary, November 1864, Civil War Collection, TSLA.

4. Ibid.

5. Ibid.

6. John K. Bettersworth, ed., *Mississippi in the Confederacy*, vol. 1: *As They Saw It* (Baton Rouge: Louisiana State Univ. Press, 1961), 357; *Troy (Alabama) Southern Advertiser*, November 18, 1864; *Montgomery Daily Advertiser*, November 15, 1864.

7. Harwell, ed., *Kate*, 238; Jason Niles Diary, November 30, 1864, Southern Historical Collection, Wilson Library, University of North Carolina, Chapel Hill (hereafter cited as SHC).

8. *Meridian (Mississippi) Daily Clarion*, October 28, 1864; Gary W. Gallagher, *The Confederate War: How Popular Will, Nationalism, and Military Strategy Could Not Stave Off Defeat* (Cambridge: Harvard Univ. Press, 1997), 115–153.

9. Steven E. Woodworth and Kenneth J. Winkle, eds., *Atlas of the Civil War* (New York: Oxford Univ. Press, 2004), 272–273; James Lee McDonough and Thomas L. Connelly, *Five Tragic Hours: The Battle of Franklin* (Knoxville: Univ. of Tennessee Press, 1983), 16–18.

10. James Montgomery Lanning Diary, October 29, 31, 1864, ADAH; E. H. Rennolds Diary, October 31, 1864, Special Collections, Hoskins Library, University of Tennessee, Knoxville (hereafter cited as Special Collections, University of Tennessee, Knoxville); Lucia R. Douglas, ed., *Douglas's Texas Battery, C. S. A.* (Tyler, Tex.: Smith County Historical Society, 1966), 146; Norman D. Brown, ed., *One of Cleburne's Command: The Civil War Reminiscences and Diary of Captain Samuel T. Foster, Granbury's Texas Brigade, CSA.* (Austin: Univ. of Texas Press, 1980), 143; George Peddy Cuttino, ed., *Saddle Bag and Spinning Wheel: Being the Civil War Letters of George W. Peddy, M. D., Surgeon, 56th Georgia Volunteers Regiment, C. S. A. and His Wife Kate Featherston Peddy* (Macon, Ga.: Mercer Univ. Press, 1981), 294–295; Vicki Betts, ed., "The Civil War Letters of Elbridge Littlejohn," *Chronicles of Smith County, Texas* 18 (summer 1979): 31; Edward Noyes, ed., "Excerpts from the Civil War Diary of E. T. Eggleston," *Tennessee Historical Quarterly* 17 (December 1958): 353; Douglas John Cater, *As It Was: Reminiscences of a Soldier of the Third Texas Cavalry and the Nineteenth Louisiana Infantry* (Austin, Tex.: State House Press, 1990), 196–199; J. Cutler Andrews, *The South Reports the Civil War* (Princeton: Princeton Univ. Press, 1970), 473–474; H. E. Sterkx, *Partners in Rebellion: Alabama Women in the Civil War* (Rutherford, N.J.: Farleigh Dickinson Univ. Press, 1970), 57–58; Mark K. Christ, ed., *Getting Used to Being Shot At: The Spence Family Civil War Letters* (Fayetteville: Univ. of Arkansas Press, 2002), 111.

11. Enoch L. Mitchell, ed., "Letters of a Confederate Surgeon in the Army of Tennessee to His Wife," *Tennessee Historical Quarterly* 5 (June 1946): 173–175; Thomas McGuire, *McGuire*

Papers, Containing Major Thomas McGuire's Civil War Letters; and Patriotic Documents and Other Letters from 1854 to the Turn of the Twentieth Century (Tusquahoma, La.: Daughters of the American Revolution, 1966), 33–35; John Crittenden to Bettie, November 10, 1864, John Crittenden Letters, Center for American History, University of Texas, Austin (hereafter cited as CAH); Brown, ed., *One of Cleburne's Command,* 144; Betts, ed., "Civil War Letters of Elbridge Littlejohn," 31; Christ, ed., *Getting Used to Being Shot At,* 109–110.

12. Thomas Hopkins Deavenport Diary, November 1864, Civil War Collection, TSLA; E. H. Rennolds Diary, October 31, November 20, 1864, Special Collections, University of Tennessee, Knoxville; George Phifer Erwin to sister, November 5, 1864, George Phifer Erwin Papers, Southern Historical Collection, Wilson Library, University of North Carolina, Chapel Hill (hereafter cited as SHC); Christ, ed., *Getting Used to Being Shot At,* 107–112; Betts, ed., "Civil War Letters of Elbridge Littlejohn," 31; Wiley Sword, *The Confederacy's Last Hurrah: Spring Hill, Franklin, and Nashville* (Lawrence: Univ. Press of Kansas, 1993), 73.

13. E. H. Rennolds Diary, November 20, 1864, Special Collections, University of Tennessee, Knoxville; Thomas Hopkins Deavenport Diary, November 8, 1864, Civil War Collection, TSLA; Christ, ed., *Getting Used to Being Shot At,* 107–112; Mitchell, ed., "Letters of a Confederate Surgeon," 175–177; Samuel King Vann, *"Most Lovely Lizzie": Love Letters of a Young Confederate* (Birmingham, Ala.: Privately Printed, 1958), 60; McGuire, *McGuire Papers,* 35–38; Craig L. Symonds, *Stonewall of the West: Patrick Cleburne and the Civil War* (Lawrence: Univ. Press of Kansas, 1997), 248; R. Lockwood Tower, ed., *A Carolinian Goes to War: The Civil War Narrative of Arthur Middleton Manigault* (Columbia: Univ. of South Carolina Press, 1983), 278.

14. Edward Norphlet Brown to Fannie, November 10, 1864, Edward Norphlet Brown Letters, ADAH; Larry Wells Kennedy, "The Fighting Preacher of the Army of Tennessee: General Mark Perrin Lowrey" (Ph.D. diss., Mississippi State University, 1976), 99–102. For other examples of reservations about advancing into Tennessee or lower morale generally, see Andrew J. Fogle to Miss, November 18, 1864, Andrew J. Fogle Letters, 9th Texas Infantry File, Simpson History Complex, Hill College, Hillsboro, Texas (hereafter cited as Hill College); Mary M. Jones and Leslie J. Martin, eds., *The Gentle Rebel: The Civil War Letters of William Harvey Berryhill, Co. D, 43rd Regiment, Mississippi Volunteers* (Yazoo City, Miss.: Sassafras Press, 1982), 110–117; Hugh Ross Rodgers to wife, November 13, 1864, Hugh Ross Rodgers Letters, Civil War Miscellaneous Collection, United States Army Military History Institute, Carlisle, Pennsylvania (hereafter cited as USAMHI).

15. E. H. Rennolds Diary, November 20, 1864, Special Collections, University of Tennessee, Knoxville; James Montgomery Lanning Diary, November 25, 1864, ADAH; Sam Davis Elliott, ed., *Doctor Quintard, Chaplain C. S. A. and Second Bishop of Tennessee* (Baton Rouge: Louisiana State Univ. Press, 2003), 95; Wirt Armistead Cate, ed., *Two Soldiers: The Campaign Diaries of Thomas J. Key, C. S. A., and Robert J. Campbell, U. S. A.* (Chapel Hill: Univ. of North Carolina Press, 1938), 154–157; Jim R. Cabaniss, ed., *Civil War Journal and Letters of Washington Ives, 4th Fla. C. S. A.* (Tallahassee, Fla.: Jim Cabaniss, 1987), 15–16; Homer L. Kerr, ed., *Fighting with Ross' Texas Cavalry Brigade, C. S. A.: Diary of Lieut. George L. Griscom, Adjutant, 9th Texas Cavalry Regiment* (Hillsboro, Tex.: Hill Junior College Press, 1976), 190; James L. Nichols and Frank Abbott, eds., "Reminiscences of Confederate Service by Wiley A. Washburn," *Arkansas Historical Quarterly* 35 (spring 1976): 78–79; Thomas Lawrence Connelly, *Civil War Tennessee: Battles and Leaders* (Knoxville: Univ. of Tennessee Press, 1979), 87–89.

16. Noyes, ed., "Excerpts from the Civil War Diary of E. T. Eggleston," 354–355; H. E. Sterkx, ed., "Autobiography and Letters of Joel Dyer Murphree of Troy, Alabama, 1864–1865," *Alabama Historical Quarterly* 19 (spring 1957): 200–201; Brown, ed., *One of Cleburne's Command*, 145.

17. McDonough and Connelly, *Five Tragic Hours*, 34–44; Woodworth and Winkle, eds., *Atlas of the Civil War*, 272–273; Herman Hattaway and Archer Jones, *How the North Won: A Military History of the Civil War* (Urbana: Univ. of Illinois Press, 1991), 643–646.

18. McDonough and Connelly, *Five Tragic Hours*, 34–59; Woodworth and Winkle, eds., *Atlas of the Civil War*, 272–273; Claudius Wistar Sears Diary, November 30, 1864, Mississippi Department of Archives and History, Jackson (hereafter cited as MDAH); J. P. Cannon, *Bloody Banners and Barefoot Boys: A History of the 27th Regiment Alabama Infantry, C. S. A.: The Civil War Memoirs and Diaries of J. P. Cannon, M.D.*, comp. and ed. Noel Crowson and John V. Brogden (Shippensburg, Pa.: Burd Street Press, 1997), 98.

19. For the definitive account of the Spring Hill Affair, see McDonough and Connelly, *Five Tragic Hours*, 36–59. For an excellent historiographical summary of the Tennessee campaign and Hood's motives, see John D. Fowler, "'The Finishing Stroke to the Independence of the Southern Confederacy': Perceptions of Hood's Tennessee Campaign," *Tennessee Historical Quarterly* 64 (fall 2005): 216–235.

20. Nannie E. Haskins Diary, November 30, 1864, Nannie E. Haskins Papers, TSLA; Woodworth and Winkle, eds., *Atlas of the Civil War*, 272–273.

21. McDonough and Connelly, *Five Tragic Hours*, 3, 60–64; Woodworth and Winkle, eds., *Atlas of the Civil War*, 272–273; Hattaway and Jones, *How the North Won*, 646–647. For a vivid first-person description of the advance, see M. H. Dixon Diary, November 30, 1864, Civil War Collection, TSLA.

22. Thomas Lawrence Connelly, *Autumn of Glory: The Army of Tennessee, 1862–1865* (Baton Rouge: Louisiana State Univ. Press, 1971), 503–504; McDonough and Connelly, *Five Tragic Hours*, 63–78; James M. McPherson, *Battle Cry of Freedom: The Civil War Era* (New York: Oxford Univ. Press, 1988), 812–813; Fowler, "The Finishing Stroke," 227–229.

23. Vann, *"Most Lovely Lizzie,"* 64–65; Connelly and McDonough, *Five Tragic Hours*, 158–160.

24. Vann, *"Most Lovely Lizzie,"* 64 (first quotation); Edward Norphlet Brown to Fannie, December 1, 1864 (second quotation), Edward Norphlet Brown Letters, ADAH; E. H. Rennolds Diary, November 30, December 1, 1864, Special Collections, University of Tennessee, Knoxville; Claudius Wistar Sears Diary, December 1, 1864, MDAH; James Marsh Morey Diary, December 1, 1864, James Marsh Morey Papers, TSLA; M. D. L. Stephens Manuscript, Department of Archives and Special Collections, University of Mississippi Libraries, Oxford; James Montgomery Lanning Diary, November 30, December 1, 1864, ADAH; Robert Franklin Bunting Papers, December 7, 1864, CAH; Hugh Ross Rodgers to wife and children, December 6, 1864, Hugh Ross Rodgers Letters, USAMHI; W. J. Watson Diary, December 15, 16, 1864, SHC.

For published wartime accounts, see Brown, ed., *One of Cleburne's Command*, 150; Elliott, ed., *Doctor Quintard*, 99; Cate, ed., *Two Soldiers*, 159–160; Cannon, *Bloody Banners and Barefoot Boys*, 99–101; Cabaniss, ed., *Civil War Journal and Letters of Washington Ives*, 17; Noyes, ed., "Excerpts from the Civil War Diary of E. T. Eggleston," 355; Jones and Martin, eds., *Gentle Rebel*, 119; Henry McCall Holmes, *Diary of Henry McCall Holmes: Army of Tennessee, Assistant Surgeon, Florida Troops, with Related Letters, Documents, etc.* (State College, Miss.: n.p., 1968), 23; Kerr, ed., *Fighting With Ross' Texas Cavalry Brigade*, 192.

25. Thomas Smyrl to Mary Jane Smyrl, December 7, 1864, Thomas Smyrl Letters, ADAH; Edward Norphlet Brown to Fannie, December 10, 1864, Edward Norphlet Brown Letters, ADAH; Connelly, *Autumn of Glory*, 506.

26. Brown, ed., *One of Cleburne's Command*, 150–151.

27. T. T. Dew to Winter Goodloe, August 20, 1904 (first quotation), T. T. Dew Letters, Civil War Miscellaneous Collection, USAMHI; William T. Alderson, ed., "The Civil War Reminiscences of John Johnston, 1861–1865," *Tennessee Historical Quarterly* 14 (March 1955): 77 (second quotation); William T. Alderson, ed., "The Civil War Diary of Captain James Litton Cooper, September 30, 1861, to January 1865," *Tennessee Historical Quarterly* 15 (June 1956): 166 (Cooper's "diary" was written from memory immediately after the war.); Sam Watkins, "*Co. Aytch*," *Maury Grays, First Tennessee Regiment; or, a Side Show of the Big Show* (1882; reprint, Wilmington, N.C.: Broadfoot, 1987), 201–206; Cater, *As It Was*, 200–201; Daniel E. Sutherland, ed., *Reminiscences of a Private: William E. Bevens of the First Arkansas Infantry, C. S. A.* (Fayetteville: Univ. of Arkansas Press, 1992), 209–213; Royce Shingleton, ed., "With Loyalty and Honor as a Patriot: Recollections of a Confederate Soldier," *Alabama Historical Quarterly* 33 (fall and winter 1971): 256–257; Edward Young McMorries, *History of the First Regiment Alabama Volunteers, C. S. A.* (Montgomery, Ala.: Brown Print Company, 1904), 87–93; William Milner Kelly, "A History of the Thirtieth Alabama Volunteers (Infantry) Confederate States Army," *Alabama Historical Quarterly* 9 (spring 1947): 160–163; Russell B. Bailey, ed., "Reminiscences of the Civil War by T. J. Walker," *Confederate Chronicles of Tennessee* 1 (1986): 69–70; Fred A. Bailey, *Class and Tennessee's Confederate Generation* (Chapel Hill: Univ. of North Carolina Press, 1987), 92–103.

28. McDonough and Connelly, *Five Tragic Hours*, 3; Hattaway and Jones, *How the North Won*, 647.

29. Jason Phillips has concluded that soldiers attempted to protect their loved ones from the truth by presenting a more positive account of the Confederate condition after the battle in letters than what they described in their diaries. However, Phillips cites *different* Confederate soldiers for the two diaries and two letters in question, and the sources cited throughout this study indicate no meaningful difference between diary accounts and letter accounts of the Battle of Franklin. (Jason Phillips, *Diehard Rebels: The Confederate Culture of Invincibility* [Athens: Univ. of Georgia Press, 2007], 113–114.)

30. Connelly, *Autumn of Glory*, 506–509; Fowler, "The Finishing Stroke," 229.

31. Mary L. Pearre Diary, December 16, 1864, Special Collections, University of Tennessee, Knoxville; Edward Norphlet Brown to Fannie, December 10, 1864, Edward Norphlet Brown Letters, ADAH; Nannie E. Haskins Diary, December 5, 18, 1864, Nannie E. Haskins Papers, TSLA.

32. Connelly, *Autumn of Glory*, 509–512; Woodworth and Winkle, eds., *Atlas of the Civil War*, 282–283. For the Schofield anecdote, see Phillips, *Diehard Rebels*, 115.

33. For a survey of soldier accounts of the Confederate retreat from Nashville, see William Dudley Gale to wife, January 19, 1865, William Dudley Gale Letters, Civil War Collection, TSLA; Stephen A. Jordan Diary, December 16, 1864, Civil War Collection, TSLA; E. H. Rennolds Diary, December 16–31, 1864, Special Collections, University of Tennessee, Knoxville; James H. Finch Diary, December 14, 1864, ADAH; James Marsh Morey Diary, December 19, 1864, James Marsh Morey Papers, TSLA; James Montgomery Lanning Diary, December 16, 18, 19, 1864, ADAH; Avington Wayne Simpson Diary, December 1864–January 1865 entries,

SHC; Brown, ed., *One of Cleburne's Command*, 153–161; Elliott, ed., *Doctor Quintard*, 106–111; Watkins, *'Co. Aytch,'* 208–210; Cannon, *Bloody Banners and Barefoot Boys*, 103–106; Cabaniss, ed., *Civil War Journal and Letters of Washington Ives*, 19; Noyes, ed., "Excerpts from the Civil War Diary of E. T. Eggleston," 356; Cate, ed., *Two Soldiers*, 170–173.

34. Several versions of the song exist. This version is taken from Clement Eaton, *A History of the Southern Confederacy* (New York: Macmillan, 1954), 282.

35. For numbers and material condition of the army, see Connelly, *Autumn of Glory*, 512–514. For specific numbers, including further losses and reinforcements, see Sword, *The Confederacy's Last Hurrah*, 426.

36. Edward Norphlet Brown to Fannie, December 24, 1864, Edward Norphlet Brown Letters, ADAH; James H. Finch Diary, December 24, 25, 1864, ADAH; Alfred Tyler Fielder Diary, December 19, 25, 26, 28, 29, 31, 1864, TSLA; Noyes, ed., "Excerpts from the Civil War Diary of E. T. Eggleston," 356–358; Claudius Wistar Sears Diary, December 15, 21, 1864, MDAH. For very similar assessments after Franklin and Nashville, see Elliott, ed., *Doctor Quintard*, 206–209; Cuttino, ed., *Saddle Bag and Spinning Wheel*, 296–297; William Pitt Chambers, *Blood and Sacrifice: The Civil War Journal of a Confederate Soldier* (Huntington, W.Va.: Blue Acorn Press, 1994), 184–186; F. Jay Taylor, ed., *Reluctant Rebel: The Secret Diary of Robert Patrick, 1861–1865* (Baton Rouge: Louisiana State Univ. Press, 1959), 248–249; Sutherland, ed., *Reminiscences of a Private*, 219–229; Holmes, *Diary of Henry McCall Holmes*, 25–27; John S. Kendall, ed., "The Diary of Surgeon Craig, Fourth Louisiana Regiment, C. S. A., 1864–1865," *Louisiana Historical Quarterly* 8 (spring 1925): 61–62; Sterkx, ed., "Autobiography and Letters of Joel Dyer Murphree," 201–202.

37. Joseph Branch O'Bryan letters to sisters, December 16, 1864, to January 4, 1865, O'Bryan Letters, TSLA.

38. Sarah Rousseau Espy Diary, December 14, 25, 31,1864, ADAH.

39. Nannie E. Haskins Diary, December 25, 1864, Nannie E. Haskins Papers, TSLA; Nimrod Porter Diary, December 14, 17, 18, 19, 24, 27, 31, 1864, Civil War Collection, TSLA. See also Rachel Carter Craighead Diary, December 1864 entries, TSLA; Stephen V. Ash, *When the Yankees Came: Conflict and Chaos in the Occupied South, 1861–1865* (Chapel Hill: Univ. of North Carolina Press, 1995), 215–225; Stephen V. Ash, *Middle Tennessee Society Transformed: 1860–1870* (Baton Rouge: Louisiana State Univ. Press, 1988), 167–168.

40. Harwell, ed., *Kate*, 245–246; Robert H. Cartmell Diary, December 6, 9, 1864, TSLA.

41. Fowler, "The Finishing Stroke," 231–233.

42. Anne J. Bailey, *The Chessboard of War: Sherman and Hood in the Autumn Campaigns of 1864* (Lincoln: Univ. of Nebraska Press, 2000), xii, 110, 169–181; Anne J. Bailey, *War and Ruin: William T. Sherman and the Savannah Campaign* (Wilmington, Del.: Scholarly Resources, 2003), 123–124; Andrews, *The South Reports the Civil War*, 468–491; Jacqueline Glass Campbell, *When Sherman Marched North From the Sea: Resistance on the Confederate Home Front* (Chapel Hill: Univ. of North Carolina Press, 2003), 36; Marli F. Weiner, ed., *A Heritage of Woe: The Civil War Diary of Grace Brown Elmore, 1861–1868* (Athens: Univ. of Georgia Press, 1997), 80, 85, 95–96, 110; Beth G. Crabtree and James W. Patton, eds., *"Journal of a Secesh Lady": The Diary of Catherine Ann Devereux Edmondston, 1860–1866* (Raleigh: North Carolina Division of Archives, 1979), 634–653, especially 648; John F. Marszalek, ed., *The Diary of Miss Emma Holmes, 1861–1866* (Baton Rouge: Louisiana State Univ. Press, 1979), 381, 385, 387, 390,

394–395; Robert Manson Myers, ed., *The Children of Pride: A True Story of Georgia and the Civil War* (New Haven, Conn.: Yale Univ. Press, 1972), 1213, 1216, 1245; William B. Styple, ed., *Writing and Fighting the Confederate War: The Letters of Peter Wellington Alexander, Confederate War Correspondent* (Kearny, N.J.: Belle Grove, 2002), 266 (quotation).

43. Campbell, *When Sherman Marched North*, 6, 25–26, 38, 59, 69–74, 91–92; Lisa Tendrich Frank, "To 'Cure Her of Her Pride and Boasting': The Gendered Implications of Sherman's March" (Ph.D. diss., University of Florida, 2001), 214–257; Lee Kennett, *Marching Through Georgia: The Story of Soldiers and Civilians During Sherman's Campaign* (New York: Perennial, 2001), 298–315. Charles Royster considers Sherman's March more successful in destroying Confederate morale, but also recognizes the importance of Confederate defeats at Franklin and Nashville to Sherman's success. See Charles Royster, *The Destructive War: William Tecumseh Sherman, Stonewall Jackson, and the Americans* (New York: Vintage Books, First Vintage Civil War Library Edition, 1993), 327–361.

44. Bettersworth and Silver, eds., *Mississippi in the Confederacy*, 2:182.

45. "Sunset at Franklin," poem by Robert Burns Mayes, Civil War Collection, reel 1, box 2, folder 9, TSLA.

7. JANUARY–FEBRUARY 1865: "WE CAN CERTAINLY LIVE WITHOUT NEGROS BETTER THAN WITH YANKEES"

1. Cora E. Watson Diary, January 1, 1865, Cora E. Watson Carey Papers, Mississippi Department of Archives and History, Jackson (hereafter cited as MDAH). Excerpts of Watson's diary are published in Robert Milton Winter, ed., *Civil War Women: The Diaries of Belle Strickland and Cora Harris Watson: Holly Springs, Mississippi, July 25, 1864–June 22, 1868* (Lafayette, Calif.: Thomas Berryhill, 2001).

2. John W. Talley to Jefferson Davis, February 9, 1865, in United States War Department, *The War of the Rebellion: A Compilation of the Official Records of the Union and Confederate Armies*, 128 vols. (hereafter cited as *Official Records*) (Washington, D.C.: Government Printing Office, 1880–1901), ser. 1, vol. 49, pt. 1, 966–967 (first quotation); T. Michael Parrish, *Richard Taylor: Soldier Prince of Dixie* (Chapel Hill: Univ. of North Carolina Press, 1992), 431 (second quotation); Malcolm Cook McMillan, *The Disintegration of a Confederate State: Three Governors and Alabama's Wartime Home Front, 1861–1865* (Macon, Ga.: Mercer Univ. Press, 1986), 116–136. For more on increasing defeatism in one southern city, see William Warren Rogers Jr., *Confederate Home Front: Montgomery during the Civil War* (Tuscaloosa: Univ. of Alabama Press, 1999), 126–144.

3. Cora E. Watson Diary, January 7, 24, February 3, 1865, Cora E. Watson Carey Papers, MDAH; Amanda Worthington Diary, January 11, 26, 1865, Worthington Family Papers, MDAH; Sarah Rousseau Espy Diary, January–February 1865 entries, Alabama Department of Archives and History, Montgomery (hereafter cited as ADAH).

4. Daniel E. Sutherland, ed., *A Very Violent Rebel: The Civil War Diary of Ellen Renshaw House* (Knoxville: Univ. of Tennessee Press, 1996), 139–150.

5. Nimrod Porter Diary, February 19, 22, 1865, Civil War Collection, Tennessee State Library and Archives, Nashville (hereafter cited as TSLA).

6. Grady McWhiney, Warner O. Moore Jr., and Robert F. Pace, eds., *Fear God and Walk Humbly: The Agricultural Journal of James Mallory, 1843-1877* (Tuscaloosa: Univ. of Alabama Press, 1997), 346; E. Grey Dimond and Herman Hattaway, eds., *Letters from Forest Place: A Plantation Family's Correspondence, 1846-1881* (Jackson: Univ. Press of Mississippi, 1993), 329-330.

7. Margaret Josephine Miles Gillis Diary, January 22, 1865, ADAH; Robert H. Cartmell Diary, January 8, 9, 1865, Robert H. Cartmell Papers, TSLA; Richard Barksdale Harwell, ed., *Kate: The Journal of a Confederate Nurse* (Baton Rouge: Louisiana State Univ. Press, 1959), 256. See also Cora E. Watson Diary, January 13, 1865, Cora E. Watson Carey Papers, MDAH.

8. Craig L. Symonds, *Joseph E. Johnston: A Civil War Biography* (New York: Norton, 1992), 340-344; Parrish, *Richard Taylor*, 430; Richard M. McMurry, *John Bell Hood and the War for Southern Independence* (Lexington: Univ. Press of Kentucky, 1982), 182.

9. Charles Roberts to wife, January 7, 1865, Charles Roberts Collection, Department of Archives and Special Collections, University of Mississippi Libraries, Oxford.

10. Joseph Branch O'Bryan to sisters, January 20, 1865, Joseph Branch O'Bryan Letters, TSLA; Alfred Tyler Fielder Diary, March 2, 1865, TSLA; Wirt Armistead Cate, ed., *Two Soldiers: The Campaign Diaries of Thomas J. Key, C. S. A., and Robert J. Campbell, U. S. A.* (Chapel Hill: Univ. of North Carolina Press, 1938), 181; Sam Davis Elliott, ed., *Doctor Quintard, Chaplain C. S. A. and Second Bishop of Tennessee* (Baton Rouge: Louisiana State Univ. Press, 2003), 213-219; Thomas McGuire, *McGuire Papers: Containing Major Thomas McGuire's Civil War Letters; and Patriotic Documents and Other Letters from 1854 to the Turn of the Twentieth Century* (Tusquahoma, La.: Daughters of the American Revolution, 1966), 39-41; William M. Cash and Lucy Somerville Howorth, eds., *My Dear Nellie: The Civil War Letters of William L. Nugent to Eleanor Smith Nugent* (Jackson: Univ. Press of Mississippi, 1977), 233-234; Ann K. Blomquist and Robert A. Taylor, eds., *This Cruel War: The Civil War Letters of Grant and Malinda Taylor, 1862-1865* (Macon, Ga.: Mercer Univ. Press, 2000), 324; Vicki Betts, ed., "The Civil War Letters of Elbridge Littlejohn," *Chronicles of Smith County, Texas* 18 (summer 1979): 33; Nathaniel Cheairs Hughes Jr., *The Pride of the Confederate Artillery: The Washington Artillery in the Army of Tennessee* (Baton Rouge: Louisiana State Univ. Press, 1997), 263; Phil Gottschalk, *In Deadly Earnest: The History of the First Missouri Brigade, C. S. A.* (Columbia: Missouri River Press, 1991), 507; William Milner Kelly, "A History of the Thirtieth Alabama Volunteers (Infantry) Confederate States Army," *Alabama Historical Quarterly* 9 (spring 1947): 164; Edmund Harrison to Jefferson Davis, January 14, 1865, *Official Records*, ser. 1, vol. 45, pt. 2, 784.

11. Thomas Lawrence Connelly, *Autumn of Glory: The Army of Tennessee, 1862-1865* (Baton Rouge: Louisiana State Univ. Press, 1971), 514-522; Parrish, *Richard Taylor*, 427-433; Mark Grimsley and Brooks D. Simpson, eds., *The Collapse of the Confederacy* (Lincoln: Univ. of Nebraska Press, 2001), 6-7; Herman Hattaway and Archer Jones, *How the North Won: A Military History of the Civil War* (Urbana: Univ. of Illinois Press, 1991), 656; Wiley Sword, *The Confederacy's Last Hurrah: Spring Hill, Franklin, and Nashville* (Lawrence: Univ. Press of Kansas, 1993), 426.

12. Nathan Bedford Forrest to Richard Taylor, January 2, 1865, *Official Records*, ser. 1, vol. 45, pt. 2, 756-757; Parrish, *Richard Taylor*, 427-433, 428 (quotation).

13. James Montgomery Lanning Diary, February 7, 1865, ADAH; Cash and Howorth, eds., *My Dear Nellie*, 234; John Q. Anderson, ed., *Campaigning with Parson's Texas Cavalry Brigade, C. S. A.* (Hillsboro, Tex.: Hill Junior College Press, 1967), 155; McGuire, *McGuire Papers*, 39-41; Joseph Branch O'Bryan to sisters, February 24, 1865, Joseph Branch O'Bryan Letters, TSLA; George

Phifer Erwin to sister, January 7, January 25, 1865, George Phifer Erwin Papers, Southern Historical Collection, Wilson Library, University of North Carolina, Chapel Hill (hereafter cited as SHC).

14. William Pitt Chambers, *Blood and Sacrifice: The Civil War Journal of a Confederate Soldier* (Huntington, W.Va.: Blue Acorn Press, 1994), 189–205; Charles Roberts to wife, January 24, 1865, Charles Roberts Collection, Special Collections, University of Mississippi Libraries; Edward Norphlet Brown to Fannie, January 1, 1865, Edward Norphlet Brown Letters, ADAH; James H. Finch Diary, January 1, 1865, ADAH; Joseph Branch O'Bryan to sisters, January 20, 1865, Joseph Branch O'Bryan Letters, TSLA; Alfred Tyler Fielder Diary, January 4, February 1, 22, 25, 1865, TSLA; D. D. Saunders to Dr. Pollard, February 5, 1865, S. A. Stout Letters, Civil War Soldiers' Letters, ADAH; Elliott, ed., *Doctor Quintard*, 114, 120, 213–214, 244; Cate, ed., *Two Soldiers*, 176–193; Blomquist and Taylor, eds., *This Cruel War*, 321–327; George Peddy Cuttino, ed., *Saddle Bag and Spinning Wheel: Being the Civil War Letters of George W. Peddy, M. D., Surgeon, 56th Georgia Volunteers Regiment, C. S. A. and His Wife Kate Featherston Peddy* (Macon, Ga.: Mercer Univ. Press, 1981), 298–304; Lucia R. Douglas, ed., *Douglas's Texas Battery, C. S. A.* (Tyler, Tex.: Smith County Historical Society, 1966), 151–156; F. Jay Taylor, ed., *Reluctant Rebel: The Secret Diary of Robert Patrick, 1861–1865* (Baton Rouge: Louisiana State Univ. Press, 1959), 250–253; Vera Dockery Elkins, ed., *Letters from a Civil War Soldier* (New York: Vantage Press, 1969), 55–57; William T. Alderson, ed., "The Civil War Diary of Captain James Litton Cooper, September 30, 1861, to January 1865," *Tennessee Historical Quarterly* 15 (June 1956): 171; Gottschalk, *In Deadly Earnest*, 499–513.

15. Joseph Branch O'Bryan to sisters, February 25, 1865, Joseph Branch O'Bryan Letters, TSLA; Betts, ed., "Letters of Elbridge Littlejohn," 34; Ray Mathis, ed., *In the Land of the Living: Wartime Letters by Confederates from the Chattahoochee Valley of Alabama and Georgia* (Troy, Ala.: Troy State Univ. Press, 1981), 122; Hughes, *Pride of the Confederate Artillery*, 263–264; Judy Watson McClure, ed., *Confederate From East Texas: The Civil War Letters of James Monroe Watson* (Quanah, Tex.: Nortex Press, 1976), 30–32; John Kent Folmar, ed., *From That Terrible Field: Civil War Letters of James M. Williams, Twenty-First Alabama Infantry Volunteers* (University: Univ. of Alabama Press, 1981), 154; Cate, ed., *Two Soldiers*, 185; Blomquist and Taylor, eds., *This Cruel War*, 326–328; John S. Kendall, ed., "The Diary of Surgeon Craig, Fourth Louisiana Regiment, C. S. A., 1864–1865," *Louisiana Historical Quarterly* 8 (spring 1925): 63.

16. John H. Marshall to wife, February 9, 12, 17, 23, 1865, John H. Marshall Letters, Special Collections Department, Mitchell Memorial Library, Mississippi State University, Starkville.

17. Joseph Branch O'Bryan to sisters, February 24, 1865, Joseph Branch O'Bryan Letters, TSLA; Chambers, *Blood and Sacrifice*, 204; Cuttino, ed., *Saddle Bag and Spinning Wheel*, 300–301; William McCole to S. A. Stout, March 7, 1865, S. A. Stout Letters, Civil War Soldiers' Letters, ADAH. See also, Douglas, ed., *Douglas's Texas Battery*, 151–152; James Montgomery Lanning Diary, February 7, 1865, ADAH; Cash and Howorth, eds., *My Dear Nellie*, 234; Anderson, ed., *Campaigning with Parson's Texas Cavalry*, 155; Charles Roberts to wife, December 24, 1864, Charles Roberts Collection, Special Collections, University of Mississippi Libraries.

18. McGuire, *McGuire Papers*, 39–41; Richard Taylor, *Destruction and Reconstruction: Personal Experiences in the Late War* (New York: D. Appleton and Company, 1879), 218.

19. James M. McPherson, *Battle Cry of Freedom: The Civil War Era* (New York: Oxford Univ. Press, 1988), 821–825; Emory M. Thomas, *The Confederate Nation, 1861–1865* (New York:

Harper and Row, 1979), 294–295; George C. Rable, *Confederate Republic: A Revolution Against Politics* (Chapel Hill: Univ. of North Carolina Press, 1994), 292; William J. Cooper Jr., *Jefferson Davis, American* (New York: Knopf, 2000), 510–513.

20. Paul D. Escott, *After Secession: Jefferson Davis and the Failure of Confederate Nationalism* (Baton Rouge: Louisiana State Univ. Press, 1978), 221–224; Charles W. Sanders Jr., "Jefferson Davis and the Hampton Roads Peace Conference: 'To Secure Peace to the Two Countries.'" *Journal of Southern History* 63 (November 1997): 803–826; Steven E. Woodworth, "The Last Function of Government: Confederate Collapse and Negotiated Peace," in Grimsley and Simpson, eds., *Collapse of the Confederacy*, 29–39.

21. Mathis, ed., *In the Land of the Living*, 121; Cora E. Watson Diary, February 13, 1865, Cora E. Watson Carey Papers, MDAH; Cate, ed., *Two Soldiers*, 195; McClure, ed., *Confederate From East Texas*, 30–32; McWhiney, Moore, and Pace, eds., *Fear God and Walk Humbly*, 346 (quotations); Rogers, *Confederate Home Front*, 136; Harwell, ed., *Kate*, 254; Avington Wayne Simpson Diary, February 17, 1865, SHC.

22. Sutherland, ed., *A Very Violent Rebel*, 142–146; Robert Franklin Bunting to the editor of the Houston *Telegraph*, February 17, 1865, Robert Franklin Bunting Papers, Center for American History, University of Texas, Austin (hereafter cited as CAH).

23. Thomas, *Confederate Nation*, 290–297; McPherson, *Battle Cry of Freedom*, 831–838; Philip D. Dillard, "'What Price Must We Pay for Victory?': Views on Arming Slaves from Lynchburg, Virginia, to Galveston, Texas," in *Inside the Confederate Nation: Essays in Honor of Emory M. Thomas*, ed. Lesley J. Gordon and John C. Inscoe, 316–331 (Baton Rouge: Louisiana State Univ. Press, 2005). For a discussion of the number of slaves and free blacks who entered Confederate military service in early 1865, see Bruce Levine, *Confederate Emancipation: Southern Plans to Free and Arm Slaves During the Civil War* (New York: Oxford Univ. Press, 2006), 125–127.

24. Major General Patrick Cleburne's Memorial to the Officers of the Army of Tennessee, January 2, 1864, *Official Records*, ser. 1, vol. 52, pt. 2, 586–592; McPherson, *Battle Cry of Freedom*, 832–833; Craig L. Symonds, *Stonewall of the West: Patrick Cleburne and the Civil War* (Lawrence: Univ. Press of Kansas, 1997), 183–191; Levine, *Confederate Emancipation*, 1–5, 16–39.

25. For various officers' responses to Cleburne's proposal, see *Official Records*, ser. 1, vol. 52, pt. 2, 595–609; Symonds, *Stonewall of the West*, 183–191; Escott, *After Secession*, 242–244.

26. Chambers, *Blood and Sacrifice*, 203; Blomquist and Taylor, eds., *This Cruel War*, 322; Rogers, *Confederate Home Front*, 137; Cash and Howorth, eds., *My Dear Nellie*, 228; Betts, ed., "Civil War Letters of Elbridge Littlejohn," 33; McPherson, *Battle Cry of Freedom*, 831–838; Escott, *After Secession*, 242–251; *Montgomery Daily Advertiser*, January 3, 1865; J. Cutler Andrews, *The South Reports the Civil War* (Princeton: Princeton Univ. Press, 1970), 483.

27. *Troy (Alabama) Southern Advertiser*, February 3, 1865; *Meridian (Mississippi) Daily Clarion*, January 18, 28, 1865; Jason Phillips, *Diehard Rebels: The Confederate Culture of Invincibility* (Athens: Univ. of Georgia Press, 2007), see chapter 4, especially 134–146. One Confederate soldier described the rumors of foreign intervention as "base" rumors. See Taylor, ed., *Reluctant Rebel*, 250. For additional examples of western Confederates rejecting rumors or consciously attempting to avoid allowing various rumors to shape their morale, see Robert W. Fort to father, April 1, 1864, Craft-Fort Papers, Department of Archives and Special Collections, University of Mississippi, Oxford (hereafter cited as University of Mississippi Archives); Harwell, ed., *Kate*, 245; John N. Fain, ed., *Sanctified Trial: The Diary of Eliza Rhea Anderson*

Fain, a Confederate Woman in East Tennessee (Knoxville: Univ. of Tennessee Press, 2004), 256, 261; Sutherland, ed., *A Very Violent Rebel*, 96–108.

28. Robert Franklin Bunting to the editor of the Houston *Telegraph,* February 17, 1865 (first and second quotations), Robert Franklin Bunting Papers, CAH; Cora E. Watson Diary, February 7, 1865 (third quotation), Cora E. Watson Carey Papers, MDAH; J. H. Stringfellow to Jefferson Davis, February 8, 1865, *Official Records,* ser. 4, vol. 3, 1067–1070; Taylor Beatty Diary, January 16, 1865, Taylor Beatty Papers, SHC.

29. For similar conclusions from an excellent recent study of wartime Virginia, see Aaron Sheehan-Dean, *Why Confederates Fought: Family and Nation in Civil War Virginia* (Chapel Hill: Univ. of North Carolina Press, 2007), especially 2, 98–100, 113, 184–187.

30. James A. Carpenter, ed., "James D. Lynch in War and Peace," *Alabama Historical Quarterly* 20 (spring 1958): 81.

31. Joseph Branch O'Bryan to sisters, January 20, 1865, Joseph Branch O'Bryan Letters, TSLA; McClure, ed., *Confederate From East Texas,* 30–32; Taylor Beatty Diary, January 16, 1865 (third quotation), Taylor Beatty Papers, SHC.

32. Sheehan-Dean, *Why Confederates Fought,* 184–187 (quotation 185); Dillard, "What Price Must We Pay for Victory?" 316–331, (quotation 328). See also Phillip D. Dillard, "Independence or Slavery: The Confederate Debate over Arming the Slaves" (Ph.D. diss., Rice University, 1999).

33. Levine, *Confederate Emancipation,* 14–15, 89–110 (quotation page 109); Escott, *After Secession,* 241–255. An earlier volume was primarily a collection of documents. See Robert F. Durden, ed., *The Gray and the Black: The Confederate Debate on Emancipation* (Baton Rouge: Louisiana State Univ. Press, 1972).

34. Levine, *Confederate Emancipation,* 115–117.

35. Quotation taken from Emory Thomas, "Reckoning with Rebels," in Harry P. Owens and James J. Cooke, eds., *The Old South in the Crucible of War* (Jackson: Univ. Press of Mississippi, 1983), 12.

8. MARCH–APRIL 1865 AND CONCLUSION

1. Robert H. Cartmell Diary, March 1, 1865, Robert H. Cartmell Papers, Tennessee State Library and Archives, Nashville (hereafter cited as TSLA).

2. Herman Hattaway and Archer Jones, *How the North Won: A Military History of the Civil War* (Urbana: Univ. of Illinois Press, 1991), 658–676; Steven E. Woodworth and Kenneth J. Winkle, eds., *Atlas of the Civil War* (New York: Oxford Univ. Press, 2004), 302–303, 316–327; Thomas Lawrence Connelly, *Autumn of Glory: The Army of Tennessee, 1862–1865* (Baton Rouge: Louisiana State Univ. Press, 1971), 520–535; T. Michael Parrish, *Richard Taylor: Soldier Prince of Dixie* (Chapel Hill: Univ. of North Carolina Press, 1992), 433–441; Robert L. Kerby, *Kirby Smith's Confederacy: The Trans-Mississippi South, 1863–1865* (New York: Columbia Univ. Press, 1972), 424–427.

3. Evan Shelby Jeffries to wife, April 15, 1865, Evan Shelby Jeffries Civil War Letters, 16th Mississippi Infantry File, Simpson History Complex, Hill College, Hillsboro, Texas (hereafter cited as Hill College); Andrew J. Fogle to Miss Loo, March 12, 1865, Andrew J. Fogle Civil War Letters, 9th Texas Infantry File, Hill College; George Peddy Cuttino, ed., *Saddle Bag and Spin-*

ning Wheel: Being the Civil War Letters of George W. Peddy, M. D., Surgeon, 56th Georgia Volunteers Regiment, C. S. A. and His Wife Kate Featherston Peddy (Macon, Ga.: Mercer Univ. Press, 1981), 309; C. T. Hardman to wife, September 2, 1864 (quotations), Hardman Family Letters, Civil War Soldiers' Letters, Alabama Department of Archives and History, Montgomery (hereafter cited as ADAH). See also Mark Lyons to Amelia, letters for March and April 1865, Mark Lyons Letters, ADAH.

4. Andrew J. Fogle to Miss Loo, March 12, 1865, Andrew J. Fogle Civil War Letters, 9th Texas Infantry File, Hill College; Evan Shelby Jeffries to wife, April 15, 1865, Evan Shelby Jeffries Civil War Letters, 16th Mississippi Infantry File, Hill College. For more on the general sentiments of western Confederate soldiers in spring 1865, see also W. H. Simrall to father, March 25, 1865, Civil War Miscellaneous, Mississippi Department of Archives and History, Jackson (hereafter cited as MDAH); Duncan McCollum Diary, March 28–April 11, 1865, MDAH; Ray Mathis, ed., *In the Land of the Living: Wartime Letters by Confederates from the Chattahoochee Valley of Alabama and Georgia* (Troy, Ala.: Troy State Univ. Press, 1981), 123; William Pitt Chambers, *Blood and Sacrifice: The Civil War Journal of a Confederate Soldier* (Huntington, W.Va.: Blue Acorn Press, 1994), 204–214; A. C. Roycroft Diary, April 9, 1865, A. C. Roycroft Papers, Hoole Special Collections Library, University of Alabama, Tuscaloosa (hereafter cited as Hoole Collections); S. V. Hughstone to wife, April 6, 1865, Sanford Venable Hughstone Letters, MDAH.

5. Grady McWhiney, Warner O. Moore Jr., and Robert F. Pace, eds., *Fear God and Walk Humbly: The Agricultural Journal of James Mallory, 1843–1877* (Tuscaloosa: Univ. of Alabama Press, 1997), 346–349; William R. Snell, ed., *Myra Inman: A Diary of the Civil War in East Tennessee* (Macon, Ga.: Mercer Univ. Press, 2000), 308; Richard Barksdale Harwell, ed., *Kate: The Journal of a Confederate Nurse* (Baton Rouge: Louisiana State Univ. Press, 1959), 259–270; Daniel E. Sutherland, ed., *A Very Violent Rebel: The Civil War Diary of Ellen Renshaw House* (Knoxville: Univ. of Tennessee Press, 1996), 151–159; Thad Holt Jr., ed., *Miss Waring's Journal: 1863 and 1865, Being the Diary of Miss Mary Waring of Mobile, During the Final Days of the War Between the States* (Chicago: Wyvern Press of S. F. E., 1964), 11–16; Cora E. Watson Diary, March and April, 1865, Cora E. Watson Carey Papers, MDAH; Sarah Rousseau Espy Diary, March and April, 1865, ADAH; Rachel Carter Craighead Diary, March 5, 1865, TSLA.

6. Sarah Rousseau Espy Diary, April 28, 1865, ADAH; Cora E. Watson Diary, April 1865 entries, Cora E. Watson Carey Papers, MDAH; William E. Sloan Diary, April 19, 1865, Civil War Collection, TSLA; Margaret B. Crozier Ramsey Diary, April 29, 1865, J.G.M. Ramsey Papers, Southern Historical Collection, Wilson Library, University of North Carolina, Chapel Hill; Snell, ed., *Myra Inman,* 309–310; Sutherland, ed., *A Very Violent Rebel,* 161–165; Harwell, ed., *Kate,* 271–276; Vicki Betts, ed., "The Civil War Letters of Elbridge Littlejohn," *Chronicles of Smith County, Texas* 18 (summer 1979): 37; Norman D. Brown, ed., *One of Cleburne's Command: The Civil War Reminiscences and Diary of Captain Samuel T. Foster, Granbury's Texas Brigade, CSA* (Austin: Univ. of Texas Press, 1980), 163–171.

7. William Fulton Letter, April 12, 1865, Hoole Collections; Kate Hopkins Oliver to Starke Oliver, May 25, 1865, Nannie Herndon Rice Family Papers, Special Collections, Mitchell Memorial Library, Mississippi State University, Starkville; A. C. Roycroft Diary, April 9, 1865, A. C. Roycroft Papers, Hoole Collections; Sam Davis Elliott, ed., *Doctor Quintard, Chaplain C. S. A. and Second Bishop of Tennessee* (Baton Rouge: Louisiana State Univ. Press, 2003), 252–253.

8. William T. Alderson, ed., "The Civil War Diary of Captain James Litton Cooper, September 30, 1861, to January 1865," *Tennessee Historical Quarterly* 15 (June 1956): 173 (quotations); Sarah Rousseau Espy Diary, May 6, 1865, ADAH; Richard Taylor, *Destruction and Reconstruction: Personal Experiences of the Late War* (New York: D. Appleton and Company, 1879), 222–226.

9. Albert Quincy Porter Diary, May 1865 entries, MDAH; United States Census Bureau, Eighth Census of the United States, 1860, Schedule 1 (Free Inhabitants).

10. See Arthur W. Bergeron Jr. *Confederate Mobile* (Baton Rouge: Louisiana State Univ. Press, 2000), 151.

11. For discussions of the meaning, character, and extent of Confederate nationalism, see, for example, James M. McPherson, "American Victory, American Defeat," in *Why the Confederacy Lost*, ed. Gabor S. Boritt, 30–32 (New York: Oxford Univ. Press, 1992); Drew Gilpin Faust, *The Creation of Confederate Nationalism: Ideology and Identity in the Civil War South* (Baton Rouge: Louisiana State Univ. Press, 1988), 2–21; Emory M. Thomas, "Reckoning with Rebels," in *The Old South in the Crucible of War*, ed. Harry P. Owens and James J. Cooke, 3–14 (Jackson: Univ. Press of Mississippi, 1983); Paul D. Escott, "The Failure of Confederate Nationalism: The Old South's Class System in the Crucible of War," in *The Old South in the Crucible of War*, ed. Harry P. Owens and James J. Cooke, 15–28 (Jackson: Univ. Press of Mississippi, 1983); Lawrence N. Powell and Michael S. Wayne, "Self-Interest and the Decline of Confederate Nationalism,"in *The Old South in the Crucible of War*, ed. Harry P. Owens and James J. Cooke, 29–45 (Jackson: Univ. Press of Mississippi, 1983).

12. For the best recent works that address the end of the war, see Mark Grimsley and Brooks D. Simpson, eds., *The Collapse of the Confederacy* (Lincoln: Univ. of Nebraska Press, 2001); Jason Phillips, *Diehard Rebels: The Confederate Culture of Invincibility* (Athens: Univ. of Georgia Press, 2007); Aaron Sheehan-Dean, *Why Confederates Fought: Family and Nation in Civil War Virginia* (Chapel Hill: Univ. of North Carolina Press, 2007); William C. Davis, *An Honorable Defeat: The Last Days of the Confederate Government* (New York: Harcourt, 2001).

Bibliography

PRIMARY SOURCES

Manuscript Collections

Alabama Department of Archives and History, Montgomery
Brown, Edward Norphlet. Letters.
Chadick, Mary Jane. Diary.
Civil War Soldiers' Letters, 1858–1909.
    Athey Family Civil War Letters.
    Cadenhead, I. B. Letters.
    Cross, William C. Letters.
    Croxton, Robert A. Letters.
    Hardman Family Letters.
    McGowin Family Letters.
    Searcy, James T. Letters.
    Snodgrass, A. Letters.
    Stout, S. A. Letters.
Espy, Sarah Rousseau. Diary.
Finch, James H. Diary.
Fitzpatrick, Phillips. Letters.
Fleming, W. V. Letters.
Gillis, Margaret Josephine Miles. Diary.
Lanning, James Montgomery. Diary.
Lyons, Mark. Letters.
Smyrl, Thomas. Letters.
Warrick, Thomas. Papers.

Hoole Special Collections Library, University of Alabama, Tuscaloosa
Bell, William Robert. Letter.
Cooper, William. Diaries.
Fulton, William. Letter.

Hundley, Daniel R. Diary.
Inge, Elizabeth Herndon. Letter.
Roycroft, A. C. Papers.

Internet Manuscripts
Berry, Carrie. Diary. http://www.americancivilwar.com/women/carrie_berry.html. Accessed February 19, 2011.
Williamson, Alice. Diary. http://scriptorium.lib.duke.edu/williamson/text.html. Special Collections Library. Duke University. Durham, North Carolina. Accessed February 4, 2006.

Mississippi Department of Archives and History, Jackson
Baker, T. Otis. Papers.
Beach, Elizabeth Jane. Letter.
Bigger, J. A. Diary.
Black. Narcissa L. Diaries.
Blakemore, Lizzie McFarland. Collection.
Brown, Maude Morrow. Manuscript.
Carey, Cora E. Watson. Papers.
Civil War Papers (Miscellaneous).
Dubuisson, Charles L., and Family. Papers.
Dunn, Mathew Andrew. Letters.
Evans, Dr. Holden Garthur. Diary.
Hughstone, Sanford Venable. Letters.
Irion Neilson, Eliza Lucy. Journal. (Irion-Neilson Family Papers.)
Martin, Anne Shannon. Diary.
McCollum, Duncan. Diary.
Nicholson, Flavellus G. Diary-Journal.
Palmer, James. Civil War Diary.
Pendleton, Jennie. Journal. (Mary E. Wilkes Shell Papers.)
Porter, Albert Quincy. Diary.
Rand, Joseph Miller. Diary.
Sears, Claudius Wistar. Diary.
Shell, Mary E. Wilkes. Papers.
Strickland, Belle F. Diary.
Worthington Family Papers.

Mitchell Memorial Library, Special Collections, Mississippi State University, Starkville
Agnew, Samuel Andrew. Diary.
Buckley, R. E. Civil War Letters.

Calhoun-Kincannon-Orr Family Papers.

Horn Collection.

Levy Family Papers.

Marshall, John H. Letters.

Oakley, John. Family Papers.

Raymond, Henry Rodney. Papers.

Rice, Nannie Herndon. Family Papers.

Sykes, William E. Letters.

Young, W. H. Letters.

Pearce Civil War Collection, Navarro College, Corsicana, Texas

Burnett, Thomas Jefferson. Papers.

Geiger, Charles A. Papers.

Martin Family Papers.

Simpson History Complex, Hill College, Hillsboro, Texas

Bates, Jesse P. Civil War Letters. 9th Texas Infantry File.

Cooper, John Daniel. Civil War Diary. 7th Mississippi Infantry File.

Davis, Fred A. Civil War Letters. 7th Mississippi Infantry File.

Fogle, Andrew J. Civil War Letters. 9th Texas Infantry File.

Harlan, Isaiah. Civil War Letters. 10th Texas Infantry File.

Jeffries, Evan Shelby. Civil War Letters. 16th Mississippi Infantry File.

Keener, Linson Montgomery. Civil War Letters. 7th Texas Infantry File.

Smith, W. E. Civil War Letters. 7th Texas Infantry File.

Watson, Henry. Civil War Letters. 10th Texas Cavalry File.

Southern Historical Collection, Wilson Library, University of North Carolina, Chapel Hill

Alston, Trudy. Diary.

Beatty, Taylor. Papers.

Coleman, D. Diary.

Erwin, George Phifer. Papers.

Gale and Polk Family Papers.

Kern, J. T. Papers.

Mercer, George Anderson. Diary.

Niles, Jason. Diary.

Ramsey, J. G. M. Papers.

Semmes, Benedict Joseph. Papers.

Simpson, Avington Wayne. Diary.

Simpson and Brumby Family Papers.

Thurman, John P. and Sallie Ecklin. Papers.

Wallace, Frances Woolfolk. Diary.
Watson, W. J. Diary.

Tennessee State Library and Archives, Nashville
Cartmell, Robert H. Papers.
Civil War Collection.
    Clark, Achilles V. Letters.
    Colville, R. W. Letters.
    Deavenport, Thomas Hopkins. Diary.
    Dixon, M. H. Diary.
    Floyd, John D. Letters.
    Franklin, Perry Morgan. Diary.
    Gale, William Dudley. Letters.
    Jordan, Stephen A. Diary.
    Mayes, Robert Burns. Poem.
    Pollard, William Mebane. Diary.
    Porter, Nimrod. Diary.
    Sloan, William E. Diary.
    Tipton, Martha. Diary.
    Wilson, Thomas Black. Reminiscences.
Craighead, Rachel Carter. Diaries.
Dyer, W. R. Diaries.
Etter, Roysdon Roberson. Civil War Diary.
Fielder, Alfred Tyler. Diary.
Haskins, Nannie E. Papers.
Henderson, Samuel. Diary.
Lindsley, John Berrien. Diaries.
Matthews, James Washington. Journal.
Morey, James Marsh. Papers.
O'Bryan, Joseph Branch. Letters.

United States Army Military History Institute, Carlisle, Pennsylvania
Civil War Miscellaneous Collection.
    Campbell, Richard Saunders. Letters.
    Cato, John A. Letters.
    Cole, William D. Letters.
    Dew, T. T. Letters.
    Hall, James A. Letters.
    Rodgers, Hugh Ross. Letters.
Herren, I. W. Letters. (Lewis Leigh Collection.)
Rabb, Hezekiah. Letters. (Micheal P. Musick Collection.)

University of Mississippi Libraries, Archives and Special Collections, Oxford
Bachman, G. W. Journal.
Bowden, William W. Letter.
Craft-Fort Papers.
Gentry, B. F. Letters.
Roberts, Charles. Collection.
Settle Family Letters.
Stephens, M. D. L. Manuscript.
Stubblefield, Charles. Collection.
Walthall, E. C. Collection.

University of Tennessee, Special Collections, Hoskins Library, Knoxville
Pearre, Mary L. Diary.
Rennolds, E. H. Diaries.

University of Texas, Center for American History, Austin
Bunting, Robert Franklin. Papers.
Crittenden, John. Letters.

Government Documents

United States Bureau of the Census. Eighth Census of the United States, 1860. Schedule 1 (Free Inhabitants). Washington, D.C.: Bureau of the Census, 1864.
United States Department of the Army. *Field Manual 22–100; Army Leadership: Be, Know, Do.* Washington, D.C.: Headquarters, Department of the Army, 1999.
United States War Department. *The War of the Rebellion: A Compilation of the Official Records of the Union and Confederate Armies.* 128 vols. Washington, D.C.: Government Printing Office, 1880–1901.

Newspapers

Chattanooga Daily Rebel, 1864.
Greensboro (Mississippi) Southern Motive, 1864.
Jackson Daily Mississippian, 1864.
Meridian (Mississippi) *Daily Clarion,* 1864–1865.
Mobile Daily Advertiser and Register, 1864.
Mobile Evening News, 1864.
Montgomery Daily Advertiser, 1864–1865.
Monticello (Mississippi) Southern Journal, 1864.
Selma Morning Reporter, 1864.
Troy (Alabama) Southern Advertiser, 1864–1865.
Tuskegee South Western Baptist, 1864.

Books

Anderson, John Q., ed. *Campaigning with Parson's Texas Cavalry Brigade, C. S. A.* Hillsboro, Tex.: Hill Junior College Press, 1967.

Barron, S. B. *Lone Star Defenders: A Chronicle of the Third Texas Cavalry, Ross' Brigade.* New York: Neale Publishing Company, 1908.

Bennett, William W. *A Narrative of the Great Revival Which Prevailed in the Southern Armies.* Philadelphia: Claxton, Remsen, and Haffelfinger, 1877.

Bettersworth, John K., and James W. Silver, eds. *Mississippi in the Confederacy.* 2 vols. Baton Rouge: Louisiana State Univ. Press, 1961.

Blomquist, Ann K., and Robert A. Taylor, eds. *This Cruel War: The Civil War Letters of Grant and Malinda Taylor, 1862–1865.* Macon, Ga.: Mercer Univ. Press, 2000.

Brown, Norman D., ed. *One of Cleburne's Command: The Civil War Reminiscences and Diary of Captain Samuel T. Foster, Granbury's Texas Brigade, CSA.* Austin: Univ. of Texas Press, 1980.

Brown, Shepherd Spencer Nerville, ed. *War Years, C. S. A.: 12th Mississippi Regiment, Major S. H. Giles, Q. M., Original Letters, 1860–1865.* Hillsboro, Tex.: Hill College Press, 1998.

Cabaniss, Jim R., ed. *Civil War Journal and Letters of Washington Ives, 4th Fla. C. S. A.* Tallahassee, Fla.: Jim Cabaniss, 1987.

Cannon, J. P. *Bloody Banners and Barefoot Boys: A History of the 27th Regiment Alabama Infantry, C. S. A.: The Civil War Memoirs and Diaries of J. P. Cannon, M.D.* Compiled and edited by Noel Crowson and John V. Brogden. Shippensburg, Pa.: Burd Street Press, 1997.

Cash, William M., and Lucy Somerville Howorth, eds. *My Dear Nellie: The Civil War Letters of William L. Nugent to Eleanor Smith Nugent.* Jackson: Univ. Press of Mississippi, 1977.

Cate, Wirt Armistead ed. *Two Soldiers: The Campaign Diaries of Thomas J. Key, C. S. A., and Robert J. Campbell, U. S. A.* Chapel Hill: Univ. of North Carolina Press, 1938.

Cater, Douglas John. *As It Was: Reminiscences of a Soldier of the Third Texas Cavalry and the Nineteenth Louisiana Infantry.* Austin, Tex.: State House Press, 1990.

Chambers, William Pitt. *Blood and Sacrifice: The Civil War Journal of a Confederate Soldier.* Huntington, W.Va.: Blue Acorn Press, 1994.

Chattahoochee Valley Historical Society, ed. *War Was the Place: A Centennial Collection of Confederate Soldier Letters.* Bulletin 5. Chambers County, Ala.: Chattahoochee Valley Historical Society, 1961.

Christ, Mark K., ed. *Getting Used to Being Shot At: The Spence Family Civil War Letters.* Fayetteville: Univ. of Arkansas Press, 2002.

Commager, Henry Steele. *The Blue and the Gray: The Story of the Civil War as Told by Its Participants.* New York: Bobbs-Merrill, 1950.

Cotton, Gordon A., ed. *From the Pen of a She-Rebel: The Civil War Diary of Emilie Riley McKinley.* Columbia: Univ. of South Carolina Press, 2001.

Crabtree, Beth G., and James W. Patton, eds. *"Journal of a Secesh Lady": The Diary of Catherine Ann Devereux Edmondston, 1860–1866.* Raleigh: North Carolina Division of Archives, 1979.

Cutrer, Thomas W., ed. *Longstreet's Aide: The Civil War Letters of Major Thomas J. Goree.* Charlottesville: Univ. Press of Virginia, 1995.

———, ed. *Oh, What a Loansome Time I Had: The Civil War Letters of Major William Morel Moxley, Eighteenth Alabama Infantry, and Emily Beck Moxley.* Tuscaloosa: Univ. of Alabama Press, 2002.

———, ed. *'Our Trust is in the God of Battles': The Civil War Letters of Robert Franklin Bunting, Chaplain, Terry's Texas Rangers, C. S. A.* Knoxville: Univ. of Tennessee Press, 2006.

Cuttino, George Peddy, ed. *Saddle Bag and Spinning Wheel: Being the Civil War Letters of George W. Peddy, M. D., Surgeon, 56th Georgia Volunteers Regiment, C. S. A. and His Wife Kate Featherston Peddy.* Macon, Ga.: Mercer Univ. Press, 1981.

Davidson, William H., ed. *Word from Camp Pollard, C. S. A.* West Point, Ga.: Davidson, 1978.

Davis, William C., ed. *Diary of a Confederate Soldier: John S. Jackman of the Orphan Brigade.* Columbia: Univ. of South Carolina Press, 1990.

Dimond, E. Grey, and Herman Hattaway, eds. *Letters from Forest Place: A Plantation Family's Correspondence, 1846–1881.* Jackson: Univ. Press of Mississippi, 1993.

Douglas, Lucia R., ed. *Douglas's Texas Battery, C. S. A.* Tyler, Tex.: Smith County Historical Society, 1966.

Durden, Robert F., ed. *The Gray and the Black: The Confederate Debate on Emancipation.* Baton Rouge: Louisiana State Univ. Press, 1972.

Elder, William Henry. *Civil War Diary (1862–1865) of Bishop William Henry Elder, Bishop of Natchez.* Natchez, Miss.: R. O. Gerow, Bishop of Natchez-Jackson, 1960.

Elkins, Vera Dockery, ed. *Letters from a Civil War Soldier.* New York: Vantage Press, 1969.

Elliott, Sam Davis, ed. *Doctor Quintard, Chaplain C. S. A. and Second Bishop of Tennessee.* Baton Rouge: Louisiana State Univ. Press, 2003.

Fain, John N., ed. *Sanctified Trial: The Diary of Eliza Rhea Anderson Fain, a Confederate Woman in East Tennessee.* Knoxville: Univ. of Tennessee Press, 2004.

Ferrell, Robert H., ed. *Holding the Line: The Third Tennessee Infantry, 1861–1864.* Kent, Ohio: Kent State Univ. Press, 1996.

Folmar, John Kent, ed. *From That Terrible Field: Civil War Letters of James M. Williams, Twenty-First Alabama Infantry Volunteers.* University: Univ. of Alabama Press, 1981.

Ford, Arthur P. *Life in the Confederate Army: Being the Experiences of a Private Soldier in the Confederate Army.* New York: Neale Publishing Company, 1905.

Franklin, Ann York, ed. *The Civil War Diaries of Captain Alfred Tyler Fielder, 12th Tennessee Regiment Infantry, Company B, 1861–1865.* Louisville, Ky.: A. Y. Franklin, 1996.

Galbraith, William, and Loretta Galbraith, eds. *A Lost Heroine of the Confederacy: The Diaries and Letters of Belle Edmondson.* Jackson: Univ. Press of Mississippi, 1990.

Garrett, Jill K., ed. *Confederate Diary of Robert D. Smith.* Columbia, Tenn.: Tennessee Division, United Daughters of the Confederacy, 1975.

Goodloe, Albert T. *Confederate Echoes: A Voice from the South in the Days of Secession and the Southern Confederacy.* Nashville, Tenn.: Publishing House of the M. E. Church, South, Smith and Lamar, 1907.

Gottschalk, Phil. *In Deadly Earnest: The History of the First Missouri Brigade, C. S. A.* Columbia: Missouri River Press, 1991.

Griffith, Lucille, ed. *Yours Till Death: Civil War Letters of John W. Cotton.* Tuscaloosa: Univ. of Alabama Press, 1951.

Harwell, Richard Barksdale, ed. *The Confederate Reader.* New York: Longmans, Green, 1957.

———, ed. *Kate: The Journal of a Confederate Nurse.* Baton Rouge: Louisiana State Univ. Press, 1959.

Holland, Katherine S., ed. *Keep All My Letters: The Civil War Letters of Richard Henry Brooks, 51st Georgia Infantry.* Macon, Ga.: Mercer Univ. Press, 2003.

Holmes, Henry McCall. *Diary of Henry McCall Holmes: Army of Tennessee, Assistant Surgeon, Florida Troops, with Related Letters, Documents, etc.* State College, Miss.: N.p., 1968.

Holt, Thad, Jr., ed. *Miss Waring's Journal: 1863 and 1865, Being the Diary of Miss Mary Waring of Mobile, During the Final Days of the War Between the States.* Chicago: Wyvern Press of S. F. E., 1964.

Hood, John Bell. *Advance and Retreat: Personal Experiences in the United States and Confederate States Armies.* Bloomington: Indiana Univ. Press, 1959.

Hudson, William Spencer. *The Civil War Diary of William Spencer Hudson.* St. Louis: Micro-Records Publishing, 1973.

Hughes, Nathaniel Cheairs, Jr., ed. *Liddell's Record: St. John Richardson Liddell, Brigadier General, C.S. A., Staff Officer and Brigade Commander, Army of Tennessee.* Dayton, Ohio: Morningside, 1985.

Jackson, Alto L., ed. *So Mourns the Dove: Letters of a Confederate Infantryman and His Family.* New York: Exposition Press, 1965.

Jamison, Henry D., and Marguerite J. McTigue, eds. *Letters and Recollections of a Confederate Soldier, 1860–1865.* Nashville, Tenn.: H. D. Jamison, 1964.

Johnston, Joseph E. *Narrative of Military Operations Directed During the Late War Between the States.* Bloomington: Indiana Univ. Press, 1959.

Jones, Mary M., and Leslie J. Martin, eds. *The Gentle Rebel: The Civil War Letters of William Harvey Berryhill, Co. D, 43rd Regiment, Mississippi Volunteers.* Yazoo City, Miss.: Sassafras Press, 1982.

Kerr, Homer L., ed. *Fighting with Ross' Texas Cavalry Brigade, C. S. A.: Diary of Lieut. George L. Griscom, Adjutant, 9th Texas Cavalry Regiment.* Hillsboro, Tex.: Hill Junior College Press, 1976.

Kirwan, Albert D., ed. *Johnny Green of the Orphan Brigade: Journal of a Confederate Soldier.* Lexington: Univ. of Kentucky Press, 1956.

Lale, Max S., and Hobard Key Jr., eds. *The Civil War Letters of David R. Garrett, Detailing the Adventures of the 6th Texas Cavalry, 1861–1865.* Marshall, Tex.: Port Caddo Press, 1964.

Lewis, Richard. *Camp Life of a Confederate Boy, of Bratton's Brigade, Longstreet's Corps, C.S.A.: Letters Written by Lieut. Richard Lewis, of Walker's Regiment, to His Mother, during the War.* Charleston, S.C.: News and Courier Book Press, 1883.

Lowe, Richard, ed. *A Texas Cavalry Officer's Civil War: The Diary and Letters of James C. Bates.* Baton Rouge: Louisiana State Univ. Press, 1999.

Marszalek, John F., ed. *The Diary of Miss Emma Holmes, 1861–1866.* Baton Rouge: Louisiana State Univ. Press, 1979.

Mathis, Ray, ed., *In the Land of the Living: Wartime Letters by Confederates from the Chattahoochee Valley of Alabama and Georgia.* Troy, Ala.: Troy State Univ. Press, 1981.

McClure, Judy Watson, ed. *Confederate From East Texas: The Civil War Letters of James Monroe Watson.* Quanah, Tex.: Nortex Press, 1976.

McGuire, Thomas. *McGuire Papers, Containing Major Thomas McGuire's Civil War Letters; and Patriotic Documents and Other Letters from 1854 to the Turn of the Twentieth Century.* Tusquahoma, La.: Daughters of the American Revolution, 1966.

McMorries, Edward Young. *History of the First Regiment Alabama Volunteers, C. S. A.* Montgomery, Ala.: Brown Print Company, 1904.

McWhiney, Grady, Warner O. Moore Jr., and Robert F. Pace, eds. *Fear God and Walk Humbly: The Agricultural Journal of James Mallory, 1843–1877.* Tuscaloosa: Univ. of Alabama Press, 1997.

Myers, Robert Manson, ed. *The Children of Pride: A True Story of Georgia and the Civil War.* New Haven, Conn.: Yale Univ. Press, 1972.

Rugeley, H.J.H., ed. *Batchelor-Turner Letters, 1861–1864, Written by Two of Terry's Texas Rangers.* Austin, Tex.: Steck, 1961.

Sexton, Rebecca Grant, ed. *A Southern Woman of Letters: The Correspondence of Augusta Jane Evans Wilson.* Columbia: Univ. of South Carolina Press, 2002.

Shelton, Perry Wayne, comp., and Shelly Morrison, ed. *Personal Letters of General Lawrence Sullivan Ross, with Other Letters.* Austin, Tex.: Shelly and Richard Morrison, 1994.

Simpson, Harold B., ed. *The Bugle Softly Blows: The Confederate Diary of Benjamin M. Seaton.* Waco, Tex.: Texian Press, 1965.

Snell, William R., ed. *Myra Inman: A Diary of the Civil War in East Tennessee.* Macon, Ga.: Mercer Univ. Press, 2000.

Styple, William B., ed. *Writing and Fighting the Confederate War: The Letters of Peter Wellington Alexander, Confederate War Correspondent.* Kearny, N.J.: Belle Grove, 2002.

Sutherland, Daniel E., ed. *Reminiscences of a Private: William E. Bevens of the First Arkansas Infantry, C. S. A.* Fayetteville: Univ. of Arkansas Press, 1992.

———, ed. *A Very Violent Rebel: The Civil War Diary of Ellen Renshaw House.* Knoxville: Univ. of Tennessee Press, 1996.

Taylor, F. Jay, ed. *Reluctant Rebel: The Secret Diary of Robert Patrick, 1861–1865.* Baton Rouge: Louisiana State Univ. Press, 1959.

Taylor, Richard. *Destruction and Reconstruction: Personal Experiences of the Late War.* New York: D. Appleton and Company, 1879.

Tower, R. Lockwood, ed. *A Carolinian Goes to War: The Civil War Narrative of Arthur Middleton Manigault.* Columbia: Univ. of South Carolina Press, 1983.

Vann, Samuel King. *"Most Lovely Lizzie": Love Letters of a Young Confederate.* Birmingham, Ala.: Privately Published, 1958.

Ward, William Walker. *For the Sake of My Country: Diary of Col. W. W. Ward, 9th Tennessee Cavalry, Morgan's Brigade, C. S. A.* Murfreesboro, Tenn.: Southern Heritage Press, 1992.

Watkins, Sam. *"Co. Aytch," Maury Grays, First Tennessee Regiment; or, a Side Show of the Big Show.* 1882. Reprint; Wilmington, N.C.: Broadfoot, 1987.

Weiner, Marli F., ed. *A Heritage of Woe: The Civil War Diary of Grace Brown Elmore, 1861–1868.* Athens: Univ. of Georgia Press, 1997.

Welker, David A., ed. *A Keystone Rebel: The Civil War Diary of Joseph Garey, Hudson's Battery, Mississippi Volunteers.* Gettysburg, Pa: Thomas Publications, 1996.

Winter, Robert Milton, ed. *Civil War Women: The Diaries of Belle Strickland and Cora Harris Watson: Holly Springs, Mississippi, July 25, 1864–June 22, 1868.* Lafayette, Calif.: Thomas Berryhill, 2001.

Wynne, Lewis N., and Robert A. Taylor, eds. *This War So Horrible: The Civil War Diary of Hiram Smith Williams.* Tuscaloosa: Univ. of Alabama Press, 1993.

Articles

Aiken, Leona T., ed. "Letters of the Offield Brothers, Confederate Soldiers from Upper East Tennessee." *East Tennessee Historical Society Publications* 46 (1974): 116–125.

Alderson, William T., ed. "The Civil War Diary of Captain James Litton Cooper, September 30, 1861, to January 1865." *Tennessee Historical Quarterly* 15 (June 1956): 141–173.

———, ed. "The Civil War Reminiscences of John Johnston, 1861–1865." *Tennessee Historical Quarterly* 13 (March 1954): 65–82; 13 (June 1954): 156–178; 13 (September 1954): 254–276; 13 (December 1954): 329–354; 14 (March 1955): 43–81; 14 (June 1955): 142–175.

Bailey, Russell B., ed. "Reminiscences of the Civil War by T. J. Walker." *Confederate Chronicles of Tennessee* 1 (1986): 37–74.

Betts, Vicki, ed. "The Civil War Letters of Elbridge Littlejohn." *Chronicles of Smith County, Texas* 18 (summer 1979): 11–50.

Bryan, T. Conn, ed. "A Georgia Woman's Civil War Diary: The Journal of Minerva Leah Rowles McClatchey, 1864–1865." *Georgia Historical Quarterly* 51 (summer 1967): 197–216.

Burgess, Mary Wyche, ed. "Civil War Letters of Abram Hayne Young." *South Carolina Historical Magazine* 78 (January 1977), 56–70.

Cadenhead, I. B. "Some Confederate Letters of I. B. Cadenhead." *Alabama Historical Quarterly* 18 (winter 1956): 564–571.

Cain, J. I., ed. "The Battle of Atlanta as Described by a Confederate Soldier." *Georgia Historical Quarterly* 42 (March 1958): 109–111.

Candler, Allen Daniel. "Watch on the Chattahoochee: A Civil War Letter." *Georgia Historical Quarterly* 43 (December 1959): 427–428.

Carleton, Mark T., ed. "A Record of the Late Fourth Louisiana Reg't, C. S. A." *Louisiana History* 10 (summer 1969): 255–260.

Carpenter, James A., ed. "James D. Lynch in War and Peace." *Alabama Historical Quarterly* 20 (spring 1958): 71–84.

Chadick, Mrs. W. D. "Civil War Days in Huntsville: A Diary by Mrs. W. D. Chadick." *Alabama Historical Quarterly* 9 (summer 1947): 199–333.

Crow, Vernon. "The Justness of Our Cause: The Civil War Diaries of William W. Stringfield." *East Tennessee Historical Quarterly* 57 (1985): 71–101.

Curry, J. H. "A History of Company B, 40th Alabama Infantry, C. S. A." *Alabama Historical Quarterly* 17 (fall 1955): 159–222.

Darst, Maury, ed. "Robert Hodges, Jr.: Confederate Soldier." *East Texas Historical Journal* 9 (March 1971): 20–49.

Fleming, Elvis E. "Some Hard Fighting: Letters of Private Robert T. Wilson, 5th Texas Infantry, Hood's Brigade, 1862–1864." *Military History of Texas and the Southwest* 9, no. 4 (1971): 289–304.

Harrison, Lowell H., ed. "The Diary of an 'Average' Confederate Soldier." *Tennessee Historical Quarterly* 29 (fall 1970): 256–271.

Haynes, Mary K., and James Wilkins, comps. "The Stanley Letters." *Papers of the Pike County Historical Society* 4 (April 1965): 1–50.

Hoole, W. Stanley, ed. "The Letters of Captain Joab Goodson, 1862–1864." *Alabama Review* 10 (July 1957): 215–220.

Jones, Charles T., ed. "Five Confederates: The Sons of Bolling Hall in the Civil War." *Alabama Historical Quarterly* 24 (winter 1962): 133–221.

Jordan, Weymouth T., ed. "Mathew Andrew Dunn Letters." *Journal of Mississippi History* 1 (April 1939): 110–127.

Joyce, Fred. "Dalton During the Winter of 1863–1864." *Southern Bivouac* 2 (June 1884): 464–465.

Kendall, John S., ed. "The Diary of Surgeon Craig, Fourth Louisiana Regiment, C. S. A., 1864–1865." *Louisiana Historical Quarterly* 8 (spring 1925): 53–70.

Kremenak, Ben, ed. "Escape from Atlanta: The Huntington Memoir." *Civil War History* 11 (June 1965): 160–177.

Lewis, Donald W. "A Confederate Officer's Letters on Sherman's March to Atlanta." *Georgia Historical Quarterly* 51 (December 1967): 491–494.

Lufkin, Charles L., ed. "West Tennessee Unionists in the Civil War: A Hawkins Family Letter." *Tennessee Historical Quarterly* 46 (spring 1987): 33–42.

Marsh, Bryan. "The Confederate Letters of Bryan Marsh." *Chronicles of Smith County, Texas* 14 (winter 1975): 9–30, 43–55.

Martin, John M., ed. "A Methodist Circuit Rider Between the Lines: The Private Journal of Joseph J. Pitts, 1862–1864." *Tennessee Historical Quarterly* 19 (September 1960): 252–269.

Maxwell, David E. "Some Letters to His Parents by a Floridian in the Confederate Army." Transcribed by Gilbert Wright. *Florida Historical Quarterly* 36 (April 1958): 353–372.

McMurry, Richard M., ed. "A Mississippian at Nashville." *Civil War Times Illustrated* 12 (May 1973): 8–11.

Mims, William J. "Letters of Major W. J. Mims, C. S. A." *Alabama Historical Quarterly* 3 (1941): 203–231.

Mitchell, Enoch L., ed. "The Civil War Letters of Thomas Jefferson Newberry." *Journal of Mississippi History* 10 (January 1948): 44–80.

———, ed. "Letters of a Confederate Surgeon in the Army of Tennessee to His Wife." *Tennessee Historical Quarterly* 5 (March 1946): 61–81; (June 1946): 142–181.

Nichols, James L., ed. "Reminiscing From 1861 to 1865: An 'Ex-Confed,' H. P. Morrow." *East Texas Historical Journal* 9 (March 1971): 5–19.

Nichols, James L., and Frank Abbott, eds. "Reminiscences of Confederate Service by Wiley A. Washburn." *Arkansas Historical Quarterly* 35 (spring 1976): 47–90.

Norrell, William O. "Memo Book: William O. Norrell—Co. B., 63d GA. Regt. Vols., Mercer's Brigade, Walker's Division, Hardee's Corps, Army of Tennessee." *Journal of Confederate History* 1 (1988): 49–82.

Noyes, Edward, ed. "Excerpts from the Civil War Diary of E. T. Eggleston." *Tennessee Historical Quarterly* 17 (December 1958): 336–358.

Osborn, George C., ed. "Civil War Letters of Robert W. Banks: The Atlanta Campaign." *Georgia Historical Quarterly* 27 (June 1943): 208–216.

———, ed. "Stephen Washington Holladay's Civil War Letters." *Tennessee Historical Quarterly* 4 (September 1945): 256–264.

Partin, Robert, ed. "The Civil War in East Tennessee as Reported by a Confederate Railroad Bridge Builder." *Tennessee Historical Quarterly* 22 (September 1963): 238–258.

Peacock, Jane Bonner, ed. "A Wartime Story: The Davidson Letters, 1862–1865." *Atlanta Historical Bulletin* 20, no. 1 (1975): 8–121.

Rainwater, Percy L., ed. "The Civil War Letters of Cordelia Scales." *Journal of Mississippi History* 1 (July 1939): 169–181.

Roher, Walter A. "Confederate Generals: A View from Below." *Civil War Time Illustrated* 18 (July 1979): 10–13.

Rountree, Benjamin, ed. "Letters of a Confederate Soldier." *Georgia Review* 18 (fall 1964): 267–297.

Shingleton, Royce, ed. "With Loyalty and Honor as a Patriot: Recollections of a Confederate Soldier." *Alabama Historical Quarterly* 33 (fall and winter 1971): 240–263.

Silver, James W., ed. "The Breakdown of Morale in Central Mississippi in 1864: Letters of Judge Robert S. Hudson." *Journal of Mississippi History* 16 (spring 1954): 99–120.

Sterkx, H. E., ed. "Autobiography and Letters of Joel Dyer Murphree of Troy, Alabama, 1864–1865." *Alabama Historical Quarterly* 19 (spring 1957): 170–208.

Still, William N., ed. "The Civil War Letters of Robert Tarleton." *Alabama Historical Quarterly* 32 (spring and summer 1970): 51–80.

Stone, Benjamin Franklin. "'My Love to Them All': The Letters of Private Benjamin Stone, C. S. A., to His Sister." *Mississippi Quarterly* 23 (spring 1970): 175–179.

Wiley, Bell Irvin, ed. "The Confederate Letters of John W. Hagan." *Georgia Historical Quarterly* 38 (June 1954): 170–200; 38 (September 1954): 268–290.

Williams, Benjamin B. "Two Uncollected Civil War Poems of Alexander Beaufort Meek." *Alabama Historical Quarterly* 25 (spring 1963): 114–119.

Williamson, John C., ed. "The Civil War Diary of John Coffee Williamson." *Tennessee Historical Quarterly* 15 (March 1956): 61–74.

Zornow, William Frank. "State Aid for Indigent Soldiers and Their Families in Tennessee, 1861–1865." *Tennessee Historical Quarterly* 13 (December 1954): 297–300.

SECONDARY SOURCES

Books

Andrews, J. Cutler. *The South Reports the Civil War.* Princeton: Princeton Univ. Press, 1970.

Ash, Stephen V. *Middle Tennessee Society Transformed, 1860–1870.* Baton Rouge: Louisiana State Univ. Press, 1988.

———. *When the Yankees Came: Conflict and Chaos in the Occupied South, 1861–1865.* Chapel Hill: Univ. of North Carolina Press, 1995.

———. *A Year in the South: Four Lives in 1865.* New York: Palgrave Macmillan, 2002.

Bailey, Anne J. *The Chessboard of War: Sherman and Hood in the Autumn Campaigns of 1864.* Lincoln: Univ. of Nebraska Press, 2000.

———. *War and Ruin: William T. Sherman and the Savannah Campaign.* Wilmington, Del.: Scholarly Resources, 2003.

Bailey, Fred A. *Class and Tennessee's Confederate Generation.* Chapel Hill: Univ. of North Carolina Press, 1987.

Barton, Michael. *Goodmen: The Character of Civil War Soldiers.* University Park: Pennsylvania State Univ. Press, 1981.

Barton, Michael, and Larry M. Logue, eds. *The Civil War Soldier: A Historical Reader.* New York: New York Univ. Press, 2002.

Bearss, Edwin C. *Decision in Mississippi: Mississippi's Important Role in the War between the States.* Jackson: Mississippi Commission on the War Between the States, 1962.

———. *Forrest at Brice's Cross Roads and in North Mississippi in 1864.* Dayton, Ohio: Press of Morningside Bookshop, 1979.

Bearss, Margie Riddle. *Sherman's Forgotten Campaign: The Meridian Expedition.* Baltimore: Gateway Press, 1987.

Bergeron, Arthur W., Jr. *Confederate Mobile.* Baton Rouge: Louisiana State Univ. Press, 2000.

Beringer, Richard E. *The Elements of Confederate Defeat: Nationalism, War Aims, and Religion.* Athens: Univ. of Georgia Press, 1988.

Beringer, Richard E., Herman Hattaway, Archer Jones, and William N. Still Jr. *Why the South Lost the Civil War.* Athens: Univ. of Georgia Press, 1986.

Bettersworth, John K. *Confederate Mississippi: The People and Policies of a Cotton State in Wartime.* Baton Rouge: Louisiana State Univ. Press, 1943.

Blair, William A. *Virginia's Private War: Feeding Body and Soul in the Confederacy, 1861–1865.* New York: Oxford Univ. Press, 1998.

Boatner, Mark M. *The Civil War Dictionary.* New York: McKay, 1959.

Boritt, Gabor S., ed. *Jefferson Davis's Generals.* New York: Oxford Univ. Press, 1999.

———, ed. *Why the Confederacy Lost.* New York: Oxford Univ. Press, 1992.

Bragg, C. L. *Distinction in Every Service: Brigadier General Marcellus A. Stovall, C. S. A.* Shippensburg, Pa.: White Mane Books, 2002.

Brinsfield, John W., ed. *Faith in the Fight: Civil War Chaplains.* Mechanicsburg, Pa.: Stackpole Books, 2003.

Buck, Irving. *Cleburne and His Command.* Jackson, Tenn.: McCowat-Mercer Press, 1959.

Bynum, Victoria E. *The Free State of Jones: Mississippi's Longest Civil War.* Chapel Hill: Univ. of North Carolina Press, 2001.

Campbell, Edward, and Kim Rice, eds. *A Woman's War: Southern Women, Civil War, and the Confederate Legacy.* Charlottesville: Univ. of Virginia Press, 1996.

Campbell, Jacqueline Glass. *When Sherman Marched North from the Sea: Resistance on the Confederate Home Front*. Chapel Hill: Univ. of North Carolina Press, 2003.

Castel, Albert. *Decision in the West: The Atlanta Campaign of 1864*. Lawrence: Univ. Press of Kansas, 1992.

Clinton, Catherine, and Nina Silber, eds. *Divided Houses: Gender and the Civil War*. New York: Oxford Univ. Press, 1992.

Cole, Garold L., comp. *Civil War Eyewitnesses: An Annotated Bibliography of Books and Articles, 1955–1986*. Columbia: Univ. of South Carolina Press, 1988.

Connelly, Thomas Lawrence. *Army of the Heartland: The Army of Tennessee, 1861– 1862*. Baton Rouge: Louisiana State Univ. Press, 1967.

———. *Autumn of Glory: The Army of Tennessee, 1862–1865*. Baton Rouge: Louisiana State Univ. Press, 1971.

———. *Civil War Tennessee: Battles and Leaders*. Knoxville: Univ. of Tennessee Press, 1979.

Cooper, William J., Jr. *Jefferson Davis, American*. New York: Knopf, 2000.

Coppock, Paul. *Memphis Sketches*. Memphis, Tenn.: Friends of Memphis and Shelby County Libraries, 1976.

Coulter, E. Merton. *The Confederate States of America, 1861–1865*. Baton Rouge: Louisiana State Univ. Press, 1950.

Culpepper, Marilyn Mayer. *Trials and Triumphs: Women of the American Civil War*. East Lansing: Michigan State Univ. Press, 1991.

Daniel, Larry J. *Cannoneers in Gray: The Field Artillery of the Army of Tennessee, 1861– 1865*. University: Univ. of Alabama Press, 1984.

———. *Soldiering in the Army of Tennessee: A Portrait of Life in a Confederate Army*. Chapel Hill: Univ. of North Carolina Press, 1991.

Davis, Stephen. *Atlanta Will Fall: Sherman, Joe Johnston, and the Yankee Heavy Battalions*. Wilmington, Del.: Scholarly Resources, 2001.

Davis, William C. *An Honorable Defeat: The Last Days of the Confederate Government*. New York: Harcourt, 2001.

———. *The Orphan Brigade: The Kentucky Confederates Who Couldn't Go Home*. New York: Doubleday, 1980.

Dornbusch, Charles E. *Regimental Publications and Personal Narratives of the Civil War: A Checklist*. 4 vols. New York: New York Public Library, 1961–1972, 1987.

Dunkelman, Mark H. *Brothers One and All: Espirit de Corps in a Civil War Regiment*. Baton Rouge: Louisiana State Univ. Press, 2004.

Durham, Walter T. *Reluctant Partners: Nashville and the Union, July 1, 1863 to June 30, 1865*. Nashville: Tennessee Historical Society, 1987.

Dyer, John P. *"Fightin' Joe" Wheeler*. Baton Rouge: Louisiana State Univ. Press, 1941.

———. *The Gallant Hood*. Indianapolis: Bobbs-Merrill Company, 1950.

Eaton, Clement. *A History of the Southern Confederacy*. New York: Macmillan, 1954.

Elliott, Sam Davis. *Soldier of Tennessee: General Alexander P. Stewart and the Civil War in the West.* Baton Rouge: Louisiana State Univ. Press, 1999.

Engle, Stephen D. *Struggle for the Heartland: The Campaign from Fort Henry to Corinth.* Lincoln: Univ. of Nebraska Press, 2001.

Escott, Paul D. *After Secession: Jefferson Davis and the Failure of Confederate Nationalism.* Baton Rouge: Louisiana State Univ. Press, 1978.

Faust, Drew Gilpin. *The Creation of Confederate Nationalism: Ideology and Identity in the Civil War South.* Baton Rouge: Louisiana State Univ. Press, 1988.

——. *Mothers of Invention: Women of the Slaveholding South in the American Civil War.* Chapel Hill: Univ. of North Carolina Press, 1996.

Fisher, John E. *They Rode with Forrest and Wheeler: A Chronicle of Five Tennessee Brothers' Service in the Confederate Western Cavalry.* Jefferson, N.C.: McFarland, 1995.

Fisher, Noel C. *War at Every Door: Partisan Politics and Guerilla Violence in East Tennessee, 1860–1869.* Chapel Hill: Univ. of North Carolina Press, 1997.

Fleming, James R. *Band of Brothers: Company C, 9th Tennessee Infantry.* Shippensburg, Pa.: White Mane Publishing, 1996.

Fleming, Walter L. *Civil War and Reconstruction in Alabama.* New York: Columbia Univ. Press, 1905.

Forster, Stig, and Jorg Nagler, eds. *On the Road to Total War: The American Civil War and the German Wars of Unification, 1861–1871.* New York: Cambridge Univ. Press, 1997.

Foster, Buck T. *Sherman's Mississippi Campaign.* Tuscaloosa: Univ. of Alabama Press, 2006.

Gallagher, Gary W. *The Confederate War: How Popular Will, Nationalism, and Military Strategy Could Not Stave Off Defeat.* Cambridge: Harvard Univ. Press, 1997.

——, ed. *The Wilderness Campaign.* Chapel Hill: Univ. of North Carolina Press, 1997.

Genovese, Eugene. *A Consuming Fire: The Fall of the Confederacy in the Mind of the White Christian South.* Athens: Univ. of Georgia Press, 1998.

Glatthaar, Joseph T. *The March to the Sea and Beyond: Sherman's Troops in the Georgia and Carolina Campaigns.* New York: New York Univ. Press, 1985.

Gordon, Lesley J., and John C. Inscoe, eds. *Inside the Confederate Nation: Essays in Honor of Emory M. Thomas.* Baton Rouge: Louisiana State Univ. Press, 2005.

Grimsley, Mark, and Brooks D. Simpson, eds. *The Collapse of the Confederacy.* Lincoln: Univ. of Nebraska Press, 2001.

Groce, W. Todd. *Mountain Rebels: East Tennessee Confederates and the Civil War, 1860–1870.* Knoxville: Univ. of Tennessee Press, 1999.

Hale, Douglas. *The Third Texas Cavalry in the Civil War.* Norman: Univ. of Oklahoma Press, 1993.

Hallock, Judith Lee. *Braxton Bragg and Confederate Defeat.* Tuscaloosa: Univ. of Alabama Press, 1991.

Hattaway, Herman. *General Stephen D. Lee.* Jackson: Univ. Press of Mississippi, 1976.

Hattaway, Herman, and Archer Jones. *How the North Won: A Military History of the Civil War*. Urbana: Univ. of Illinois Press, 1991.

Haughton, Andrew. *Training, Tactics, and Leadership in the Confederate Army of Tennessee: Seeds of Failure*. Brookfield, Vt.: Frank Cass, 2000.

Horn, Stanley F. *The Army of Tennessee: A Military History*. New York: Bobbs-Merrill, 1941.

———, ed. *Tennessee's War: 1861–1865*. Nashville: Tennessee Civil War Centennial Commission, 1965.

Howell, H. Grady, Jr. *Going to Meet the Yankees: A History of the "Bloody Sixth" Mississippi Infantry, C. S. A*. Jackson, Miss.: Chickasaw Bayou Press, 1981.

Hughes, Nathaniel Cheairs, Jr. *General William J. Hardee: Old Reliable*. Baton Rouge: Louisiana State Univ. Press, 1965.

———. *The Pride of the Confederate Artillery: The Washington Artillery in the Army of Tennessee*. Baton Rouge: Louisiana State Univ. Press, 1997.

Jimerson, Randall C. *The Private Civil War: Popular Thought during the Sectional Conflict*. Baton Rouge: Louisiana State Univ. Press, 1988.

Johnson, Ludwell H. *Red River Campaign: Politics and Cotton in the Civil War*. Baltimore: Johns Hopkins Univ. Press, 1958.

Jones, James Pickett. *Yankee Blitzkrieg: Wilson's Raid through Alabama and Georgia*. Athens: Univ. of Georgia Press, 1976.

Kennett, Lee. *Marching Through Georgia: The Story of Soldiers and Civilians During Sherman's Campaign*. New York: Perennial, 2001.

Kerby, Robert L. *Kirby Smith's Confederacy: The Trans-Mississippi South, 1863–1865*. New York: Columbia Univ. Press, 1972.

Laine, J. Gary, and Morris M. Penny. *Law's Alabama Brigade in the War Between the Union and the Confederacy*. Shippensburg, Pa.: White Mane Publishing, 1996.

Levine, Bruce. *Confederate Emancipation: Southern Plans to Free and Arm Slaves During the Civil War*. New York: Oxford Univ. Press, 2006.

Lindermann, Gerald. *Embattled Courage: The Experience of Combat in the American Civil War*. New York: Free Press, 1987.

Lonn, Ella. *Desertion during the Civil War*. 1928. Reprint; Lincoln: Univ. of Nebraska Press, 1998.

Losson, Christopher. *Tennessee's Forgotten Warriors: Frank Cheatham and His Confederate Division*. Knoxville: Univ. of Tennessee Press, 1989.

Lundberg, John R. *The Finishing Stroke: Texans in the 1864 Tennessee Campaign*. Abilene, Tex.: McWhiney Foundation Press, 2002.

Martin, Bessie. *A Rich Man's War, a Poor Man's Fight: Desertion of Alabama Troops from the Confederate Army*. Tuscaloosa: Univ. of Alabama Press, 2003.

Maslowski, Peter. *Treason Must Be Made Odious: Military Occupation and Wartime Reconstruction in Nashville, Tennessee, 1862–1865*. Millwood, N.Y.: KTO Press, 1978.

McDonough, James Lee, and Thomas L. Connelly. *Five Tragic Hours: The Battle of Franklin.* Knoxville: Univ. of Tennessee Press, 1983.

McMillan, Malcolm Cook. *The Disintegration of a Confederate State: Three Governors and Alabama's Wartime Home Front, 1861–1865.* Macon, Ga.: Mercer Univ. Press, 1986.

McMurry, Richard M. *Atlanta 1864: Last Chance for the Confederacy.* Lincoln: Univ. of Nebraska Press, 2000.

———. *John Bell Hood and the War for Southern Independence.* Lexington: Univ. Press of Kentucky, 1982.

McPherson, James M.. *Battle Cry of Freedom: The Civil War Era.* New York: Oxford Univ. Press, 1988.

———. *Drawn with the Sword: Reflections on the American Civil War.* New York: Oxford Univ. Press, 1996.

———. *For Cause and Comrades: Why Men Fought in the Civil War.* New York: Oxford Univ. Press, 1997.

———. *What They Fought For, 1861–1865.* Baton Rouge: Louisiana State Univ. Press, 1994.

McPherson, James M., and William J. Cooper, eds. *Writing the Civil War: The Quest to Understand.* Columbia: Univ. of South Carolina Press, 1998.

McWhiney, Grady, and Perry D. Jamieson. *Attack and Die: Civil War Military Tactics and the Southern Heritage.* University: Univ. of Alabama Press, 1982.

Mitchell, Reid. *Civil War Soldiers: Their Expectations and Experiences.* New York: Viking, 1988.

Moore, Albert Burton. *Conscription and Conflict in the Confederacy.* New York: Macmillan, 1924.

Nelson, Larry E. *Bullets, Ballots, and Rhetoric: Confederate Policy for the United States Presidential Contest of 1864.* University: Univ. of Alabama Press, 1980.

Noe, Kenneth W., and Shannon H. Wilson, eds. *The Civil War in Appalachia: Collected Essays.* Knoxville: Univ. of Tennessee Press, 1997.

Owens, Henry P., and James J. Cooke, eds., *The Old South in the Crucible of War.* Jackson: Univ. Press of Mississippi, 1983.

Parks, Joseph. *General Leonidas Polk, C. S. A.: The Fighting Bishop.* Baton Rouge: Louisiana State Univ. Press, 1962.

Parrish, T. Michael. *Richard Taylor: Soldier Prince of Dixie.* Chapel Hill: Univ. of North Carolina Press, 1992.

Phillips, Jason. *Diehard Rebels: The Confederate Culture of Invincibility.* Athens: Univ. of Georgia Press, 2007.

Potter, David M. *The South and the Sectional Conflict.* Baton Rouge: Louisiana State Univ. Press, 1968.

Purdue, Howell, and Elizabeth Purdue. *Pat Cleburne, Confederate General: A Definitive Biography.* Hillsboro, Tex.: Hill Junior College Press, 1973.

Rable, George C. *Civil Wars: Women and the Crisis of Southern Nationalism.* Urbana: Univ. of Illinois Press, 1989.

————. *Confederate Republic: A Revolution Against Politics.* Chapel Hill: Univ. of North Carolina Press, 1994.

Ramsdell, Charles W. *Behind the Lines of the Southern Confederacy.* Baton Rouge: Louisiana State Univ. Press, 1944.

Rogers, William Warren, Jr. *Confederate Home Front: Montgomery during the Civil War.* Tuscaloosa: Univ. of Alabama Press, 1999.

Roland, Charles P. *The Confederacy.* Chicago: Univ. of Chicago Press, 1960.

Royster, Charles. *The Destructive War: William Tecumseh Sherman, Stonewall Jackson, and the Americans.* New York: Vintage Books, First Vintage Civil War Library Edition, 1993.

Schroeder-Lein, Glenna Ruth. *Confederate Hospitals on the Move: Samuel H. Stout and the Army of Tennessee.* Columbia: Univ. of South Carolina Press, 1994.

Shattuck, Gardiner H., Jr. *A Shield and a Hiding Place: The Religious Life of the Civil War Armies.* Macon, Ga.: Mercer Univ. Press, 1987.

Sheehan-Dean, Aaron, ed. *The View from the Ground: Experiences of Civil War Soldiers.* Lexington: Univ. Press of Kentucky, 2007.

————. *Why Confederates Fought: Family and Nation in Civil War Virginia.* Chapel Hill: Univ. of North Carolina Press, 2007.

Silver, James W. *Confederate Morale and Church Propaganda.* Tuscaloosa, Ala.: Confederate Publishing Company, 1957.

Simkins, Francis B., and James W. Patton. *The Women of the Confederacy.* Richmond: Garrett and Massie, 1936.

Smith, John David, ed. *Black Soldiers in Blue: African American Troops in the Civil War Era.* Chapel Hill: Univ. of North Carolina Press, 2002.

Sterkx, H. E. *Partners in Rebellion: Alabama Women in the Civil War.* Rutherford, N.J.: Fairleigh Dickinson Univ. Press, 1970.

Storey, Margaret M. *Loyalty and Loss: Alabama's Unionists in the Civil War and Reconstruction.* Baton Rouge: Louisiana State Univ. Press, 2004.

Stouffer, Samuel A., et al. *Studies in Social Psychology in World War II.* 4 vols. Princeton: Princeton Univ. Press, 1949.

Sword, Wiley. *The Confederacy's Last Hurrah: Spring Hill, Franklin, and Nashville.* Lawrence: Univ. Press of Kansas, 1993.

Symonds, Craig L. *Joseph E. Johnston: A Civil War Biography.* New York: Norton, 1992.

————. *Stonewall of the West: Patrick Cleburne and the Civil War.* Lawrence: Univ. Press of Kansas, 1997.

Tatum, Georgia Lee. *Disloyalty in the Confederacy.* Lincoln: Univ. of Nebraska Press, 2000.

Thomas, Emory. *The Confederate Nation, 1861–1865.* New York: Harper and Row, 1979.

Trudeau, Noah Andre. *Out of the Storm: The End of the Civil War, April–June, 1865.* Boston: Little, Brown, 1994.

Walker, Peter F. *Vicksburg: A People at War.* Chapel Hill: Univ. of North Carolina Press, 1960.

Waugh, John C. *Last Stand at Mobile.* Abilene, Tex.: McWhiney Foundation Press, 2001.

Weigley, Russell F. *A Great Civil War.* Bloomington: Univ. of Indiana Press, 2000.

Weitz, Mark A. *A Higher Duty: Desertion among Georgia Troops during the Civil War.* Lincoln: Univ. of Nebraska Press, 2000.

———. *More Damning than Slaughter: Desertion in the Confederate Army.* Lincoln: Univ. of Nebraska Press, 2005.

Wesley, Charles H. *The Collapse of the Confederacy.* Chapel Hill: Univ. of North Carolina Press, 1934.

Wiley, Bell I. *The Life of Billy Yank: The Common Soldier of the Union.* Baton Rouge: Louisiana State Univ. Press, 1952.

———. *The Life of Johnny Reb: The Common Soldier of the Confederacy.* 1943. Reprint, Baton Rouge: Louisiana State Univ. Press, 1978.

———. *The Plain People of the Confederacy.* Baton Rouge: Louisiana State Univ. Press, 1943.

———. *The Road to Appomattox.* Memphis, Tenn.: Memphis State College Press, 1956.

Williams, David. *A Rich Man's War: Class, Caste, and Confederate Defeat in the Lower Chattahoochee Valley.* Athens: Univ. of Georgia Press, 1998.

Williams, David, Teresa Crisp Williams, and David Carlson. *Plain Folk in a Rich Man's War: Class and Dissent in Confederate Georgia.* Gainesville: Univ. of Florida Press, 2002.

Wills, Brian Steel. *A Battle from the Start: The Life of Nathan Bedford Forrest.* New York: HarperCollins, 1992.

Woodworth, Steven E. *Jefferson Davis and His Generals: The Failure of Confederate Command in the West.* Lawrence: Univ. Press of Kansas, 1990.

———. *While God Is Marching On: The Religious World of Civil War Soldiers.* Lawrence: Univ. Press of Kansas, 2001.

Woodworth, Steven E., and Kenneth J. Winkle, eds. *Atlas of the Civil War.* New York: Oxford Univ. Press, 2004.

Articles

Ambrose, Stephen E. "Yeomen Discontent in the Confederacy." *Civil War History* 8 (September 1962): 259–268.

Amos, Harriet E. "'All-Absorbing Topics': Food and Clothing in Confederate Mobile." *Atlanta Historical Journal* 22 (fall–winter 1978): 17–28.

Andrews, J. Cutler. "The Confederate Press and Public Morale." *Journal of Southern History* 32 (November 1966): 445–465.

Ash, Steven V. "Sharks in an Angry Sea: Civilian Resistance and Guerilla Warfare in Occupied Middle Tennessee, 1862–1865." *Tennessee Historical Quarterly* 45 (summer 1986): 217–229.

Bailey, Fred A. "Class Contrasts in Old South Tennessee: An Analysis of the Non-Combatant Responses to the Civil War Veterans Questionnaires." *Tennessee Historical Quarterly* 45 (winter 1986): 273–286.

Bond, Phillip. "The Alabama State Artillery." *Alabama Historical Quarterly* 20 (summer 1958): 312–338.

Breeden, James O. "A Medical History of the Later Stages of the Atlanta Campaign." *Journal of Southern History* 35 (February 1969): 31–59.

Brock, Darla. "Our Hands Are at Your Service: The Story of Confederate Women in Memphis." *West Tennessee Historical Society Papers* 45 (1991): 19–34.

Cain, Marvin R. "A 'Face of Battle' Needed: An Assessment of Motives and Men in Civil War Historiography." *Civil War History* 28 (1982): 5–27.

Crane, Conrad. "Mad Elephants, Slow Deer, and Baseball on the Brain: The Writings and Character of Civil War Soldiers." *Mid-America* 68 (October 1986): 121–140.

Daniel, W. Harrison. "An Aspect of Church and State Relations in the Confederacy: Southern Protestantism and the Office of Army Chaplain." *North Carolina Historical Review* 36 (January 1959): 47–71.

———. "Protestantism and Patriotism in the Confederacy." *Mississippi Quarterly* 24 (spring 1974): 117–134.

Davis, Granville. "An Uncertain Confederate Trumpet: A Study of Erosion in Morale." *West Tennessee Historical Society Papers* 38 (1984): 19–50.

Delfino, Susanna. "'To Maintain the Civil Rights of the People': The Tribulations of Duff Green, Iron Manufacturer in Civil War East Tennessee." *Journal of East Tennessee History* 72 (2000): 49–61.

Escott, Paul D. "'The Cry of the Sufferers': The Problem of Welfare in the Confederacy." *Civil War History* 23 (September 1977): 228–240.

Faust, Drew Gilpin. "Altars of Sacrifice: Confederate Women and the Narratives of War." *Journal of American History* 76 (March 1990): 1200–1228.

———. "Christian Soldiers: The Meaning of Revivalism in the Confederate Army." *Journal of Southern History* 52 (February 1987): 63–90.

Fowler, John D. "'The Finishing Stroke to the Independence of the Southern Confederacy': Perceptions of Hood's Tennessee Campaign." *Tennessee Historical Quarterly* 64 (fall 2005): 216–235.

Freemon, Frank R. "The Medical Support System for the Confederate Army of Tennessee during the Georgia Campaign, May–September 1864." *Tennessee Historical Quarterly* 52 (spring 1993): 44–55.

Gallagher, Gary. "Home Front and Battlefield: Some Recent Literature Relating to Virginia and the Confederacy." *Virginia Magazine of History and Biography* 98 (April 1990), 135–168.

Glatthaar, Joseph T. "The 'New' Civil War History: An Overview." *Pennsylvania Magazine of History and Biography* 115 (July 1991): 339–369.

Grimsley, Mark A. "In Not So Dubious Battle: The Motivations of American Civil War Soldiers." *Journal of Military History* 62 (January 1998): 175–188.

Hallock, Judith Lee. "The Role of the Community in Civil War Desertion." *Civil War History* (June 1983): 254–265.

Horton, Paul. "Submitting to the 'Shadow of Slavery': The Secession Crisis and Civil War in Alabama's Lawrence County." *Civil War History* 44 (June 1998): 111–136.

Kelly, Maud McClure. "John Herbert Kelly: The Boy General of the Confederacy." *Alabama Historical Quarterly* 9 (spring 1947): 6–112.

Kelly, William Milner. "A History of the Thirtieth Alabama Volunteers (Infantry) Confederate States Army." *Alabama Historical Quarterly* 9 (spring 1947): 115–167.

Knowlton, William A. "Morale: Crucial, But What Is It?" *Army* 33 (June 1983): 34–40.

Kondert, Nancy T. "The Romance and Reality of Defeat: Southern Women in 1865." *Journal of Mississippi History* 35 (May 1973): 141–152.

Little, Robert D. "Southern Historians and the Downfall of the Confederacy." *Alabama Review* 3 (October 1950): 243–262; 4 (January 1951): 38–54.

Lufkin, Charles L. "Divided Loyalties: Sectionalism in Civil War McNairy County, Tennessee." *Tennessee Historical Quarterly* 47 (fall 1989): 169–177.

Maslowski, Pete. "A Study of Morale in Civil War Soldiers." *Military Affairs* 34 (December 1970): 122–126.

McMurry, Richard M. "Confederate Morale in the Atlanta Campaign of 1864." *Georgia Historical Quarterly* 54, no. 2 (1970): 226–243.

McNeill, William J. "A Survey of Confederate Soldier Morale during Sherman's Campaigns through Georgia and the Carolinas." *Georgia Historical Quarterly* 55 (spring 1971): 1–25.

McPherson, James M. "'Spend Much Time in Reading the Daily Papers': The Press and Army Morale in the Civil War." *Atlanta History* 42, nos. 1–2 (1998): 7–18.

Norton, Herman. "Revivalism in the Confederate Armies." *Civil War History* 6 (1960): 410–424.

Norton, Wesley. "The Role of a Religious Newspaper in Georgia during the Civil War." *Georgia Historical Quarterly* 48 (June 1964): 125–146.

Partin, Robert, ed. "The Sustaining Faith of an Alabama Soldier." *Civil War History* 6 (December 1963): 425–438.

Prim, G. Clinton, Jr. "Born Again in the Trenches: Revivals in the Army of Tennessee." *Tennessee Historical Quarterly* 43 (fall 1984): 250–272.

———. "Revivals in the Armies of Mississippi during the Civil War." *Journal of Mississippi History* 44 (August 1982): 227–234.

Rable, George. "The Battlefield and Beyond." *Civil War History* 53 (September 2007): 244–251.

———. "Despair, Hope, and Delusion: The Collapse of Confederate Morale Reexamined." *North and South* 4, no. 4 (2001): 60–72.

Reid, Richard. "A Test Case of the 'Crying Evil': Desertion among North Carolina Troops during the Civil War." *North Carolina Historical Review* (summer 1981): 234–262.

Sanders, Charles W., Jr. "Jefferson Davis and the Hampton Roads Peace Conference: 'To Secure Peace to the Two Countries.'" *Journal of Southern History* 63 (November 1997): 803–826.

Silver, James W. "Propaganda in the Confederacy." *Journal of Southern History* 11 (November 1945): 487–503.

Sutherland, Daniel. E. "Getting the 'Real War' into the Books." *Virginia Magazine of History and Biography* 98 (April 1990), 193–220.

Symonds, Craig. "General Joseph E. Johnston's Civil War: A Conversation with Historian Craig Symonds." Interview by Mark Snell. *Civil War Regiments* 6, no. 1 (1998): 107–120.

Towles, Louis P. "Dalton and the Rebirth of the Army of Tennessee." *Proceedings of the South Carolina Historical Association* (2002): 87–100.

Watson, Samuel J. "Religion and Combat Motivation in the Confederate Armies." *Journal of Military History* 58 (January 1994): 29–55.

Weitz, Mark A. "'I Will Never Forget the Name of You': The Home Front, Desertion, and Oath Swearing in Wartime Tennessee." *Tennessee Historical Quarterly* 59 (spring 2000): 38–59.

Wetta, Frank J. "Battle Histories: Reflections on Civil War Military Studies." *Civil War History* 53 (September 2007): 229–235.

Winter, William F. "Mississippi's Civil War Governors." *Journal of Mississippi History* 51 (May 1989): 77–88.

Theses and Dissertations

Bryan, Charles Faulkner, Jr. "The Civil War in East Tennessee: A Social, Political, and Economic Study." Ph.D. diss., University of Tennessee, Knoxville, 1978.

Dillard, Philip D. "Independence or Slavery: The Confederate Debate over Arming the Slaves." Ph.D. diss., Rice University, 1999.

Frank, Lisa Tendrich. "To 'Cure Her of Her Pride and Boasting': The Gendered Implications of Sherman's March." Ph.D. diss., University of Florida, 2001.

Gardner, Sarah Elizabeth. "'Blood and Irony': Southern Women's Narratives of the Civil War, 1861–1915." Ph.D. diss., Emory University, 1996.

Kennedy, Larry Wells. "The Fighting Preacher of the Army of Tennessee: General Mark Perrin Lowrey." Ph.D. diss., Mississippi State University, 1976.

Maslowski, Peter. "A Study of Morale in Civil War Soldiers." Master's thesis, Ohio State University, 1968.

Williams, James Levon. "Civil War and Reconstruction in the Yazoo Mississippi Delta, 1863–1875." Ph.D. diss., University of Arizona, 1992.

Index